Memoirs of a Scientology Warrior

Mark 'Marty' Rathbun

Edited by Russell Williams & Mike Rinder

Cover art and design by Evie Cook

Dedicated to the dedicated

ISBN 13: **978-1484805664**
ISBN 10: **1484805666**

CONTENTS

PREFACE

"Use the shotgun", Kerry Riley advised in his thick Oklahoman drawl, "it's better they be picking shards of glass out of their foreheads for a spell till the Sheriff arrives than to have corpses on your hands." Kerry preferred that I use my double-barrel, over-under shot gun - "use the heavier buckshot, not that chicken-shit bird shot" - when the Mexican Mafia started surveiling my home in preparation for a drive by shooting. One of their offshoots had tagged my car port with their death sentence – three pitch fork prongs up, with stars above each one, signifying I am soon to arrive in one of three places: jail, the hospital or the morgue. That is how the lead investigator for the San Patricio County District Attorney's Office interpreted it anyhow. Until I helped deliver some hoods to jail, I would continue to guard my wife's slumber at night, sitting in our carport with my shotgun across my knee.

The deputy chief of the local police department was puzzled by all this. He wanted to know what I'm doing in South Texas investigating gangs for Riley's tri-county "conscience of the Coastal Bend" newspaper when I was once an international executive in Los Angeles. I reminded the man that I sort of made it my mission when the Crips nearly killed a six year old girl with a Russian assault rifle during a drive by shooting, and it seemed apparent that local law enforcement, including himself, were too intimidated to do anything effective about it. He smirked as if unaffected by my swipe at his lack of courage and added, "a man with your history could do a lot better than this." Without acknowledging the implication that he had looked into my past life - I replied, "you may be right on that score".

I pulled away in my pickup truck, turned up Wyclef Jean's cover of *Knocking on Heaven's Door* and drove into the shadows of another steamy, gulf coast summer night: "*I remember playing my guitar in the projects, a product of the environment, pour some liquor for those who passed away.*"

"Good question" I thought, "what am doing in a place like this?" I contemplated the answer as I drove an isolated stretch of highway. I'm investigating gangs because they are the bullies in this county – shooting up innocent folk – that's easy. That's what I do, that's what I've always done. I've got to defend to the death in order to survive. "*My dad taught me the American dream, baby, you can be anything you want to be, if I did it, y'all could do it.*"

But, the cop's unasked question nagged me, "how could you be here doing that when you are dead?" If he had looked my name up on the Internet – as he obviously had - a number of sites, including Wikipedia, listed me as deceased. But, I was breathing and creating chaos in San Pat county to boot. That was after the Church of Scientology had effectively pronounced me dead. That's what happens when you up and leave unannounced, even after twenty-seven years of service. Excommunicated – can't speak to another living Scientologist, or any professional contact you may have made during that time. Those are the rules and I had agreed to play by the rules. So, yeah, I guess I am dead. *"I feel a dark cloud coming over me, so poor, so dark, it feels like I'm knocking on heaven's door."*

Then I thought about the "why South Texas?" part of the question. Easy. It is the furthest point geographically in the contiguous US from the two main Scientology centers I worked at for almost three decades. There is unlimited space, and plenty of uncorrupted coast line. After nearly a quarter century of fighting Scientology's legal and public relations battles, all I was looking for was a little peace of mind. And I found where to get it. *"Would someone take these guns away from here, take these guns from the street, Lord, I can't shoot my brothers anymore."*

As I pulled up to my little bungalow on the bay, I admitted to myself that I was certain only about the last answer, why South

Texas. Then, the dichotomy hit me - if I came here for peace, what on earth am I doing at war again? I walked out onto the small deck behind the house and lit a menthol. I looked at the moon reflecting off the wind swept water, then at the stars. I felt melancholic, but did not know why. I was contemplating who I really was. I found myself humming Clef's tune, and singing lightly its final lyrics, *"Please put down your heat, Oh Lord, To my brothers that's on the corner, Oh God, Ay, get out quick or you too will be knocking on heaven's door."*

CHAPTER ONE

THE ZEN OF BASKETBALL

Zen: A total state of focus that incorporates a total togetherness of body and mind. Zen is a way of being. It also is a state of mind. Zen involves dropping illusion and seeing things without distortion created by your own thoughts. – The Urban Dictionary

Caveat emptor (buyer, beware). I may be crazy – and this book of my recollections therefore may just be laced with delusion.

It all depends on whether you buy into the genetic theory of mental health. That is the school of thought that maintains we are simply organisms, unthinkingly carrying on the genetic, cellular commands we are born with. That is the very theory that L. Ron Hubbard eschewed in developing Scientology. Scientology is predicated upon the idea that the spirit (called *thetan* in Scientology) and its considerations are senior to the mind and the body, and that ultimately each of us is capable of sanity and of becoming the captain of his own destiny – irrespective of genetic or biological make-up.

The church of Scientology has apparently done away with such core Hubbard principles. Corporate Scientology leader David Miscavige sent my former wife to Clearwater Florida to visit reporters Tom Tobin and Joe Childs of the *St. Petersburg Times* (now *Tampa Bay Times*) in mid 2009. She came with a script to read to the reporters, one no doubt carefully crafted by Miscavige himself. It would be corporate Scientology's answer to an interview I had given, exposing a culture of violence created by Miscavige at the highest levels of his church.

In embarrassed, halting phrases my former wife told the reporters that I had a family history of insanity and the "church" was concerned that I had picked up the insanity gene. When the reporters attempted to make some sense of the relevance of those claims, my former wife, on cue, stood, turned and walked from the room, noting with finality, "This is not a deposition; I'm not here to answer questions." When official Scientology spokesperson Tommy Davis was confronted with the claims I'd made about violence in the church, he shouted, with veins popping from his neck, "Marty Rathbun is a fucking lunatic. He's psychotic!"

Miscavige came up with this brilliant public relations move based on an analysis of my church counseling folders. Those folders note, in meticulous detail, every significant event of my life, and of many prior lives as well. It is a policy of the corporate Scientologists to find bits of embarrassing confession from a former member's past, and then allude to one of these bits publicly. The hope is that the target will quail, for fear of any more particulars being revealed.

In order to erase any influence such attempted blackmail might otherwise have, let's get right to the heart of Miscavige's allusion to the matter he seems to believe is my Achilles' heel.

Insanity runs deep in my family. My mother received multiple electro-convulsive shock therapy treatments while pregnant with me. I found that out through Scientology counseling which probes into pre-natal, and even previous lifetime, incidents of the being. I told my Scientology counselor that I recalled my mother being taken off to a private psychiatric facility while I resided in her womb. When she was hit with electro-convulsive shock I, the spirit, was hurtled out of the body and witnessed the rest of the 'treatment' from above looking down at the psychiatrists and his assistants and my mother's body strapped to the table. When the violence was over, I contemplated leaving and finding another mother and another fetus to occupy. But, my conscience struck me and I decided I would weather the storm, stick around and help the mother I had initially chosen. When I was in my early thirties I told my aunt about these recollections and her jaw dropped. My descriptions of the facility and the surrounds and the event were accurate in all details. And that, in essence, is Scientology Inc.'s blackmail on me: I am a lunatic by virtue of carrying my mother's genes, complicated and compounded by my fetal electro-shock experience.

Back to my recollections, pre-Scientology. When I was five years old my mother jumped off the Golden Gate Bridge. She did not survive the impact and her body washed up on shore a couple of days later. My mother's suicide had a definite effect in shaping my later life. In the wake of this loss, some of my most lasting childhood memories were of avoiding social situations because of the pain inflicted by older boys teasing me about my mother "kicking the bucket." My two older brothers never recovered. After living tortured childhoods both went insane in their early twenties. Scott, eight years my elder, has been institutionalized for "schizophrenia" most of his adult life. Bruce, four years older than I, was locked up in mental institutions several times, and finally was stabbed to death after a bar room brawl at the age of twenty-seven.

That I avoided the fates of my brothers, I mostly credited to having been younger and thus more naïve. I never believed my mother committed suicide. I remained proud of her after her death. I knew she was an artist and an athlete. I had seen pictures of her in Acapulco, Mexico, where she stood atop a huge cliff overlooking the Pacific Ocean. She told me, and my aunts confirmed it, that she had been the first woman to dive from the highest rocks – a feat theretofore only attempted by men.

Since nobody wanted to explain to a five-year-old what was wrong with his mom, I was left to create my own reality. No matter what anybody said, I held firm to the idea that my mom hadn't committed suicide. No, she had attempted to conquer the Golden Gate Bridge just as she had vanquished the high cliffs of Acapulco. Our collie, Chipper, to whom I was then most inclined to confide, acknowledged this as a perfectly rational explanation. And so it held with me for nearly half a century.

I think my impressions of my mom were also influenced by the fact that I was with her through most of the time she was enduring her personal hell. Here again, being a small child had its benefits. She had enough control not to trip out on an infant and pre-schooler. She would have her psychotic episodes, then run off with me in the car, calm down, and express her thoughts to me as we drove down the redwood-lined roads of Marin County.

I can't remember what those thoughts were, exactly. The

significances were not important. What was important was that she vented them and calmed herself down. She would cry for 20 minutes or more; then, when she ran out of tears, she would start talking – and I'd listen. When she was done, at a loss for words, all I could think to do was to hug her. I got the idea she thought it was safe to talk to me.

I guess I was kind of like a good dog. A good dog is there for you when nobody else wants to be. He'll understand (or seem to) when no one else can or will. A good dog doesn't invalidate your thoughts, doesn't analyze and judge your words. A good dog just listens and acknowledges – non-verbally of course, with a lick or a nuzzle-up with the snout. Sometimes, given its inability to speak and limited facial expressions, you miss the acknowledgment unless you are really tuned in to the dog's wavelength. I guess that is why I always liked dogs. I have always told my innermost thoughts to my dogs. And not a one of them ever condemned me, no matter how off the wall my views might have been. Dogs are the best listeners God ever created.

With my father Slade busy making ends meet, I never had much supervision as a kid. Even though he'd go at it with my older brothers, he and I always seemed to get along. I think he considered me to be sort of like a good dog. Even though he wasn't around much, I loved him. I was grateful to him for providing for me and carrying on despite his own pain and survivor's guilt. I was loyal to him and listened to him attentively. Once in a while he took to confiding in me, even though I was his youngest son. He'd get into fights with my brothers, chase them out of the house, then settle down with a six pack of Coors talls and a pack of menthols. And after maybe a couple of 16-ouncers the old man would start philosophizing. He'd get so into his thoughts that he'd light up his next smoke before the last one was put out. His philosophy was simple and pretty easy to follow and agree with. He was for loyalty, honesty, hard work, and overcoming the odds. After about four beers he could get melancholic and blame himself for Bruce and Scott; sometimes when he had too much to drink he'd even take on some measure of blame for mom's fate. I got pretty good at hearing him out and seeing he got to bed on a little bit of an up. All I ever really did was listen. If that was a virtue, I attribute it to Chipper, who was perhaps my best early childhood mentor.

When I was 12, my dad got married for the third time and we moved to Laguna Beach. I had always tried to help dad create a family, through two stepmothers who my brothers just would not friendly up to. By becoming enemies of my brothers, those stepmothers alienated even me. With Scott off to college and a life of his own, I tried to get Bruce, a high school introvert by then, to give the second stepmother a break. When I attempted to open up a discussion about our real mother and the hurt her loss had laid in, he would withdraw even harder. When I would persist, he would take me into the garage to settle it with the family's traditional dispute-resolution tools: boxing gloves. Being the quiet type and built like a bull, he would give me the Sonny Liston stare-down and then coolly delivered a brutal lesson: do not communicate, particularly about the past, and least of all about mom.

My father had taken to drinking every night, and my latest stepmother was a wine and valium addict from the day she moved in. I got the idea I couldn't influence anyone in the family to pull together and become a family. I was just a pushy runt as far as they were concerned. At one point I decided that the best thing I could do was go out and prove myself in the world; then they might listen. I had to get out and live my own life. Here once again was the decision to create a world of my own.

If there was ever a place where one could create his own world, it was Laguna Beach in 1969. It was still an eclectic artist colony back then. It had yet to become commercialized and made the exclusive province of the wealthy. As a scrawny, scrappy, unsupervised kid with no friends, I gravitated toward the Boys Club overlooking old Main Beach. Main Beach was like a collection of bits of the most colorful parts of the entire world, somehow drawn into the orbit of an area the size of a couple of football fields. It was the center of the universe as far as I was concerned. The rich kids in town were repelled by Main Beach. They considered it a dirty, panhandling tourist trap and held to their private coves toward the north and south ends of town.

Main Beach was located at the intersection of the only two roads into and out of Laguna. An old Swede with long white hair and beard stood on the corner of the two highways, waving to everyone who visited. Eisler Larsen was his name, and he had taken on the unofficial title of Greeter. I loved Eisler because, even though he could barely speak English, he would listen to me and acknowledge me as though he were a big old cheerful dog.

The Boys Club looked down over Main Beach's famous half-mile-long boardwalk, bordered by a wide strip of white sand beach on one side and the Pacific Coast Highway on the other. Two or three times a day a band of a dozen or more Hare Krishnas would bob and weave past the courts and down the boardwalk – chanting, banging drums and playing small hand cymbals. They wore light-orange, flowing robes. Their heads were shaved and they sported white paint lines from hairline to eyebrows. At first I thought they were pretty freaky, and joined other boys in lampooning them. We dressed in swim fins, diving goggles and snorkels, with towels wrapped around our torsos. We followed the Krishnas down the boardwalk as if we were part of their ritual. I soon felt guilty and stopped participating, since the Krishnas were friendly and thoughtful people. Even though I was one of those ridiculing them, they invited me to their temple for free organic lunches. I sometimes even adopted their rhythmic chant to break the boredom during my long walks between home and Main Beach. It seemed to give me measure of equanimity.

On the weekends an old Mexican man dressed in a dirty white classic show caballero outfit would set up shop along the boardwalk. He was saving souls through Jesus. He was of robust build, with an enormous stomach, very dark skin and a big, shiny gold tooth. He mainly targeted homeless hippies who would gather to grope through his bakery boxes full of free day-old donuts. I let the old man try to save me a couple of times, when I was hungry for some of those hard donuts. He really got a charge out of putting his hand on my forehead, looking to the sky and contacting the spirit of Jesus. The old guy would holler at Jesus, begging for forgiveness on my behalf. When he got real excited, he would slip from English into Spanish for a few beats. I glanced up a few times but never saw what he saw. But I did read the little "sayings of Christ" booklet he handed out. Many times I'd read from it on the way home, and gain some degree of solace.

Every day during the summer I arrived at the beach early and stayed late, to help the proprietors of George's Beach Rentals set up and break down their umbrella, beach chair and surf raft stand. They would let me use the rafts for free, and I earned tips by helping tourists set up their umbrella encampments on the beach. I usually made enough to buy a Buzz Burger or two – 24 cents each at the A&W Root Beer stand. Those burgers and bags of sunflower seeds (big enough to last all day) became my summer diet.

There was never a dull day on Main Beach. Since Laguna was the gay capital of Southern California at the time, and inland tourists didn't cotton to same sex relations, interesting geo-political-sexual dynamics often broke out, as tourist families and clusters of gays staked out their beach territories. There was an avid volleyball set who camped around the sand courts from dawn till dusk, drinking beer and playing tournaments. Itinerant musicians frequented the board walk, playing for change. In those days many street musicians were very talented.

The real center of Main Beach, though – both geographically and in terms of attention – was the basketball court. Four-on-four half-court was the game of choice. At the height of summer there were multiple teams waiting to take on the winners of the current game. Current and former high school and college players from all around Southern California came to play at Main Beach.

I had become pretty skilled at handling a basketball, since the game had served me as an escape during most of my childhood. I could run off to any playground and concentrate on basketball for hours, taking attention off family dramas. But since I was less than five feet tall and weighed in at less than 100 pounds, in my first couple of summers I couldn't convince many players to accept me as a teammate. Between games I would get out on the court for the shoot-around while the new team was warming up. I would stand under the basket, grab balls as they came through the hoop or bounced off the rim, and squeeze in as many shots as I could. I would fire the ball to older boys and men warming up. I got to know the best players by name. And after many weeks of my persistent presence, some of them got to know mine. That was mainly because they wanted me to return the balls I'd retrieved. I worked on snapping quick, strong passes, hoping I might impress someone with my ability to get them the ball in the open. After a while, I would sometimes be allowed to be fourth man. This usually happened early in the morning or toward sundown, when not enough players had shown up to have a real game, or too many had left. Because no one wanted to pass me the ball, I began to develop a quick dash to recoup loose balls; that was the only way I'd see any action.

Basketball became my Zen. Home was dead – but basketball was alive. Working on skills, concentrating on angles and getting the ball to the hoop were physical and mental disciplines that increased my focus. They took my attention off my faults, shortcomings, and worries. I began to really enjoy the art of it. The poetry of the motion. And especially the communication. I wanted to play someday on the Main Beach center court, in the thick of the afternoon competition. Maybe one day play on the high school varsity team; maybe even get a college scholarship. I got myself a ball and seldom went anywhere without it. When I was thirteen I got a job as a score keeper for men's basketball leagues at the high school, with the recreation department. That netted me a key to the gym. For the next four years I spent most evenings after school alone in the old girl's gymnasium, working on my ball handling and shooting.

I tried to emulate some of the more accomplished players at the beach. But, more than anyone, I tried to play like professional star Earl "The Pearl" Monroe. I could relate to The Pearl because he didn't have great jumping ability, but he more than compensated for it with his ball handling skills. The Pearl had more class and rhythm than any other player in the world. He could see the entire court, even when he wasn't looking at it through his eyes. He could throw a pass with ease and great precision in one direction while looking in the opposite direction. The President could command a nation, rich men could have everything money could buy, teachers were okay and to be admired, but The Pearl was in a zone, a spiritual place where mind ruled over matter, all with a relaxed look on his face and an easy bounce in his step. I spent virtually all my free time for the next four years at the beach courts, the Boy's Club or in the gym. I worked on Pearl's moves, behind-the-back passes and dribbling, between-the-leg dribbling and no-look passes. I practiced spinning the ball on the fingers of my hands in the gym, on the beach, and on the streets to and from home.

One day at the age of 14 I got my break at the Beach. I was scrambling for rebounds between games and throwing passes to the group of men and older boys warming up. One guy in his twenties stood out. He was tall and wiry, had long, brown, wild (almost matted) sun-bleached hair, and a long, reddish beard. He looked like a homeless hippy. I threw him a crisp one-hand bounce pass from 20 feet away. He rapidly spun, hair flying in all directions, and flashed toward the basket, rose up above the rim and gently dropped the ball in. "Nice pass, kid," he said as he turned and ran back toward the top of the key. I came alive with that acknowledgment. For two years nobody had noticed me. I might as well have been a statue.

Then the bearded man got 20 feet out and turned and looked at me. I nodded to the left indicating he should make a slashing drive to his right. As the man made his move, I looked out at and dribbled the ball toward the highway and away from the court. I rapidly flipped the ball with my right hand under my left arm behind me. The ball rocketed off the asphalt and bounced crisply and did a 45-degree ascent from the ground. The hippy, airborne, intercepted it en route to the hoop and laid it in. The big guy looked at me and started laughing, "What's your name?" "Mark," I answered. He immediately announced, in his hoarse, cackling voice, "We'll take the kid – let's get it on." Most of the regulars looked surprised; a couple sneered.

Why the man asked my name, I'll never know – because from there on out, to him I was "The Kid."

I called my new mentor "Crazy Legs," shortened to "Crazy" once I got to know him better, because he spun and moved like a whirling dervish, his legs flailing and seemingly out of control. The chaos of Crazy's body confused defenders and made him an effective scorer. He played with reckless abandon and enjoyed every second of it. Crazy played crazy, lived crazy, and by societal standards I supposed he might be considered crazy.

We got our butts kicked in the first game, mainly because the other side exploited our weakness on defense, namely me. But I impressed Crazy with my ball handling, willingness to take elbows from the bigger players, and my creative passing. Crazy was a street baller. But he was different than the rest of them. Winning was nice, but the Zen of basketball trumped victory.

Crazy could enter that telepathic zone where I could send the ball exactly where he was intending to go, without any verbal coordination. If we got into that hallowed space even for a few brief moments during a game, Crazy didn't care what the final score was. "It's the zest for the ride that matters, kid," he told me. "A roller coaster makes one person vomit, makes another person terrified, and thrills somebody else. The roller coaster doesn't treat anyone any differently from anyone else. The roller coaster stays the same. It's what each person brings to it that makes the difference. Just like life."

I didn't get invited to play much that summer. But then I'd see Crazy approaching from a half mile off, bouncing down the boardwalk, singing out loud and taking in the beach scene, and I knew I'd get another chance. Crazy wore a pair of blue jean cut-offs, sandals and no shirt. He'd have his dirty Converse hi-top canvas sneakers hanging around his neck and shoulders, suspended by their laces. Crazy never wore any socks, even on the court. Crazy never got into fights. And he pissed a lot of people off with his reckless moves. But when somebody squared off with him, Crazy would break out into a broad smile, and announce unabashedly, "I love you brother!" It worked; I never saw anybody throw a punch at Crazy. After a while, it seemed like more players tolerated Crazy, and by the end of the summer Crazy was just about the most popular guy on the courts.

After weeks of intermittent games with Crazy, we began to win once in a while. Sometimes we'd even hold the court for two or three games before some former college players would come to restore order. Crazy didn't stay to socialize. He'd hold the court for as long as he could, then down a can or two of cold beer and disappear down the beach.

Crazy always had a few words of encouragement for me. After a loss I'd apologize for some sloppy defense. "Kid, don't focus on the negative. It was a hell of a ride, wasn't it?" he'd say with a smile. "Some day they'll be coming for miles just to watch you deal that ball, kid, believe me. But don't get too caught up in it; stay focused on the ride," Crazy said – then guzzled a half a can of beer, crushed the can, shot it into the trash receptacle, turned and headed down the boardwalk. Another time it was,"You'll grow into those feet, then they'll take notice. As long as you keep following the rhythm, just keep following the rhythm," while taking off his canvas sneakers. Then without another word he ran and dove into the surf. Still another was, "Kid, you got rhythm; that's something that can't be taught. The rhythm is what makes the ride worthwhile," then he flipped his sneakers around his neck and took off.

One day Crazy explained the rhythm to me in more depth. He said it was another way of saying the Tao – the Way, from Lao Tzu's *Tao Te Ching*. He wanted me to understand that rhythm was like the Tao: a universally present and connected spiritual energy that made the entire cosmos operate. If you could attune to it, you could overcome bigger bodies and bigger forces and have fun doing it. He said that that was the Zen of basketball. Zen is focus and concentration of such intensity that one steps, without effort, into the stream of the Tao. The most lasting and memorable lesson Crazy taught me from the *Tao* related to the basketball position he was validating me for beginning to master: point guard. The point guard handles the ball, sets up the plays and initiates the offense. He is the equivalent of the football quarterback. Crazy told me the greatest honor a point guard can achieve is invisible effectiveness – just like the Tao. It is the ability to do what needs to be done to make the other four teammates look good bringing out the best in each of them and making all five operate as one. He related it to the Tao's principles of leadership:

When the master governs, the people are hardly aware he exists…

The Master doesn't talk, he acts. When his work is done, the people say, 'Amazing: we did it all ourselves…

This prompted me to find myself a copy of the *Tao* and read it. It didn't all add up, but sometimes a line or phrase seemed to make sense of things for me. It had much the same effect as the "Sayings of Jesus" pamphlet had, years before.

I wondered where Crazy appeared and disappeared from, as he never mentioned where he lived. I never asked him because I didn't want to embarrass him if he was living in a tent or something.

One night late that summer I was bouncing my basketball while walking past the old American Legion Hall. There was loud rock music blaring and the place was packed with long-haired guys and braless women. I went up to the entrance to take a peek. There was a band up on a dais playing to a wood floor full of hippie types, dancing in wild fashion. Once I got my fill of looking at the sea of juggling breasts, I began to turn to leave.

Out of the corner of my eye, in the middle of the floor, I caught a glimpse of something familiar. It was Crazy's wild hair, several inches above the crowd and gyrating to the beat. I edged my way through the crowd toward Crazy. He looked like he was deep in some hypnotic trance, but he was smiling as usual. I tapped him on the shoulder. Crazy turned and beamed in surprise. "Hey Kid!" he yelled. Then he pulled up a bota bag that was draped over his shoulder. "Open wide!" he screamed. I opened my mouth, and nearly drowned in a stream of red wine shooting from the bag.

Crazy was surrounded by three shapely hippy women. They seemed infatuated with him. "Here, have some more!" he shouted as he took aim with the bota bag. That was enough to make me light-headed. I began to sway with the music. After a while and several more wine shots, I felt like Crazy himself, my legs dancing and kicking in all directions, women's bodies grinding against mine. I began to feel the bliss of vanishing inhibition. After a while, one of Crazy's woman friends took me outside behind some bushes, pulled out a joint, and taught me how to smoke weed. After that the evening went from sensuous and adventurous to completely surreal. Back in the hall, we were going at it as hard as we did on the court, but this was directionless, wild, free. The environment became more fluid, then disjointed, then finally came blackness.

I awoke just before dawn. There were ivy leaves in my face. As much as I was startled and confused, I couldn't move my body. I could shift my eyes, though, and I saw that my entire body was engulfed in ivy. I was lying in a bank of it. Had I died and gone to some other world? I mustered enough strength to crane my neck, and recognized that I was in the front yard of an unfamiliar house. Shocked, I moved my head off the ground to see a neighborhood I had never seen before. It seemed like it took an eternity just to get up on my butt to try to make sense of where I was. It was difficult, because the entire street and every house on it were slowly rotating around me.

The only thing I could think of was an overwhelming desire for a Dr. Pepper. Somehow I thought it was the only thing that could save me. I finally got on my feet and stumbled to a liquor store. Dr. Pepper did save me; my consciousness slowly but surely returned. While the initial hangover was hell, oddly enough I felt re-booted and refreshed once back on the court and sweating again. I decided the occasional high created a good balance with athletics.

The rest of that summer I continued to hoop with Crazy. He continued to be an enigma, playing his heart out, laughing the entire time, citing snippets of wisdom from the *Tao* and the Buddha, then disappearing down the beach.

After that summer I never saw Crazy again. I reckoned he'd probably drifted up to Venice Beach or San Francisco, Oregon or maybe even Mexico. It didn't really matter much. Up easy, down hard; peaks and valleys are of no great import, as long as you don't lose the rhythm and zest for the ride. I had learned some lessons – though some were contradictory – and spent the next couple years applying them.

CHAPTER TWO

OUT OF BODY, OUT OF MIND

I felt my soul or something coming right out of my body, like you'd pull a silk handkerchief out of a pocket by one corner. – Ernest Hemmingway

My Tao, Zen, basketball and drug lessons got me nowhere in building any family stability. My early teens were pretty wild. I spent more time away from home than at home. I always had jobs during summers and lots of weekends. They included car parking, restaurant table bussing, grocery delivery, sports refereeing, landscaping, and handyman work. That bought most of my clothes and food during my teenage years. It also bought me a great deal of independence. If things got too thick at home, sometimes I would hitchhike hundreds of miles up the coast to camp out at Big Sur, where the Central California Mountains hit the surf. While I kept playing organized basketball in the fall and winter in high school, I worked, body surfed, played sports, and smoked pot during spring and summer.

By my junior year in high school I was promoted to the varsity team. I almost didn't play. I was losing hope of achieving much of anything with basketball. My body and my hands were too small. My interests were heading more in the direction of philosophy, drugs and the opposite sex. Then a coach and teacher of mine started putting conscience into the equation. He reminded me that almost the entire varsity team would be made up of the group I had led as captain of the freshman and junior varsity teams the years before. The only reason we were going to varsity as juniors was that the class ahead of us had but one decent player. To leave my friends alone would be abandoning them to slaughter. The coach said he did not want to see me become another pot-head surfer when I had so much potential. I reconsidered.

We were the smallest basketball team from one of the smallest high schools in Southern California. The varsity coach was one of the smaller men who had played college basketball. Coach relished being the little guy facing the bigger guy. It was the story of his life. Jerry Fair stood about five feet, seven inches tall. He had wispy dark hair, combed back from his receding hairline. He was serious most of the time, and intense. Being an old-school, hard-work-overcomes-all Midwesterner, Fair was a friendless loner in bohemian Laguna Beach. Being a scrawny junior who had had his share of being humiliated by bigger, stronger and faster types up to that point in life, I started listening to the man.

Coach's training regimen was designed to make us tough as nails. "If you are smaller and weaker in body, you overcome that by being bigger mentally. You do that by getting in the best possible physical condition. Your goal is to outlast anyone, no matter how big, how fast, or how strong. As University of Texas football coach Daryl Royal once said, 'The best a man can do is to do the best that he can do.' Honest to God fellas, if you give me your best I'd give up my left nut for you. I guarantee you one thing: if you have that attitude, you'll never walk out of the gym with your head down." As much as I had heard Fair was a madman disciplinarian, this sounded reasonable to me; seemed like a little more serious take on Crazy's view – that it doesn't much matter whether you win or lose, what counts is how you tackle the ride.

Coach had us all read Maxwell Maltz's *Psycho-Cybernetics*, a book on how to condition your mind into a servo-mechanism that guides you toward achieving your aims. It was a sort of slightly more technical take on 2006's *The Secret,* and its Law of Attraction. That is, you get what you focus your mind on. The book's meditative exercises seemed to help me concentrate better.

Basketball practice at Laguna Beach High in the mid-seventies looked more like football practice. Coach would have us stand in the defensive position and have another player run full speed into our chests. "Taking a charge," in basketball vernacular. Coach valued a charge taken – a foul assessed against the offensive side with the ball being awarded to our side – more than any offensive play, no matter how spectacular. Coach validated reckless courage. He spent more time teaching us how to dive on the hard wood floor for a loose ball than on putting balls through the hoop. "Shooters are a dime a dozen. A guy who will sacrifice his body for his team, he is golden." We played man-to-man defense, full court, full time. From the first practice in the fall to the last game in late winter, our bodies were decorated with raspberries, from ankles to faces. And when healing burn scabs broke, which they did regularly, we'd be smeared with blood. We wore fresh blood with pride.

Since we had nobody who could perform a dunk, the way we got the crowd excited was to slide on the floor, full speed, face first to save a loose ball. The momentum of our bodies colliding with the wooden grandstands detonated a thunderous exploding sound.

We learned to check our egos at the door and become a living, breathing entity of five. Coach valued an assist – a pass that leads to an immediate basket – above the most accomplished scoring shot. That was consistent with my Tao leadership lessons. I took more satisfaction in dishing a good pass than in scoring; and if there was anything I could do, it was handle a basketball.

We were a small group of nobodies, first-time varsity players. Most of the guys shared my fear of getting blown out and embarrassed, so we made exceptionally rapt pupils for Coach. I was about the only gym rat on the team in a school whose best athletes gravitated toward beach-town sports like water polo, tennis and volleyball.

But we did have one baller – a student who moved to our town from West Virginia that year. Mickey Allen was a graceful beast. He was a smaller version of Charles Barkley, ten years ahead of Charles Barkley. Mickey had almost exaggerated African-American facial features, but with skin more pale than my own. With his afro like Jimi Hendrix, a pair of high tension springs as legs, a dignified-if-radical goatee , and an easy-going, confident swagger, most people had the idea Mickey was about 25 years old. Mickey had class. He got that from his older brother Joe. Joe was a Marine Corps pilot and did double duty as Mickey's father, since their dad was nowhere to be found. Even though Mickey looked like an intimidating political radical, he was a straight-A student and one of the nicest guys I had come to know, up to that point in my life.

Through all the torture of Coach's brand of sacrifice ball, Mickey made basketball fun for me. He was a point guard's dream as a teammate. Since we focused almost entirely on aggressive defense, our entire offense consisted of "steal the ball and get it down the court before the other side could get set up." It was a practical necessity, too. Given our lack of height, we'd never get a shot off with a traditional offense playing against virtual trees.

Mickey had playground basketball sense and creativity. After a lot of practice, Mickey and I could occupy a certain wavelength that no one else seemed to know the password to. I always knew where he was on the court, and where he intended to go – and vice versa. We could take off at a full sprint the length of the court, with Mickey out of my range of sight – and I would know exactly where he was going to be. Mickey made me look better than I was. I could go up for a shot in the face of a larger defender, never intending to shoot but instead to dish the ball into seeming thin air – only to have Mickey appear from nowhere, effortlessly grab the ball without losing stride and take it up for a score.

When Mickey and I went into our zone, I actually did feel like Earl the Pearl. I could throw passes around my back, over my head, and across my shoulder, while looking and travelling full-speed in the opposite direction from Mickey. And nine times out of ten, Mickey would be there and deliver the score with a panache all his own. Mickey and I developed "the shining" – the ability to communicate to one another telepathically.

The other side didn't know all that when we quietly rambled into the Fallbrook High School gymnasium in November, 1973. Fallbrook had reason to be confident. They hadn't lost a home game in two years. To make matters worse, their 1950s, wood-walled, stuffy cracker box of a gymnasium was packed to the rafters with fans on the verge of hysteria. The gym was so small that their dozen cheerleaders spent more time on the court than off, serving as moving obstacles every time we brought the ball down toward our basket. They even had a couple of dogs as mascots on the court. The Fallbrook boys averaged a two inch height advantage at every position. They looked pretty smug during warm-ups.

Once the game started, however, they soon realized that they had run into a buzz saw. Every ball that was below shoulder height for more than a second was pounced on by swarms of our obnoxious, persistent, skinny-armed swipes. Every loose ball immediately attracted two or more diving bodies from our side. Sometimes one flying body would just manage to keep a ball from going out of bounds, with another flying body tipping the ball into the middle of the court to keep it out of the opponents' hands, while our remaining three bodies piled into a mid-court scrum to finally secure it.

The bigger opponents couldn't even rule the paint (the key – the zone under and close to the basket, usually painted to contrast it with the rest of the natural-wood court). Mickey had a hand on any ball that entered that area, and an immovable body on every big man who tried to get in close for the easy shots. Our "poetry in motion" was like gangster rap.

We were so exhausted from perpetual motion that during time outs, Coach would have us lie on our bellies in a semi-circle, watching intently as he crouched to draw X's and O's on his mini chalk board, laid on the floor before us. The game was a barn burner – dozens of lead changes, neither side ever going ahead by more than a basket or two. We were handicapped by height and skill, while Fallbrook was handicapped by having to struggle like salmon swimming upstream just to get the ball down court where they could take advantage of their skills.

After four quarters of full-out abandon, we had somehow managed to wind up tied with a clearly superior group of athletes. On the verge of delirium from exhaustion, we entered overtime operating on sheer adrenaline and will.

Overtime was the same see-saw battle. The deeper the exhaustion, the more our will became apparent, almost tangible. The entire experience began to take on a surreal shade. The building, the floor, the backboards, the players, the ball – everything physical – began to seem less solid. It was almost as if I could perceive the molecular, moving, impermanent nature of the physical universe. Some Eastern philosophy I had read began to make sense: nothing is permanent in the world but the spirit. The mover unmoved, the creator of energy became perceivable – the spirit; because after all, we were having to create energy to keep those bodies operating. We had burned far more calories in a couple of hours than our bodies had taken in for days. It was truly a test of will, the physical (including bodies) becoming less and less important and real.

With fifteen seconds remaining in overtime, we were down by one point and Fallbrook had the ball. It looked like we had been checkmated. However, with our five bodies worn to their cores, the collective intention of my teammates seemed even more tangible. Perhaps we were too tired to think about anything else but that shared will that had gotten us this far; the only thing remaining after all physical energy and consideration of mechanics had been depleted.

Somehow I was certain we would, as an entity, with that combined intention, create another chance. That intention was the only thing I was aware of at that moment. It was so strong, and so unsullied by any other intention or consideration, that it seemed to be carrying our bodies forward.

At the very edge of my peripheral vision I saw the dark flash of my teammate Mike Serrano jetting toward a space between the Fallbook man with the ball, and one of his teammates. Simultaneous with the ball leaving the opponent's hands, Mike magically arrived between the two players – with the ball in *his* hands. Nine seconds remaining.

I instinctively flashed to the top of the opponents' key – as I was trained to do, as the point guard – to receive the pass in transition from defense to offense. Seven seconds remaining.

I flew down the middle of the court toward our basket, ahead of everyone but two defenders. I wasn't looking at anything in particular. I was *perceiving* everything. As I dribbled full speed, I sensed my two trailing teammates, Mickey on my right and Frank Wright on my left, sprinting just behind me along the sidelines, just as they were trained to do.

I planted my feet just above the top of the key, 18 feet from the basket and dead-center between the sidelines. As I grasped the ball, committing to keep my body in that position, I saw the eyes and the bodies of the defenders turning from me to Mickey and Frank. Two seconds remaining.

At that moment something happened that I had never experienced before. Something that I would devote a good deal of the rest of my life to attempting to re-experience. The deafening crowd roar disappeared. All bodies seemed to move in extra-slow motion. Two seconds seemed like a lifetime.

My head was looking forward, but I "saw" Mickey and Frank a couple of steps behind me. They weren't going to make it in time for my pass. I saw the remaining players behind me, each of them, and their relative positions on the court. All the while I saw what was in front of me. I felt the shining coming from behind me, a final, direct, emphatic telepathic message from Mickey, Mike, Frank , coach and the rest of the team: "Shoot!"

Instinctively, I launched the shot from my position, twenty feet directly in front of the basket. I could perceive a single, clean intention – mine, joined by 10 other teammates on the court and on the bench – willing the ball toward the basket. The buzzer sounded a fraction of a second after the ball left my fingers. The ball arched high in the air and its parabolic journey seemed suspended – a two-second flight feeling like two minutes. I was not looking *up* at the basket; I was looking *down* at it. Even as the ball rotated, I could read the brand label. The ball headed straight into the basket, striking nothing but net.

As my teammates ecstatically ran toward me, my body stood right where it had been when I'd thrown up the shot. When my teammates jumped on me, tackled me to the floor and buried my body with theirs in celebration, I remained 10 feet above them, looking downward to watch the entire scene. Right where I was when I had seen the entire court, 360 degrees, moments earlier. There was no time, there was no energy, no space, no matter. I was exterior to my body.

We continued to surprise opponents, winning more than we lost through December. During a holiday invitational tournament, we began to make people notice by marching to the semi-finals. Never had my morale been so high, never had my confidence in the future been so strong.

That triumphant 6 weeks ended in a single, frightening instant. In the semis we were once again beating a higher-rated opponent. On a full-speed fast break, I made a drive toward the hoop. Just before I arrived, I dished a no-look pass to Mickey, who was slashing to the basket. Pop! "Awwwww," Mickey roared, as he collapsed in a helpless heap on the baseline. Mickey, the guy who made collision ball worth the sacrifice, was down and couldn't get back up. I knew it was bad, and I felt nauseous. As I served as a human crutch to get Mickey back to the locker room, I knew he was gone for the season –

if not forever. (Back then, knee surgery was invasive and potentially career-ending.) We lost in the finals, but took solace in playing a far superior team to the final seconds. And that is how the rest of the season went without Mickey – not bowing to anybody, but only winning as many as we lost.

I wondered over the next year why it was that Mickey was the one who was crippled. All the rest of the starters, including myself, were partiers. While Mickey liked drinking some beer once in a while, the rest of us were smoking pot and drinking far more regularly. As captain of the team, I was getting the notice of a lot of girls. I started having regular sexual liaisons, in addition to getting high. What made it worse was that the more profligate I became, the holier became Mickey. He turned to Christianity and hung with a Bible-study group, and girls known to be virgins. He and I drew apart socially and as teammates.

My brother Bruce was discharged from the Army in the spring leading up to my high school senior year. He had been stationed in Germany, acting as a Military Policeman at a US base there. He was deposited in the Veterans Administration psychiatric ward in Oakland. The report my dad got was that Bruce had been thrown in the drunk tank one too many times after starting bar room brawls. Then he started fighting the Army jail guards. He was diagnosed as mentally ill and discharged.

My dad didn't know what to do. I thought I did. I thought Bruce would be proud of me. I thought my ability to lead and inspire was so great that I could overcome my previous failures to get Bruce into communication. I hopped in my car and drove all night long to Oakland, to see Bruce.

Upon arriving at his ward, I found Bruce heavily drugged and apathetic. The only thing I knew about institutional mental health was what I had read in Ken Kesy's *One Flew over the Cuckoo's Nest.* Two things from that book resonated with me. Number one, if left to rot in the hospital, Bruce would ultimately wind up a vegetable. Number two, the thing that seemed to work with super-introverted nut cases was extroversion. Bruce was like a helpless child. I talked with him for a couple hours, trying to sell him on the therapeutic nature of getting out and living life, travelling, surfing, learning, getting interested. I took him for some walks to get his attention out of his head. Bruce gradually became more coherent. He finally agreed to start coming off the drugs and get himself back home.

Life became increasingly serious and difficult when Bruce returned. I pretty much forsook my friends and my own social life, trying to get him out and interested in the world. We went body surfing, played some hoops, took long walks, and took a couple of road trips to Northern California. But try as I did, I couldn't seem to get Bruce to extrovert much.

No matter what we did, Bruce just would not become very animated; he would not originate communication. The more I outflowed communication with no live response, the more I felt like a battery being drained of its energy. The more I failed, the more introverted *I* became. At one point I tried to get Bruce to face our shared childhood demons and the circumstances of the death of our mother. Big mistake. Bruce snapped, dragged me out of our shared bedroom, shoved my body against the walls and punched me until I managed to escape.

Mickey played our senior year season, but he was a shadow of himself. He wore a big, constricting metal brace on his leg. I tried to will his leg to heal, but in the end he had very little mobility and less jumping ability. I had worked hard over the summer to improve my own jumping ability. But by the time the season started, both my knees were so sore I could barely get off the ground. An orthopedic surgeon diagnosed me with tendonitis in both knees, and advised I sit out the season. I opted to tough it out, while secretly self-medicating with alcohol and dope. As I went, so went the team. I and we became a tremendous disappointment. Coach Fair, who once spoke of me becoming the greatest player in the school's history, now resented me as a good boy gone bad. The downward slide from hard-won success to total failure was a painful ride.

I suspected that karma was in play. I spent years wondering how and why it turned out the way it had. Had I taken on Mickey's bad knee as my own shot knees, because I knew in my heart of hearts I deserved it more than he? Had my own lack of discipline and journey into the high life betrayed and doomed the rest of my teammates? Had I taken on Bruce's demons through my failure to draw them out of him? Had I caught whatever it was that possessed his tortured mind? Would I ever get a second chance, with the stars once again aligning for my success, the way they had a year earlier?

The question that burned the most, though, was: would I ever again escape the four walls of my skull, the way I had transcended that night in the Fallbrook gym? Would I ever regain the shining, share telepathic communications, and experience the power of clean, clear intention? It was noisy and pressure packed in my head, and it seemed the more I tried to extrovert, the harder I wound up introverted.

I thought about Crazy. I had lost not only my rhythm but also my zest for the ride.

CHAPTER THREE

DHARMA BUMS

Dharma Bums*: 1958 novel by Jack Kerouac. The book largely concerns duality in Kerouac's life and ideals, examining the relationship that the outdoors, bicycling, mountaineering, hiking and hitchhiking through the West had with his "city life" of jazz clubs, poetry readings, and drunken parties.* –Wikipedia

I spent two years studying in the University of California (UC) system. The first three semesters were in UC Santa Barbara. The highlights of my time there were making the junior varsity basketball team (and beating out a scholarship player in the process), writing for the radical alternative paper, and hearing Timothy Leary, Eldridge Cleaver and Cesar Chavez of the United Farm Workers speak.

My final semester was spent at UC Santa Cruz. The highlights there were experimenting with hallucinogens, being arrested for participating in the shutting down of the administrative building in support of the United Farm Workers, and extracurricular studies in Eastern philosophy.

In the summer of 1977 I left school with a backpack and 25 dollars in my pocket. I was not prepared to declare a major and did not believe my one long-term dream was being served by continuing. I wanted to write. I had taken a writing class in my final semester. It was the epitome of dilettante-ism, in my view. A touchy-feely professor had the students imaging dreamy thoughts and putting them to paper. He frowned upon realism and writing about events that had actually occurred. To me, all this went against the best in American literature – Twain, London, Hemingway, Steinbeck were all about living life and divining meaning from experience. That, I decided, was for me.

My intention was to hitchhike, do itinerant labor and write. I would leave with 25 dollars and make it around the entire world, gaining a wealth of experiences to draw from. When I let my dad know I was off to pursue my life's dream, he asked sincerely and quietly, "You haven't flipped like your brothers, have you?"

A college friend Steve and I hitchhiked up to Oregon. Our first job was for Oren Ditner, a portly middle-aged redneck who called himself the watermelon king of Oregon. Every Monday morning we met Ditner and a cattle truck trailer full of watermelons in Klamath Falls, in south-central Oregon. As Ditner made deals with supermarkets, we'd pull into the lot with two big-rig cattle trailers full of melons. Steve and I would pitch melons to one another, stacking them in great pyramids in front of the markets. At night we camped out in the straw-bedded cattle trailers. We would bathe in the Willamette River around sundown. We camped, we sang Dylan, we read Jack Kerouac and beat poets, and we wrote.

The route ended on Fridays, near Portland to the north. Steve and I would hitchhike back to Klamath Falls over the weekends to meet another truck full of melons on Mondays. It was an idyllic scene, for the first couple of weeks. Then I caught Ditner cheating on the melon counts, short-changing the grocers. Our subsequent argument ended with me walking down the road with my backpack and my last week's pay.

I had enough cash to survive until later in the summer, when we were to start another job we had already lined up in northern California. I spent the next six weeks backpacking in the Coastal Range Mountains along the Oregon coast. I tried various Eastern meditation techniques, with mixed results: sometimes feeling I'd nearly reached the feeling of leaving the body, which I was striving so hard to recover. At other times feeling isolated and alone, and at still others feeling like my head was being squeezed in a vise.

Then I read Jiddu Krishnamurti's *You Are the World.* Krishnamurti frowned on formal meditation as an escape from confronting the environment and the world as it is. He referred to mediation while concentrating on a mantra or objects or thoughts (as is done in most forms of meditation) as a form of evading the world as it is. His views aligned with some of great Zen Buddhist masters of China and Japan, who suggested that mind-quiet, full perception of the here and now was achieved by letting go and simply being where one was, fully. Krishnamurti suggested that if one simply developed the discipline of observing, and not following distracting thoughts, one would see a world he had been missing his entire life. It was not difficult to do this in such a wide-open, beautiful environment as the Oregon coastline. After practicing the lack of effort required for detaching for some time in that environment, the way I looked at the world was shifting. I became far more extroverted and more concerned with living things other than myself. I felt I was beginning to be able to perceive life force – the massless spirit of living things, as opposed to their physical bodies. I began to get short glimpses of my previous full-blown out-of-body experience. After those weeks in the mountains I never again had the inclination to take drugs, nor did I take any.

In late summer I hitchhiked to Clear Lake, California, and reunited with my buddy Steve. The lake is a large, relatively shallow body of water. It is in the center of pear country, with orchards stretching for miles. Steve and I decided we would stay in the migrant workers' camp while working at Mt. Konocti pear packing plant. The migrant camp was simple – rows of dusty camp spaces and tents, punctuated by fire pits. There was a handful of dilapidated junker cars scattered around the camp. There were unevenly-ripped sheets of canvas nailed to oak trees and anchored with heavy odds and ends on the dusty ground. Folks were clad in dirty, worn-out Salvation Army second-hands. Steve and I were the only Anglos in the place. The rest of the inhabitants were Spanish speaking, Mexican and Mexican-American migrant workers. We were accepted, and we both considered it just the type of adventure we were seeking.

The Mt. Konacti plant was a beehive of activity from the crack of dawn until sunset. Huge conveyer belts rumbled, loaded with pears automatically culled for size. Pears that made the mass grade were shunted onto other belts that passed rows of women, predominantly Latinas, who lightly held their hands inches above the belt so the pears would roll; this revealed defective fruits, which were then removed. The pears that made the quality grade moved on toward another group of women, who carefully enveloped each one in a sheet of paper with the Mt. Konakti label. Then, gently but rapidly, they placed them in boxes, in neat rows. Behind the ladies a group of men, also predominantly Latinos, put tops on the boxes as they were filled, and then lifted and stacked the boxes on wooden pallets several yards away.

A team of a dozen forklift operators, all Anglo, swooped in to lift the pallets as they filled, then swung out of the packing plant sheds into a large cement yard where double flat-bed trailer big-rigs awaited. When a trailer was nearly filled, its driver would be alerted so that the second he had a full load, he pulled out with his bounty, headed for distributors all across the country.

Steve and I, being Anglo, got forklift gigs. The head of the forklift corps was none other than the handsome, well-built Roland Wages. Or, as he used to announce on pay day, "I'm Rollin' in the Wages." Roland was from a different class of migrant worker. He had a real trailer, but it was parked down at a cleaner campground, miles away. Roland took great pride in his neat jeans, western shirt, and spit-shined cowboy boots. He was even more proud of his thick, jet-black, neatly-trimmed hair. He would take an exaggerated split-leg posture and dramatically use both hands and arms to comb his well-greased bangs straight back – several times a day. Roland was dead certain he was God's gift to women. He was about our age, but his culture was 1950s all the way.

Roland had no use for a couple of Kerouacian dharma bums like Steve and me, but he'd save his overt contempt for those lower in the pecking order: those of darker skin and limited English. Despite having to answer to the reincarnation of Elvis (two kings in one summer was a bit much for me) the forklift races were a riot. The drivers would regularly bet on who could fill a truck the fastest, and the pavement was black with skid marks from the radical short cuts we'd maneuver. Once I nearly rolled mine; however, instinctively putting out a foot to break my anticipated fall, I became perhaps the first man in history to run over his own toe with a forklift.

One hot afternoon at the lunch break, all employees gathered around the back of the plant, where pear tossing trials were held. The following weekend, the winner was to represent Mt. Konocti at the

Clear County Fair competition between all plants in the area. For 20 minutes the migrant workers fought it out among themselves. Then, strutting from the packing shed came Roland, making a big production of unbuttoning and stripping off his shirt to reveal his tight-fitting wife-beater t-shirt. "Move aside, boys," he announced, as he strode toward a stack of pears. "Billy," he said to his side-kick, "run out to that big ol' oak and spot this one. Roland Wages is about to shatter the Mt. Konocti record." Billy complied, dashing nearly a hundred yards to the end of the clearing, where a huge, lone oak stood. None of the previous pears had come close to the tree.

Roland took several light practice throws, then performed a dramatic wind up. Unlike the previous contestants, Roland took several strides – including three large ones past the throwing line that had been clearly etched into the dirt. He gracefully scampered back behind the line, then dramatically pointed to the missile he had launched. The crowd went silent as the pear sailed, landed 30 yards from the tree and rolled at a fast clip toward it. Billy chased it down, turned around and hollered back, "Rolled right up to the damn root system. Its a new record!" A cheer went up from Roland's entourage. Roland smiled at the workers. "Anyone want to take one final shot at that? Be my guest." Nobody dared go against the foreman.

On an impulse, I stood up and headed toward the pear pile. With no warm-up, I took three large strides and put every fiber I had into the heave. The pear had a far lower trajectory than Roland's, but it was travelling at twice the speed. Splat! The pear landed right in the center of the trunk of the oak tree and exploded. My shoulder was on fire, and pain shot down through my arm to my fingers. It took everything I had to not show it was affecting me. I turned around and calmly looked at Roland. He looked at me as if he wanted to kill me. Mumbling something to his crew, he turned and they all took off together. As soon as Roland was out of sight, I grasped my right shoulder with my left arm and let out a scream.

Even though I had just inflicted an injury that would nag me for most of the rest of my life, I felt contented around the migrant campfire that evening. We drank beer with the co-workers, and they treated me with a great deal of affinity – after all, I had put Roland in his place. That happy moment of road-adventure pleasure was suddenly interrupted by an administrator from the plant calling out my name out. When he located me he said, "Your father wants you to call him; he said it's an emergency." And just like that, I was awakened from my living dream. I phoned my dad from the pay phone in front of the packing shed. I'd never heard him so shook up. He was grief stricken.

"It's your brother Bruce. He flipped again. Mark, for crying out loud, I'm at the end of my rope. I can't do anything else for him."

"What happened?"

"He started another brawl, then fought the cops, and now he's locked up in a hospital for the criminally insane, outside of Portland. I hope you understand. I've done all I can do. I'm done with it."

"Oh, Jeez, What about Scott, can't he do anything?"

"No, you know he couldn't care less. For Christ's sake, he pushed him into this whole mess. They were doing a job for me up there, and were living together in an apartment. You know Scott, he'd needle Bruce non-stop."

"Yeah, I know."

"But I'll tell you – I can't do another thing. I've tried to have him live here, I've tried to employ him. I can't do another damn thing. I'm done."

"Don't worry Dad, I'll take care of it"

"What are you going to do?"

"I don't know...first thing I'm going to do is go see him...then I'll take it from there."

"Jesus, I'm sorry Mark – there just isn't anything else I can do."

"Don't worry dad, I'll take care of it," I reassured him.

He ended the call with a word of warning, "You take care of yourself. If you feel yourself being dragged down, get the hell out of there, do you hear me? Last thing I need is you flipping."

It took me two days of hitchhiking to get to Portland, so I had plenty of time to reflect.

I had mixed feelings. On the one hand, Bruce had seemed to find a way to drag me down whenever I was in pursuit of my own dreams. On the other hand, I felt a tremendous sense of empathy for him, and felt I had an obligation. When our mother died, Bruce had taken me under his wing. He was a gregarious nine-year-old, and adventurous kids flocked to him. He would regularly lead expeditions through the foothills surrounding Mt. Tamalpias, and up the mountain itself, near our home in Mill Valley. We'd leave early in the morning and sometimes not return until after dark. Bruce protected me like a she-gator protects her young. Hazing of me by the older boys was strictly prohibited. When we moved to Southern California three years later, Bruce went from extrovert to introvert almost immediately. He never had another close friend, and he never participated in extracurricular school activities.

When I arrived in Portland, I first met with my eldest brother Scott in his one-bedroom apartment, in an old tenement building by the railroad yard. Scott held a degree in psychology, and I thought he might have some useful input on the task ahead of me. Even though I was aware Scott reveled in driving Bruce to the edge, his level of disinterest in Bruce's plight was disappointing. Although Bruce had been in the joint for three days by then, Scott had not even bothered to visit him.

"What am I supposed to do? He's not my problem." he explained.

I countered, "You're a psychology graduate, Scott. You must have some idea how to deal with this."

"Oh, the little savior marches into Portland to save the fucking day! I'll give you my psychological evaluation: you've got a goddamn Jesus Christ complex. Now, *that* is classified as a mental disorder."

"No, I didn't ask what I could do, I asked what *you* could do. You're the second coming of Sigmund Freud, aren't you?"

"If you think a merry prankster like yourself can suddenly walk in and perform miracles, you've eaten one too many peyote buttons."

"For Christ's sake, Scott! I just want to help, and I'm asking what you can contribute to the effort. And you are attacking me."

"There is no help for a guy like that. He's fruit loops, loony tunes, flip city. If I were you, I'd go back to granola munching and bear wrestling in the mountains." He let out a howl – he had an irritating habit of laughing at his own strings of one-liner insults. I recognized I would have to go this adventure alone.

CHAPTER FOUR

CUCKOO'S NEST

One Flew Over the Cuckoo's Nest (1962) is a novel written by Ken Kesey. Set in an Oregon asylum, the narrative serves as a study of the institutional process and the human mind, as well as a critique of Behaviorism and a celebration of humanistic principles. – Wikipedia

It was dark when I walked up the long driveway toward the entrance to Dammasch State Hospital for the Criminally Insane. I couldn't put my finger on what it was exactly, but I had an eerie feeling that I had been there before. There was heaviness and tension in the air that seemed to get thicker the closer I approached. The front door was locked. I lit a Camel and thought about what Scott had said; maybe he was right, maybe I am powerless to accomplish anything here.

A few minutes passed before a janitor came out the front door. I persuaded him to at least let me into a sparsely-furnished lobby area where I might be able to contact the orderly of my brother's wing, via intercom. After several calls I finally located Arnold, the psychiatric nurse on duty in Bruce's ward. He said it was past visiting hours, but he was on his way out to go home and he'd see me in the lobby.

Arnold was a diminutive psychiatric graduate student in his mid to late twenties. He had a patchy dark beard, thick glasses and greasy, black, medium-length hair. His skin was pale and his eyes were pink around the edges. He was an introvert and of a very serious demeanor. He struck me as someone who, by personality and personal bearing, was the least-qualified candidate imaginable for supervising 30 mad men's recovery.

Arnold confirmed my brother was on his ward, but he knew next to nothing about him, except that he had been under sedation since he arrived. He said that I would have to return during visiting hours the next afternoon to see him. I related some of my history, how my brother had no one else, and what I'd gone through to arrive there. I pleaded with him to please give me five minutes, just to let my brother know I was there for him. Arnold reluctantly agreed, warning me that should I stir up the ward in any way, Arnold would be held to account. I promised him I'd slip in and out like a church mouse.

Arnold led me down sterile, dark corridors to a nursing station. Its thick glass windows looked out onto a large open room. We walked through the room, around a pool table that sat in the middle, and past a group of 20 chairs that faced an elevated television screen. Arnold unlocked another door, which had a small window protected by heavy metal mesh. Inside were 30 beds, neatly but narrowly spaced. Two dim night lights afforded murky vision. Arnold said he was not sure which one was Bruce, but warned me not to wake anyone. I walked softly down the rows of beds, noting face after face. Though each man was deep in sleep, every one bore a countenance of hopelessness. I had the feeling I was walking through a morgue.

Finally, I found Bruce. I sat at his bedside, gently grabbed his hand and squeezed. "Bruce, it's me, Mark." Bruce's breathing sputtered for a moment, then one eye opened. It was the most chilling moment of my life up to that point: he showed no recognition whatsoever. Zero. His eye was a pitch-black pit, no sparkle of life anywhere.

"Bruce, I'm here to get you out, my brother."

He just stared upward, lifeless. Not a single body movement, not a single sign of life beyond his troubled breathing. He closed his eyes and went back to sleep as if nothing had happened.

I leaned down and hugged him, but there was no response whatsoever. I whispered in his ear, "Bruce, I swear to you, I'm getting you out of here." Bruce looked up at me for a second and mumbled, "Oh, uh-huh," then closed his eyes again.

As I followed Arnold back through the corridors, I was numb. When we got back outside, Arnold noticed tears crawling down my face. "I understand," is all he said.

"What did you all do to him, shock him back to the stone ages?" I asked.

"No, Mark, he's on Stelazine is all. For violent types it is considered necessary."

"No, there is no drug that can do that – he's gone, his lights are out. He didn't even recognize me."

"Well, Stelazine is pretty powerful. Some call it the chemical straitjacket."

"Well Arnold, I want him off that stuff."

"The doctor prescribes, I have no power over that."

I pressed Arnold to tell me the program laid out for my brother's recovery. He could only answer with vague generalities about "maintenance" and "control." "Cure" and "rehabilitation" were conspicuously absent from the soliloquy. Ultimately, after continued pressure, Arnold acknowledged that he was frustrated; his only job seemed to be administering medications, and calling for orderlies if they didn't seem to "bite" sufficiently. He said he was touched by my level of concern, and that he seldom saw family visit patients, let alone demand results. He promised he would help me if he could find any way to do so.

As we walked across an empty parking lot toward Arnold's car, I said, "Arnold, I gotta tell you, this place really gives me the creeps. I could swear I've been here before, but I know I haven't."

Arnold replied, "Mark, did you ever see the film *One Flew Over the Cuckoo's Nest?"*

"Yes, and I read the book twice."

"Well, this is where they filmed the movie, maybe that's it."

Over the next several afternoon visits, I realized Arnold was right. It was just like *Cuckoo's Nest* in several respects, with one big exception: in the *real* Dammasch, some roles were reversed from the book and movie. In Ken Kesey's book, Nurse Ratched was the villainous, unmerciful control freak, getting in the road of the well-meaning psychiatrist. In real life, it was the meek, well-meaning psychiatric nurse, nervously navigating around the arbitrary dictates of the unsympathetic psychiatrist.

Dr. Stern – as I'll call him eponymously, since I cannot recall his real name – operated like the Wizard of Oz. Hiding behind a maze of administrators, it took several days before I was able to speak with him – and even then, only by phone.

I asked, "Doctor, what has he got?"

"How old are you?" came the non-sequitur, cold response.

"I'm twenty."

"So you are his younger brother. How you could be considered guardian is beyond me."

"Ok, my father sent me – he's in California. I'm all my brother has got. What disease did you diagnose him with?"

"I haven't. He hasn't had a full evaluation yet."

"Can we do something to cut back on the drugs? I can't reach him – he acts like a zombie."

"I'm afraid not."

"But doctor, if you haven't diagnosed him, how can you have him strapped down in the chemical straitjacket?"

"Where did you hear that term, 'chemical straitjacket?'" he snapped.

"Hell, I don't know."

"Well, using such pejorative labels is counter-productive."

"Look, I'm sorry, I didn't mean any disrespect. It's just that I've seen him for five days running and I have yet to see any sign he recognizes me. It is frightening – I've never seen my brother in worse shape. He's dying in there. Please, I just want to help."

"You are going to have to wait for the full evaluation. Friends and family have no say in medication decisions."

"Sir, I understand. But it occurred to me, isn't his heavily-drugged state going to throw a monkey wrench into the evaluation process?"

"I've got to go. Your brother is not my only patient. Good bye."

By comparison, Arnold – despite his personality betraying a bundle of worrying nerves – was like a breath of fresh air. The first week with my brother was depressing. It would take me an hour to persuade him to shuffle along the wall with me for a short walk around the ward. Once up, he would sometimes mumble distress at some distraction in the environment. I would steer him to the window and start directing his attention to anything I could – the trees, the groundskeeper cruising on his lawn mower, anything. He would calm down. That is as far as I got that first week. But I persuaded Arnold to lighten up on his medication so I could reach him more. Arnold was terrified about the consequences he would face should it be found out. But after I told him some stories about how Bruce had taken care of me in childhood, and how I'd handled him after the VA hospital incarceration, he agreed – "But just a little less, for starters."

The next week was better. Bruce could not discuss anything more significant than environmental distractions like Eddie jerking off in the middle of the TV room. Eddie was at it, stroking his hard penis so loudly that several others watching the TV were getting restless. Eddie took pleasure in drawing their ire. "Oh yeah, baby!'" he screamed, "whoo-haaa!" Bruce started to wake up, "I'll kill the fucking weasel if he doesn't knock it off." When it looked like Bruce was about to snap, I instinctively grabbed a pool cue, walked in front of the TV and called out, "Hey, fast Eddie, you want to stroke a hard stick? Come in the rec room and I'll kick your sad, lunatic ass in pool!" The patients started laughing and chiding Eddie.

"Oh yeah?" Eddie yelled back, standing, "You and what fucking army? Let's get it on."

"Not till you tuck your dick back in your pants."

Eddie stuffed his penis back in and walked toward the pool table with his boner covered by his pajamas. The ward gathered around the table. Eddie was on fire, telling war stories about his purported pool exploits. We played a sloppy game of eight ball that went on for half an hour. But Eddie, Bruce, and several others were gathered around, having a hell of a time. I caught a glimpse of Arnold looking up from his paperwork several times. He seemed interested in the activity, but didn't seem to want any responsibility for it, in the event things got out of hand.

After I'd let Eddie beat me, Bruce played the winner. I refereed; which was necessary with all the balls knocked off the table, and accidentally knocked into holes by unsteady hands. Every dispute turned into a raucous argument, but ultimately, I made the final call. Several others lined up for "next game." After two hours the ward was still, the inmates exhausted. Arnold came in with no orderlies accompanying him – which was a first. He announced it was time to wash up for dinner. Arnold was helping recalcitrant patients out of their chairs, and gently pushing them along to the sinks – another first. It seemed that my exercising of the patients wore them out and made them mellow enough for Arnold to directly interact with. When I finished saying good bye to my brother and began to leave the ward, Arnold caught up to me and grabbed my arm. "Mark, thank you." "Arnold, thank you", I replied as I left.

I had enough savings from summer work to put down a first-and-last-month payment on a studio apartment on the southwest side of town. It wasn't much. The fourth-floor apartment looked straight across at an expressway, less than one hundred yards away, and it was loud. I told Bruce it was better than it was – like it had a view – to get him to want to come out with me. After a couple of weeks of Arnold's cooperation with reducing his drugs, Bruce was able to attain conditional release. He was ordered to report in to the University Medical Center Emergency Room if he had the slightest relapse. He was not allowed to drive, and had a prescription.

The environment I had arranged did not help Bruce much. He would wrap his head in pillows and roll around restless most nights. Still, we did make progress with taking long walks, and then hikes in the hills surrounding Portland. When my money began to run out, I started job hunting.

While I was away one day looking for a job Bruce connected up with a fellow in the apartment complex who gave him some street drugs to supplement the psych meds. Bruce started getting more erratic. Then one day when I came home, Bruce was gone. I went to the druggie down the hall and asked what had happened. He told me Bruce had taken some amyl nitrate, freaked out and wound up in the emergency room. I ran several miles to the ER, only to learn Bruce had already been transferred back to Dammasch. I was distraught. After several miles of walking, I decided I was incapable of dealing with insanity – and that if I did not remove myself from the environment soon, I too would go insane.

I had 25 dollars to my name – just as I had when I'd left college several months earlier. I decided that was it; I was going to the Greyhound station downtown, go south as far as 25 dollars would take me, and then hitchhike to Mexico. I would do field work as an illegal immigrant south of the border. I thought that might be a far more rewarding adventure than the current one.

CHAPTER FIVE

INTRODUCTION TO SCIENTOLOGY

Scientology: An applied religious philosophy dealing with the study of knowledge, which through the application of its technology can bring about desirable changes in the conditions of life. – L Ron Hubbard

That evening, I strode down the south sidewalk of Salmon Street in my shorts and big hiking boots. My thumbs were tucked under the shoulder straps of a large yellow backpack that contained all my earthly possessions. Looking across the street at the Church of Scientology Mission of Portland, I surveyed the intersection ahead for Scientology's street promoters. I used to get a kick out of playfully jawing with them as I passed. On the opposite corner I spotted the bearded fellow who coordinated the street group.

"Hey, Bud!" I yelled. Bud turned, smiled and waved.

"You won't have me here to kick around anymore," I hollered.

"Where you headed?"

"Mexico way. Good luck with saving the world."

Bud chuckled, then turned around to continue briefing one of his new "body routers." Their job was to route bodies into the Mission for some orientation, and hopefully a course sign-up. I was always on the move, so never stopped to talk to the Scientology body routers for long. They seemed like friendly folks, though, and we'd trade pleasantries from time to time.

As I crossed the Salmon/Broadway intersection, one block from the Greyhound station, I saw Mark on the corner I was headed for. Mark was about my age, and wore big, black-framed eye glasses. Mark seemed more analytical and conservative than I, which is probably why I never had much interaction with him. He smiled at me as I passed. I stopped and said, "Mark, I gotta catch a bus, so you're not going to sell me anything – but since I don't see any other potential customers around, can you take a moment to tell me what it is you all do in there?"

"Sure," Mark said, "basically, we specialize in communication."

"No kidding?"

"Yeah, I mean you can break down just about any problem in human relations to a problem in communication."

"You know, I've just been through some pretty heavy shit and I think you all might be onto something."

"Well, a lot of people seem to be able to turn their lives around just by doing our introductory communication course." Mark gave me a short description of what the "Comm Course" consisted of. We rapped for about 20 minutes on that corner, talking about what I had been through with my brother and how that related to failures of communication.

Then I asked, "How much do you charge for this Comm Course?"

"Fifty bucks," he replied.

"Too bad. I only have 25 bucks, and about 1,500 miles to travel."

"Well, I think I can get you enrolled for 25, if you pay cash."

I laughed, "You think a rambler like me carries a check book?"

We went to the Mission to close the deal. Mark threw in a complimentary copy of *Dianetics: The Modern Science of Mental Health*, by Scientology's founder L. Ron Hubbard. The "mental health" subtitle obviously piqued my interest. I found a lot of the fundamentals in the book to be in alignment with the experiences I'd had with Bruce. For example, Hubbard talked about what he called "the three valid therapies": health (diet, exercise), change of environment, and education. That was what I had sort of naturally been trying to do with Bruce – and with some results. But this cat Hubbard had the whole business codified. Just like that, I was beginning to think I was back in the ball game. I decided that with this book, some communication skills, and some folks who knew something about the mind to consult, man, I could bring my brother back to life.

The first step of the communication course was to learn how to comfortably occupy a position in space while facing another person. The first gradient (that is, the first step in a gradually increasing series of steps) was to face another student who was seated across from one, three feet away – both students with eyes closed. I found the exercise therapeutic – especially after a few weeks of bouncing around in a mental institution. It was like the purest form of Zen meditation. No tricks or vias, such as mantras and the like. Instead the idea was to simply be there – and eventually to conquer, through non-effort, every urge or influence the mind and body might toss out, to get you to do something *other* than simply be there comfortably.

The next gradient was to assume the same positions, but this time to comfortably face the other person with one's eyes open. Any fidget, movement, twitch, eye watering, or other physical movement under the sun, moon and stars received a "flunk" from the supervisor. Like most all Scientology courses, there was no "teacher" – just a "supervisor" who made sure drills were being done correctly, and helped students out when needed. To me this new drill was sort of an exercise, aimed at accomplishing what Krishnamurti advised: to train oneself to simply observe, with no additives whatsoever.

They called these drills the "TRs" or training routines. Back then, even students fresh off the street were made to do these drills in the fashion Hubbard called "the hard way." The supervisors were friendly, but tough – insisting you do the drills "by the book," and persist until you'd mastered each one. The supervisors were trained to always coach the drill on a gradient – one small step at a time, with a "win" at each step, improving all the while. I liked the discipline and the challenge – they recalled my basketball training days.

The most irritating and painful reactions would turn on and off while doing the drill – but you had to keep at it regardless, until you could do it comfortably for up to an hour or more at a time. At one point my shoulder hurt as if I were reliving the moment of the Mt. Konocti pear-tossing injury. But every time I shifted my body in the slightest to take some pressure off the aching shoulder, the coach or supervisor was on me at once with a crisp, "Flunk. You moved your shoulder. Start!"

Eye watering, eye soreness, reliving of other earlier accidents – it all turned on during the TRs. But after many hours of drilling, with encouragement from coach and supervisors (including reference to some of Hubbard's writings, like the principle that "the way out is the way through," all those pains and discomforts would dissipate and finally disappear. All manner of mental pictures would arise, many packing a sensation of mass or creating drowsiness.

The original intention behind the drills was to instill people training to be auditors (Scientology counselors) with some good discipline, and to give them an understanding of the elements of communication. But whether the student intended to become an auditor or not, once in a while something really remarkable would occur during TRs done "the hard way."

During a particularly grueling drill session on TRs, it seemed like every injury or accident I had ever suffered surfaced to torment me again. This went on for an hour or more, but each time some new pain or discomfort appeared, I paid no attention to it. Instead, I continued to do nothing but comfortably face the person in front of me. And invariably the pains disappeared. After 20 more minutes of simply sitting there comfortably, I began to feel as though my forehead had disappeared. Instead of looking through two peephole windows (my eyes) I was looking through a magnificent wrap-around aquarium glass. Though this was startling, I didn't want to risk reacting – and having to start the drill all over again. So I continued to follow the instructions: "Do nothing other than sit comfortably, facing the student in front of you."

The aquarium glass continued to grow until it was as if there was no obstruction or limitation to my vision whatsoever. I felt myself slowly rising above my own head. I continued to rise until I was looking down from where the ceiling met the wall behind my chair. I could see everything in the room. I could see the top of my head, I could see the three supervisors – two of whom were thoroughly outside my line of sight within the head. Being a skeptical sort, I mentally noted objects in the room, assuming I'd wind up back in my head. I wanted to prove to myself this was not some kind of hallucination. Here was the identical phenomena I had experienced in the Fallbrook gym: the clean separation of *me,* the spirit, from the body – with full perception of my surroundings. However, rather than lasting mere seconds, this time it was sustained for minutes.

The supervisor walked over to me. "That's it," he said. "How are you doing?"

I replied, "I am up on the ceiling looking down at this entire course room."

Very gently he said, "Okay. Pass. You can stay there for as long as you like, or come down whenever you feel like it."

From the way the supervisor reacted, it was clear this occurrence came as no surprise. I noticed my twin (student drilling partner) was looking puzzled. "Exteriorization," as I learned this phenomenon was regularly referred to in Scientology, was not something he had experienced or thought possible. I began to worry about explaining it to him, and almost simultaneously I found myself assuming a viewpoint around my head – although not necessarily just from within it.

I tried to get back up the wall, but I couldn't. The harder I tried, the more I went in. Finally I quit trying, and moved naturally into a comfortable position, as if hovering partially in and partially out of my head. My peripheral vision was extended far beyond normal. I turned my head and looked around the course room to verify the items I had spotted were in their proper places. A clipboard, a portrait of Hubbard on a wall, an unused chair positioned at a particular angle. It all checked out. I continued to sit there in peaceful awe after the course was dismissed. The supervisor came over and sat in front of me, smiling.

"Man, does this happen with everyone?" I asked.

He said, "I think ultimately with most people, but not necessarily on the TRs."

"What percentage on the TRs, do you think?" I asked.

"Well, there are different degrees. Were you able to see from up there?"

"Yes, in fact I noted objects in the room, then later verified they were where I had seen them when I was out of the head."

"Well, that's called 'exterior with full perception.' It's not too common. Maybe 30 to 50 percent of students will get some level of feeling exterior. But I'd say – what are there, like 27 people on course now? Two others currently on course have reported full exteriorization like yours. It isn't the purpose of the drill, but if you really apply yourself, it happens."

"Man, I read that stuff about thetan (Scientology word for spirit), mind, and body being three separate entities, and it made sense. But to experience it so clearly..."

"Yeah, well, enjoy your win. Well done."

I really liked the firm but caring discipline exercised by the course supervisors. They were trained to push the students and clearly invalidate wrong procedure, while at the same time validating the person himself by commending what he was doing right. There was a group spirit and camaraderie among the course staff, like that of a good ball team. It was, in a way, the meeting of the two most important and consistent lessons of my life: the quest for the spiritual, with the structure and agreement of team sports. This view was later reinforced by Hubbard books, which described Scientology as being the marriage of the spiritual philosophy of the East with the methodical, scientifically disciplined approach of the West.

After the class was over, I stayed around the Mission thumbing through books. A staff member showed me some Hubbard references about exteriorization. The phenomenon was so common during the course of Scientology practices that an entire body of work had been developed about it.

Finally, at about 11:30 that night, the last staff started to turn out the lights and clear out. The streets of Portland were empty, and wet from recent rain. The traffic lights from intersection after intersection cast incredibly beautiful mosaic patterns across the roads. I walked the three miles to my apartment.

As I was passing by a big park, I began noticing my perceptions were intensely keen. It was almost like being on acid, but far more natural, and the perceptions were far more real. I began moving above my head again. Without resisting, I continued to stride along, simply enjoying the cool, clean air going in and out of my lungs. I started seeing the park on my side of the road, and the buildings on the other, from what seemed to be 10 feet above my body.

I had walked for several blocks before I started trying to figure it all out again; when I did that, I came back down. Amazing – it requires absolutely no effort, and that is a skill in itself. Put the slightest bit of attention on mechanics or effort, and the phenomenon is gone.

I would come to learn that the Comm Course and its TRs were originally developed by Hubbard to train Scientology counselors, called "auditors." He coined "auditor" from its Latin root *audire*, meaning "to listen." An auditor's essential function is to listen.

More than any other factor, Hubbard clearly distinguished Scientology counseling from other forms, both religious and psychological, by its communication discipline – and that is what the TRs were all about. That discipline begins with gaining the ability to sit comfortably for as long as a counseling session might go, listening without reacting, evaluating or invalidating, overtly or covertly.

The gradient of difficulty is then increased to performing the "being there" drill while one's coach (drilling partner) throws out every insult and distraction he can think of, all to make one flinch, laugh, or react in any way. Once that step is mastered, the next drill works on developing the ability to speak clearly, naturally and with sufficient attention to get a spoken communication across to the coach (or, in an auditing session, to the person one is counseling).

Next, one drills on the ability to duplicate and understand communications from the person being counseled, and then acknowledging in such a fashion that the person is completely assured that you've heard and understood. In the next two drills, all the elements of the earlier drills are combined, and new elements added, to drill a mock auditing session, with communication flowing smoothly and with certainty, back and forth. Critical in this training is overcoming the impulse to be *interesting*, instead being fully *interested* in the other person and what he or she has to say.

It all sounds simple. And it is, in theory. With these drills you are training someone to perfect the art of communicating effectively, with simplicity and compassion. But when you break that seemingly simple activity down into its elements and drill them, it takes quite a bit of discipline and conscientious work to master and finally combine them all, naturally and effortlessly.

Over the next several weeks I would learn how the TRs fit in to the entire Scientology program. The TRs are the bedrock upon which the technologies and Dianetics and Scientology function. The term "technology" is used in Scientology to denote the methodology of auditing a person from a state of no knowledge of the subject on up to the highest spiritual states attainable through Scientology counseling. In practice, Scientology's technology is differentiated from its policy. "Policy" is used to refer to Scientology writings on the subjects of groups, organizations and their effective functioning and administration. Policy is sometimes referred to as Scientology administrative technology.

Ultimately, for legal purposes, the church of Scientology defined all of L. Ron Hubbard's writings and recorded spoken words on Scientology (whether about technology or administrative policy) as constituting the "scripture" of Scientology.

The foundations of Scientology are set forth in L. Ron Hubbard's book, *Dianetics: The Modern Science of Mental Health. Dianetics* introduced the idea that the human mind could be viewed as consisting of two main parts. First, there is the *analytical mind* – the part of the mind we consciously use, day in and day out, to carry out rational, survival activities. Dianetics postulated that, unless interfered with, the analytical mind is an infallible computer.

The second major portion of the mind is called the *reactive mind.* Here is found the interference that fouls the analytical mind, pushing us into irrational and reactive behavior and undesirable emotional and mental states. Hubbard postulated that all of our more base, animalistic irrationalities, urges and drives are dictated by this reactive mind.

According to Dianetics theory, humans evolved a reactive mind during tooth-and-claw times, when constant stimulus-response reactivity was vital to survival. The reactive mind records all perceptions during moments of unconsciousness and pain – when the organism's survival is most severely threatened, and immediate action is necessary to avoid further pain and possibly death.

Later on, if circumstances and perceptions similar to those in the earlier painful incident appear (similar stimuli) the reactive mind responds by forcing the person to behave as he or she did in the original incident – based on the crude reasoning that if the person survived by behaving that way before, the same behavior now should also result in survival. Such "reasoning" and action might sometimes work for lower animals (where the mechanism originally developed), but for a human – a highly-developed and intelligent organism – it is far more of a liability than a survival aid.

The liability of the reactive mind was magnified enormously as humanity developed language. That is because the reactive mind's stimulus-response character takes the words perceived during an incident of pain and reduced consciousness literally, and later feeds them back to the person. This creates, in effect, a post-hypnotic-suggestion. In this way the reactive mind overrides or influences the analytical mind, causing the individual to think and act irrationally.

The technology of Dianetics involves mentally returning to and recounting the moments of pain and unconsciousness in our lives. This is done so thoroughly as to nearly, in effect, *relive* them. The idea is that our resistance to fully viewing such incidents allows them to remain in place – with the force they contain (such as the mentally recorded force of a blow to the head, many years before) enabling them to dictate later actions. Such an incident of pain and unconsciousness is called an "engram." When completely viewed, the emotional or mental "charge," or force, is relieved. Dianetics is, in essence, a formalized, regimented regression therapy.

Each time we relieve such an incident, the memory of the occasion becomes available to the analytical mind. This in turn increases our rational or analytical memory and potential, as well as our outlook and abilities. When we relieve enough of these painful incidents, and have restored our hidden memories to the analytical mind, we achieve a state called "Clear." The term comes from the button on a calculator which clears a previous computation, so that the machine can be used to address a new problem. And that is the goal of Dianetics: to clear the mind of the wrong answers that have been entered into it through painful past experiences.

The activity of relieving engrams is one of the objectives of Dianetics and Scientology counseling (auditing). As mentioned earlier, the counselor is called an auditor. The person being counseled is called a preclear (someone on the route to achieving the state of Clear).

As Dianetics was more extensively practiced and its results were analyzed by Hubbard, matters became a bit more complicated. The further practitioners of Dianetics regressed down the mind's track of incidents (called the "time track") and the more awareness and perception was returned to the analytical portion of the mind, the further back in time the auditor and preclear could venture. Before long, Dianeticists were reporting contact with incidents that had occurred in previous lifetimes. This led to the conclusion that people are not simply genetic entities. The "I" – the being viewing and reporting on these incidents stored in the mind, evidently transcended and outlived the genetic body, carrying on after death to start the cycle of birth-life-death all over again in a new body. The "I" had occupied many different bodies, over many lifetimes. It was resolved that this "I" must be what had been referred to in other subjects as the spirit.

So as to avoid confusion of this discovery with terms and ideas from other subjects, Hubbard coined the term "thetan" to describe the spiritual being. He took 'thetan' from the Greek letter *theta*, which has traditionally been used to symbolize the concept of "thought" or "spirit." In Hubbard's philosophy, then, the thetan is the spiritual being – the essence and true identity of any person.

Dianetics proceeded from the fundamental premise that the lowest common denominator of life was the urge to survive. With the discovery and validation of the existence of the thetan, it was recognized that the spiritual essence of a person was not *of* the physical universe – not truly subject to the concepts of time or survival. It became apparent that the lowest common denominator of life could no longer be said to be survival. After all, a thetan was not inherently part of the create-survive-destroy cycle of the physical universe – a concept understood in spiritual circles since before the time of the Buddha, Siddhartha Gautama. The thetan could not *help* but survive; it was immortal.

An entirely new echelon of axioms was conceived, beginning with the premise that the essential and common purpose of life was the creation of an effect. This led to the idea that the effects that life force could create were uncharted and presumably unlimited. Out of this new work, a "post-graduate" study of Dianetics evolved.

Coined from the Greek *scio,* "knowing," and the Latin *logos,* "study of," the word "Scientology" was born. Hubbard, not presuming to have all the answers, but ever curious and eager to learn more of them, postulated that Scientology would be an unadulterated, non-politicized, and incorruptible search for ultimate truth, meaning, and immortality. Whereas Dianetics approached an individual from the perspective of removing negatives (incidents of pain and unconsciousness, and the reactive mind itself), Scientology approached the individual more with a view toward rehabilitating and regaining native and inherent spiritual abilities.

Scientology auditing theory and practice are built upon the assumptions set forth in the first ten Axioms of Scientology:

Axiom One: Life is basically a static. (Definition: A life static has no mass, no motion, no wavelength, no location in space or in time. It has the ability to postulate and to perceive.) (Definition: In Scientology, the word 'postulate' means to cause a thinkingness or consideration. It is a specially applied word and is defined as causative thinkingness.)

Axiom Two: The static is capable of considerations, postulates and opinions.

Axiom Three: Space, energy, objects, form and time are the results of considerations made and/or agreed upon or not by the static, and are perceived solely because the static considers that it can perceive them.

Axiom Four: Space is a viewpoint of dimension. (Space is caused by looking out from a point. The only actuality of space is the agreed-upon consideration that one perceives through *something, and this we call space.)*

Axiom Five: Energy consists of postulated particles in space. (One considers that energy exists and that he can perceive energy. One also considers that energy behaves according to certain agreed-upon laws. These assumptions and considerations are the totality of energy.)

Axiom Six: Objects consist of grouped particles and solids.

Axiom Seven: Time is basically a postulate that space and particles will persist. (The rate of their persistence is what we measure with clocks and the motion of heavenly bodies.)

Axiom Eight: The apparency of time is the change of position of particles in space.

Axiom Nine: Change is the primary manifestation of time.

Axiom Ten: The highest purpose in the universe is the creation of an effect.

Scientology evolved over the next two decades, through Hubbard's continual experimentation and exploration, seeking the most workable route to bring a thetan to the highest attainable levels of truth, awareness and ability.

Hubbard likened his creation of a gradient approach toward enlightenment to the building of a bridge across a chasm, from a lower plane of existence to a higher one. He called the prescribed

Scientology route for spiritual improvement 'the Bridge.'

In crossing this bridge, initially one addresses the things that are currently fixating one's attention and holding one back in life. A variety of short study courses are offered, to help one tackle such problems. Alternatively (or additionally) one can partake of a short program of auditing called "Life Repair," specifically addressing, through auditing sessions, self-imposed barriers that are ruining one's life. Continuing in auditing, an individual would next embark upon the Scientology Grades – six echelons of gradient spiritual enlightenment.

The first grade is called ARC Straightwire. Some explanation is needed here, to make the grade's name understandable. First, there is "ARC" - an important fundamental of Scientology philosophy. "A," "R" and "C" stand for Affinity (liking; the degree of closeness or liking one feels for a person or thing), Reality (agreement; the degree of agreement one has with another regarding any idea, object or circumstance) and Communication (the interchange of ideas, perceptions or even objects between people; perception of the environment could also be considered as communication). These are the components that define and describe the activity of life force (theta).

It is interesting and useful to note that as affinity, reality and communication increase and improve, so does understanding. So to increase a being's understanding (and capability), all one needs to do is raise his affinity, his reality and his communication with respect to any given person, subject or situation. If one raises any *one* of the three (A, R or C) the other two automatically rise as well. That translates to greater understanding. And with greater understanding comes increased ability to interact, to bring about desirable changes, and to build A, R, C and understanding even higher.

Next there is the term "Straightwire." This refers to the concept of stringing an imaginary wire from a thetan (in the present time) to his memory banks (his mental recordings of the past) – and thus recovering memories which have been "lost," buried or suppressed. ARC Straightwire auditing consists of simple mental exercises designed to increase a person's ability to face his own past, incident by incident. These mental exercises are known in Scientology as "processes." In an auditing session, the auditor (Scientology counselor) works with the preclear (person being audited) to run one or more processes.

An individual process consists of a series of commands (questions or directions) which the preclear is able to understand and answer or carry out. In ARC Straightwire processes, the preclear is asked to recall various types of experiences from his past. ARC Straightwire auditing has the effect of increasing the preclear's understanding of his own mind and of the environment. It also tends to bring about remarkable improvements in the person's memory and ability to recall.

As ARC Straightwire processing was developed and extensively practiced, it was found that it uniformly led to a realization by the preclear that he or she would not get any worse as a spiritual being. When the preclear originates, in one way or another, having come to such a realization, ARC Straightwire is ended off as complete.

Having finished ARC Straightwire, the preclear proceeds to Grade 0. At that grade the subject of communication is intensively addressed. The idea is that once a person can comfortably *face* his past and his present, he can learn to *communicate* with them. The processes of Grade 0 bring about the understanding that virtually anything can be resolved with communication. The processes at this level increase one's willingness to communicate to, and receive and understand communication from, other people and his environment. Grade 0 processes are continued until such time as the preclear originates the ability and willingness to communicate with anyone, on any subject.

Grade 1 deals with the subjects of help and problems. The first part of this grade involves processes that increase an individual's ability to comfortably face and change (control) the physical environment (the world of matter, energy space and time – shortened to "MEST" in Scientology parlance). These are called Objective Processes. In this type of process, the auditor first guides the preclear to observe the physical environment (increasing awareness) and then to comfortably bring about changes in that environment. An intensive or two (auditing is administered in 12 ½ hour blocks of auditing, called "intensives") of Objective Processes usually is sufficient to assist the individual to a much clearer recognition of the difference between himself (as a spiritual being) and the physical universe (MEST), and a greater ability to handle and control physical objects (including his own body) without unpleasant mental reactions or interference. A fair number of preclears have reported experiencing the phenomena of exteriorization during Objective Processing.

Once Objective Processes are complete, the auditor and preclear run a number of processes addressing the common – and upsetting – experience of failed attempts at help. This includes "help" directed toward the preclear that failed or even resulted in harm, as well as failures or rejections of the preclear's attempts to help others. These processes rehabilitate the person's own ability to help, and to accept help.

The final leg of Grade 1 addresses the subject of problems. A problem is first defined as two opposing or conflicting intentions, purposes, or forces. To get an idea of this, imagine two gushing water hoses, pointed at one another, resulting in a turbulent mass of water, seemingly suspended in mid-air where the flows collide. Mentally and spiritually, a persistent problem is quite similar to that churning, suspended mass. Unresolved problems suspend *mental* mass and energy in time. In the problems processes of Grade 1, the preclear examines problems, past and present, from this perspective. The processing is continued until the preclear experiences and expresses a tremendous degree of relief, along with the ability to recognize the source of problems and, by doing so, routinely make them vanish with little or no effort.

Grade 2 addresses the source of hostilities and sufferings in life. It is often referred to as the "confessional grade," since its processes are almost entirely concerned with the commission of transgressions (harmful acts) and the karmic results of such acts. In Scientology, the pattern or progression of such acts and their spiritual consequences is referred to as the overt act-motivator sequence. An "overt act" is defined as a destructive act committed by one person against another or others. It is an act contrary to what the thetan considers pro-survival conduct – a transgression against what he conceives to be good and right. When one has committed an overt act (often simply called an overt), he considers it inevitable that he will receive some sort of payback – some sort of personal harm, in retribution for what he has done. If he does ***not*** soon receive such a payback, he will rationalize and *imagine* that the victim of his original transgression *started* the chain of events by *first* committing an overt against him. This twist, in the person's mind, is purely an effort to justify his own transgression. He considers the imagined harm received as his rightful motivation for the harm he caused – his "motivator." As this phenomenon was further explored and described, *any* harmful action received came to be called a motivator – regardless of whether or not it was preceded by an overt act of the person's own. Whoever might have started things off, though, a hellish, brutal cycle would ensue, with each overt leading to a retaliatory overt, which in turn motivated a new overt – on and on, all seemingly justified, righteous and inescapable.

Complicating this senseless, unnecessary mess is this: After committing an overt act, one also tends to withhold himself from the target of his overt and generally from life. Considering what he has done to be harmful, and being natively, basically *good* as a spiritual being, he tries to keep himself from doing any further harm. He also begins to punish himself (sub-consciously) for overts that are not "repaid" by motivators. Caught in this complex web, we accumulate many hostilities and sufferings in life. Through Grade 2 processing, one is able to gradually recall and recount his own secret overt acts, as well as those others have committed against him. By doing so, one begins to recognize the mechanism and to free himself from its effects. Ultimately, one recognizes the Overt Act-Motivator sequence as the primary source of hostilities and sufferings. As might be expected, an auditor at this level must be able to create a completely non-judgmental, non-accusative atmosphere in a session, so that the preclear feels safe in confronting and divulging his past transgressions.

In his numerous recorded lectures on this level, Hubbard contends that Grade 2 auditing proves over and over that thetans are basically good. In case after case, the preclear recognizes that he punishes *himself* for his own transgressions, well before others even learn of them (let alone punish him for them). Ultimately, the theory behind the level is that once a person makes a clean breast of his misdeeds in life, he will, of his own accord, tend to lead a more ethical, pro-survival existence. Rather than withhold his transgressions, he will take responsibility for them and then move on in life, rather than pin himself back into the self-constructed Hades of the overt act - motivator sequence.

Grade 3 deals first with cleaning up upsets one has experienced in the past. Next it tackles a thetan's ability to tolerate and effectuate *change.* Having transcended the muck of the overt act-motivator sequence (essentially putting one in a position of causation in the matter of Karma), and having learned to tolerate and effectuate changes in life, a being attains greater recognition of the power of the spirit and its seniority over the physical universe. The end phenomenon of Grade 3 (that is, the event or realization that indicates that the level is complete) is a realization by the preclear that he or she is free from upsets of the past, and has the ability and willingness to face the future and all the change that entails.

At Grade 4 one handles deeply ingrained defense mechanisms the person has set up to automatically make himself *right* while making others *wrong.* It is this level of the bridge where the focus shifts: from *removing disability* to *rehabilitating ability.* The processes of Grade 4 result in a preclear moving out of fixed conditions, and into the ability to do new things. For most of the '60s and '70s, it was prescribed that the Scientology Grades be applied *after* Dianetics auditing. However, after much consideration, Hubbard finally resolved that over all, the best and most consistent results were to be achieved if the Scientology Grades are completed *before* one embarks on Dianetics processes.

He reckoned this sequence was the best for a couple of reasons. First, the Grades were discovered and developed to resolve the most common barriers to bringing a person up to the state of clear through Dianetics. Not surprisingly, these same barriers are also the barriers to living life to its fullest. As one improved his outlook and increased his abilities in life through the Grades, one also built up his spiritual "horsepower" – and thus his ability to confront and erase the considerable and potentially daunting mental energies and masses of the reactive mind. And so the Dianetics processing had originally been developed before Scientology, it became the final step on the bridge to the state of Clear.

Scientology processes – the Grades – are predominantly *recall* processes. That is, the preclear is asked to remember or bring to mind incidents from his past, and inspect them in the present. The processes are continued until the preclear has what is referred to as a "cognition" – a new realization about life. Recall processes such as those of the Scientology Grades are said to create stages of "release." A release is a separation of the thetan from a part of the reactive mind.

Dianetics processing is different. Dianetics involves "running" (thoroughly inspecting and re-inspecting) past incidents of pain and unconsciousness. Such incidents are referred to as "engrams." Again, "running an engram" means return to and thoroughly viewing an incident of pain and a greater or lesser degree of unconsciousness. Running engrams through Dianetics processing does not *release* the preclear from the incidents. Rather, it *erases* them – causes them to vanish completely from the reactive mind, along with all their power to influence the preclear, physically, mentally or spiritually.

Dianetics directly attacks the reactive mind engram bank and systematically relieves it of its mass and force upon a thetan. Usually, in the course of several intensives of Dianetics auditing, a person has a major realization, coming to terms with the relationship between the spirit, the mind and the physical universe. This has been described as a most profound, personal revelation, which brings tremendous feelings of equanimity, compassion, and understanding. The expected end phenomenon – the realization that marks attainment of Clear – is that one has truly reached an unrepressed and self-determined state of being.

Beyond Dianetics and clearing, there are further stages of auditing know as the "Operating Thetan" or "OT" levels. Originally, Hubbard defined the idea of the OT Levels as an orientation of a cleared being to operation as a spiritual entity, separate from and independent of the body. Certain OT levels that were once part of the official Scientology bridge did seek such an objective, in their entirety. However, that changed and the bulk of the processes on the OT Levels are now concerned with handling energies and masses that are not part of the body, but are somehow connected to the thetan and body, and exerting physical, mental and spiritual influences. Scientology doctrine holds that it is spiritually and potentially physically detrimental for someone who is not yet Clear to examine the writings and processes of the OT Levels.

I learned this general description of the auditing line-up while studying basic courses in Portland. At the time, I didn't know whether I would ever become a professional auditor. Because I hadn't yet achieved Clear, I didn't learn any of the details of the OT Levels – it would be some years before I would finally study them. But I did know one thing for certain: Everything I was learning and mastering on the TRs communication course would help me to help my brother.

CHAPTER SIX

THE GREAT ESCAPE

Sometimes simply taking a long walk with a psychotic, giving him some exercise until he is very tired, will help you in gaining the few minutes of communication you must have with him. – L. Ron Hubbard

I secured a job as short order cook at Dave's Deli, Portland's kosher lunch spot of choice for the downtown business set. I would come in early in the morning to prep, then cook omelets, eggs and pancakes for the breakfast customers. Then the owner, Abe Salzstein, his wife, his son-in-law Phil Cohen and I would prepare for the onslaught. Between 11:30 and 1:30 folks would line up to the buffet and counter for lunch. The line regularly stretched 40 feet to the front door and then extended dozens of yards more down the sidewalk. I enjoyed the job; the communication was fast and furious. Phil made the Reubens, pastramis, and chopped livers. I'd make the burgers and melts. Abe would keep the matzo ball and cabbage borscht urns full, running behind Phil and me. His wife handled the register at the end of the line. We would feed a couple hundred people a day, and fast.

I would get off by 3 p.m. each day, which allowed me to take the bus to Dammasch to see my brother two weekday evenings. I'd also go all day on Sundays. All day Saturday and the other three weekday evenings I'd be on Scientology courses down at the mission.

After course was over, about 10 p.m., my course supervisor John would help me find Hubbard references for dealing with insane people. For the most part, the works were expansions on the themes of the three valid therapies – health (diet, exercise – and in this case, weaning off drugs), exercise, and education. They included procedures (called "processes" in Scientology) that served to extrovert a person's attention. Hubbard's material was spiked with spirited rants about the atrocities of modern mental health practices, particularly heavy sedation, electro-convulsive shock therapy, and brain surgery. After my experiences with the system, those criticisms resonated with me.

When I went back to Dammasch I felt a new level of confidence. Arnold was happy to see me, but in his inimitable nervous fashion he became anxious about my bold plan to convert the entire ward from a holding tank into a rehabilitation activity.

"Mark, one thing you need to realize is that it is going to be a lot more difficult this time. Because Bruce was committed a second time, he can't just walk out when you and he feel it's time."

"What do you mean, Arnold?"

"He is going to have to face a hearing, and until the psychiatric board rules in his favor, I'm afraid he is stuck."

"I understand. Look, we'll do this on a gradient."

"You've also got Dr. Stern to contend with. He feels like you pressured him, and now that Bruce is back he feels somewhat vindicated."

"What did he say?"

"Nothing, I'm just telling you what I sense; it's my assessment of the situation."

"Well, you know what? What kind of attitude is that? Arnold, does anyone here give a fuck about curing anybody? This place is a hell hole – for God's sake, everybody in this ward looks just the way they did the day I first walked in here."

"Look, you've got to realize nobody's got anybody. Do you know there has not been a single visitor for a single one of my 30 patients since we met?"

He was right, and that was perhaps the saddest part of the entire experience. It would become much harder as I came to establish personal relationships with several of the patients. First order of business was establishing exercise time for the ward. We reserved the gym for the two weekday evenings I visited each week.

"I'm going to teach you sons of bitches something about the *real* American pastime, basketball," I announced in the rec room.

"Basketball's for coloreds," protested Eddie.

"You know something Eddie? You got a big mouth and nothing to back it up. Basketball is the real deal – no props, no bats, no pads, no helmets, no nothing. It's man to man. And I think you're scared. Tell you what, we're heading to the gym, you just stay here and knit or something."

Eddie jumped out of his chair defiantly, "I'm gonna kick your ass."

"You and what army, Eddie?" I replied as the ward boys followed me and Arnold to the gym.

The gym was so small there was less than a foot between the out-of-bounds line and the walls surrounding the court.

"All right, split it up." I started physically moving bodies into two groups of roughly 15 each. "All you guys, take your shirts off." I gathered them at center court, with the shirts on one side and the skins on the other. "All right, skins, you go that way," I indicated by pointing, "and shirts, that's your basket over there." I picked two guys to jump, lined them up face to face and tossed the ball up. Both swung their arms with all their might, both missed, and the ball bounced off the floor.

Eddie grabbed the ball, tucked it under his arm like a football and started running for the basket. Bruce sprinted after Eddie, and just as Eddie began to plant a foot to take off for the basket, Bruce grabbed him in a bear hug. Bruce lectured, "Eddie, first of all, wrong basket. Second, you gotta dribble – you can't run with the ball."

I smiled at hearing the only decisive utterances that had come from my brother's lips in two months. A huge argument broke out. I grabbed the ball and tossed it toward the other basket. "Ball's in play." Most of the ward dropped the fight and tore out after the ball. And so it went, 45 minutes of tearing up and down the court. Nothing was out of bounds – we created the game as we went. The walls were used to ricochet the ball – sort of a mix between basketball and handball. Even though the ball seldom went in the basket, everyone soon lost track of the score, and didn't care. They were running, sweating, and screaming at the top of their lungs. It was like a pack of hyperactive kids let loose on the playground. And when it was time to head back to the ward, there was a collective calm about the group that was obvious. Arnold had stood in the corner looking on nervously for most of the period. I noticed him several times crack and then suppress a smile, when something particular wacky went on between the patients.

After several exercise sessions, one night Arnold told me he needed to speak with me. I met him at a coffee shop after he got off work. "Mark, I don't want to talk out of school, but I have to tell you there has been a marked improvement with the ward since you started team activities. I get the feeling you have some kind of insight or some methodology you are applying. I need to know what is going on." I proceeded to tell Arnold about Dianetics and the three valid therapies. He said he had heard some good things about Dianetics, but also that Hubbard was somewhat of a charlatan. Whatever it is, he wanted to learn more. I promised to bring him the book *Dianetics* the next time I showed up, and I did.

Arnold became progressively more cooperative with my plans. On Sundays he arranged outings. We'd take the institution's bus on half-day trips. Even though the bus windows were obstructed with metal mesh protection, drives along northern Oregon country roads afforded the patients some extroversion. Our final destinations were always parks, where the patients could get out and get space and walk – we never went to populated areas such as museums and the like.

As far as education went, I mainly applied that step to my brother. I taught him how to give himself what they call a "locational," in Scientology. The idea was to locate oneself in the physical universe. It was simple: I told him that whenever he began to feel like he was simmering or introverting, to get his attention out of his head. "Go look out the window – just look at things *away* from yourself. Pick up a pool stick and knock some balls around the table. Get your attention out of your head."

It wasn't quite that easy with Bruce because of the continued heavy medication. Again, I was able to obtain some cooperation on the side from Arnold to lighten up on the dope. But Bruce remained under the influence of psychotropic medication, which made for a bit of a roller-coaster ride.

Nonetheless, Bruce did improve. He could talk in a sensible fashion, provided one had the patience to spend quite some time while he found the words to articulate his thoughts. The TRs came in handy on that count. If we played pool, walked, shot some baskets, maybe after a couple hours he would originate something out of the blue, like, "I think I could hold a job." Then we'd talk for a couple of minutes, mainly me trying to validate the original idea while Bruce tried to talk himself out of it. It wasn't much, but it was progress. Finally, after several weeks, one day Bruce told me straight up, "I gotta get out of here." Arnold advised that I had to convince Dr. Stern to convene the board for a hearing.

It took several days to finally get the good doctor on the phone. "Bruce would like to leave, doctor. Can we arrange one of those board hearings?" The doctor proceeded to explain to me the great hurdles he would have to clear at the hearing – not only would he have to establish to the psychiatrists' satisfaction that Bruce was sufficiently sane, but his family would have to establish that sufficient external supports were in place – financial, moral, et cetera.

The conversation became circular on point one, because the doctor could not establish a clear standard for what constituted sanity. I got the impression he was attempting to blow me off. From the pay phone at Dave's Deli I pressed the doctor hard, demanding the hearing and promising to research and enforce my brother's legal rights, should he attempt to deny us fairness. At that, Dr. Stern said he would set a date for the hearing. But he ended off the conversation with an ominous warning: "I hope you realize that you may find yourself under greater scrutiny than your brother – after all, you do claim to be his only external support."

By then I was onto the graduate portion of the Communication Course. This consisted of drills known as the Upper Indoctrination Training Routines. Had it not been for these advanced drills, I do not think I could have stood up to the institutional intention I was facing.

The Upper Indoctrination drills dealt with the subject of intention itself. The first part of one drill entailed putting one's intention into material objects. This drill has been criticized – and misunderstood – as "yelling at an ashtray." In fact, the student does speak toward an ashtray, and then raise his voice at it. But the purpose of the drill is to step outside of the physical universe mechanics of sound, so as to distinguish and perceive *intention* as something separate from the intention's "carrier wave" – the voice. Having earlier experienced non-verbal transmission of intention while playing basketball, the concept was real to me. After several hours of communicating intention to a material object, I developed a keen perception of the intention I was able to project, separate and apart from the carrier wave, the sound waves issuing from my mouth.

Another of the Upper Indoctrination drills involved ordering another person – one's study partner (or "twin") – to perform simple tasks. The command "Look at that wall" is given, while pointing to the wall across a room, with no furniture in between. Once the twin complies, the student then commands, "Walk over to that wall." When the twin complies, the next orders are "Touch that wall" and then "Turn around." With that final command completed, the entire series is repeated. The twin is acknowledged each time he complies with a command.

The drill is done on a gradient. At first there is no resistance offered. Once the student can deliver the commands and acknowledge compliance naturally, the twin begins to resist. This might start with verbal attempts to throw the student off. It graduates into physical resistance, requiring the student to physically enforce compliance with his commands. The student finally progresses up to overcoming even physical resistance with intention alone. Well coached, the student gradiently becomes more aware of and more in control of the direction and execution of his own intention.

When it came time for the final pass on the final drill, the executive director of the mission, Ed Petty, came into the room. He was an Operating Thetan (OT), having reached the highest levels of Scientology's bridge, or grade chart of spiritual awareness and ability. Ed was an impressive individual. He was clearly in the present and exuded a great deal of confidence and calm. At first Ed tried to divert my attention and make me laugh. He was very adept at this, but I did not react and kept performing the drill. Ed stayed at it and made me continue drilling for several minutes. He did not relent until something remarkable happened. Ed began to perform my commands before the words arrived. I knew he was receiving the intention a microsecond before the mechanics of speech could catch up to it.

We went through several cycles of the drill with me conveying the intention of the command without uttering anything. I would intend the commands across to Ed, and he would comply, right on cue. I noticed that in order to achieve this telepathic transmission of thought, I had to be so thoroughly in the present that I had no attention whatsoever on the mechanics of my own body. I had transcended them. Like exteriorization, it required transcendence from the mechanics of effort. Clear, clean intention was of spirit, not of body. To me, this was the attainment of my long quest for developing the ability to exercise exteriorization and the pure, clean, unobstructed intention I had experienced in the Fallbrook gymnasium years before.

When I graduated the Communication Course I felt on top of the world. The timing couldn't have been better. I needed to get focused on the upcoming hearing and on making preparations to receive Bruce. I had saved up enough from work that I could afford to rent living quarters for my brother and me. John, the course supervisor, had pointed out that the "change of environment" step was going to be critical. The last noisy apartment I'd had, situated by the freeway and frequented by drug dealers, was not the ideal environment for someone recovering from acute schizophrenia. Then a monkey wrench of sorts got thrown into the works, by the folks I most credited with helping me.

I was sent to see the registrar – the person who signs people up for services. Such a visit was routine for everyone graduating from a course. In fact, it was required that graduates see the registrar immediately upon course completion. Judy was in her late twenties, blonde, wore a slick business dress, and had brilliant, piercing eyes. The no-nonsense certainty of her demeanor lent her a lot of altitude. The framed training certificates on the wall behind her desk helped, too. She said that John had briefed her on the situation with my brother. She had researched the matter and had come up with the exact package I needed.

First, she said, I would need to enroll on the Student Hat Course. That would teach me how to study effectively, and would speed my progress through the rest of my courses in Scientology. Then I would need to enroll on the Hubbard Dianetic Auditor Course. I would have to purchase all the basic Dianetics and Scientology books for the course, and buy an electrometer (also called an e-meter), the mental resistance detection machine that makes Dianetics and Scientology counseling so precise.

Judy was very convincing. I told her that this all sounded fine, but I was not there to advance myself as much as to advance my brother. She informed me that I would not have a snowball's chance in hell of pulling my brother out of the soup without professional auditor training. After being shown a number of Hubbard writings to support her assertion, I finally agreed that her course of action sounded good.

Then she pulled out her calculator, and punched buttons while talking under her breath about discounts I qualified to receive. The total for the whole package was $2,000. I told Judy that was out of the question – I had more pressing obligations, what with preparing a suitable environment for my brother. She continued to press and I continued to object. Finally we called in the man at the mission I trusted most, the course supervisor John. John came in and the two skillfully ganged up on me. They convinced me that it was important to invest in the health of the mission, as they would be there ultimately to help my brother.

I wound up buying the Student Hat, a meter and the books for $1,500 – more than the totality of my savings – holding off on the auditor course until a later time. I would have to phone my father to borrow a few hundred in order to purchase the package. This made me feel degraded, since I had not asked him for money since I was 12 years old. I doubted that I had wisely spent what meager resources I had, in light of what I would need to do to help Bruce recover. But I rationalized that it was not for me, I was doing this to save my brother. I would get him to the mission and he would have the same transcending and empowering experience that I had.

For the first time, I walked out of the Mission with an uneasy feeling. The Scientologists I had met to date were the most caring folks I had ever encountered. While everyone has their own distinct level of spiritual attainment and understanding, the traits common to just about every Scientologist I had met were a reality that we are all spiritual beings, and that one's conduct on the whole should be geared toward helping others to have that same realization. What bothered me was that this basic goodness seemed to be tainted by financial considerations. I would later learn that by working with Judy to sign me up, John would earn a 10 percent commission on every service and product I purchased from the mission. It was not the individual Scientologist that I lost any affinity for. Instead, it seemed that individuals' good intentions were being clouded by an organizational system I understood little about.

Mild disappointment aside, for the next two weeks I put my attention fully on preparation for Bruce's hearing. I spent a lot of time at Dammasch preparing Bruce, and working on Arnold to cut back on the meds. Money was tight, but I managed to find a decent-fitting set of somewhat business-like threads from a St. Vincent De Paul thrift store. I needed to be presentable.

Finally, the day of the hearing arrived. I was ushered into a conference room in the administrative wing at Dammasch. Four psychiatrists sat across the table. Dr. Stern was about what I'd expected. A stern, pale-looking, forty-something fellow with thinning hair and a flannel three-piece suit. His colleagues were of much the same ilk. To make matters worse, when Bruce was escorted in, he looked like he was recovering from electroshock – disoriented and very introverted. Painfully shy to begin with, he apparently was overwhelmed with the inquisitorial set-up. It was Bruce and I on the one side, the four psychs on the other, Arnold at one end of the table observing, and a note taker at the table's other end.

I recognized that the group's counter-intention to my intention of freeing my brother was intense. I applied my Scientology lessons, though. I did not react. I did not get angry. I did not try to muster force. Instead, I arrived completely in the present, calmly perceiving exactly what lay before me. I focused my intention effortlessly toward attainment of my goal: Bruce walking out of that institution at my side.

A woman psychiatrist read some introductory statements about the purpose of the hearing, a short description of Bruce's institutional history, his chronic schizophrenic behavior, and a couple of complimentary statements about his recent conduct from his psychiatric nurse, dear old Arnold. She went on to read Dr. Stern's recommendations for further incarceration at the hospital, but noted that in keeping with Oregon law and state guidelines, given that Bruce and his family wished that he be released, the board was required to hear the case and make the final decision. With that we proceeded.

"Bruce, we would like to ask you some questions," said one of the psychiatrists.

Bruce was staring blankly at the floor. I extended my right leg, and very lightly nudged the side of Bruce's foot with my shoe. He looked up at me, and I nodded toward the psychs, indicating he should look at them. Bruce looked up at the fellow addressing him.

"Bruce, does this phrase have any meaning to you? 'If you live in a glass house, don't throw rocks.'"

"I don't know," Bruce mumbled.

"Well," continued the psychiatrist, "do you think there is anything to be learned from that statement?"

Bruce was again looking at the floor. There was silence for several seconds.

"Bruce, do you understand the question?" the psychiatrist nudged.

"I don't know what you want to hear," Bruce finally responded.

"Well, we want to hear what you think; don't try to anticipate what is a right or wrong answer."

"Bruce, seems like everyone is out to get you, doesn't it?" Stern jabbed.

I spun my chair around and faced Stern. "Doctor, this is the first time we've met face to face. I must tell you I am getting the impression that you are the one person in this room attempting to trip my brother up. And I don't know that that is appropriate, given that you have been entrusted with his care and recovery." Stern look aghast, slammed his notebook shut, looked haughtily at the other psychiatrists and announced it appeared the hearing was now over.

The one female psychiatrist on the panel smoothly restored order. "Let's all just settle down for a moment. I think that we need to understand that Mark's passion for his brother is not necessarily a negative. At the same time, Mark, I think you need to put some faith in the objectivity of the panel. We all have Bruce's best interests in mind." I nodded in agreement. Dr. Stern did not. He pouted, with his closed notebook held close to his chest.

My bout with Stern seemed to wake Bruce up. He began to speak more directly and decisively. He answered a series of questions much like the first. "What does 'the grass is always greener on the other side' me to you?" "What does 'a rolling stone gathers no moss' mean to you?" and the like. Despite Bruce's lack of communication skills, the fact that he was an intelligent, decent person began to manifest in his answers.

Stern and I continued to spar, which kept Bruce alert. At one point I sensed Bruce was about to pounce on Stern physically, but he calmed down when I nonchalantly gave him a brotherly pat and rub on the shoulder. The woman psychiatrist patiently kept the train on the rails.

By part two of the interview, the external supports section, the woman psychiatrist was mildly defending my lack of monetary means, at one point even pointing out that to discriminate on the basis of poverty could raise some thorny legal issues.

Finally, much to Arnold's joy – and to Dr. Stern's chagrin – the board ruled that Bruce could be released, to go live with me in Portland.

CHAPTER SEVEN

WHO'S ZOOMIN' WHO?

Zoom: To fool, as in "Who's zoomin' who?" (Aretha Franklin) – The Urban Dictionary

As low as my morale had dropped when Bruce was re-incarcerated, it rose to its highest apex when we busted him loose. We rented a basement apartment under a home in a quiet neighborhood, on the northwest side of Portland. The surroundings were fairly peaceful, but even this was not the ideal place for a recovering mental patient. There was no light, save for a small window at ground level, half blocked by the dirt of a front-yard garden. It was cold, and we had no access to hot water or central heat. We had a cave, in essence, but I rationalized that it was a nice cave, and unfortunately it was all I could afford after my purchases at the mission.

For the next couple of weeks Bruce and I did a lot of walking, hiking and playing basketball. At night I went to the mission to study on the Student Hat Course. I told Bruce about the course's theory that there are only three fundamental barriers to learning on any level or in any subject. In a nutshell, they were these: First, the skipped gradient – moving to more advanced levels or lessons of a subject without having first mastered earlier, more fundamental steps along the way. Next there was lack of mass – not having the mass of the subject under study (the physical objects, or at least some representation of them such as photos or diagrams) so they could be viewed, touched, and worked with. Finally there was the misunderstood word. This was the most treacherous barrier – going past words or symbols one did not fully or correctly understand. I found these principles very workable, as did Bruce.

Bruce took to reading my Dianetics and Scientology books at home while I was on course. I did not want to push Bruce in any direction, knowing his reluctance to intermingle with people socially and his extreme fear of rejection. At the same time, I hoped he would come to originate a reach for help from the mission, somewhere along the line.

Life was not a walk in the park. Bruce was extremely introverted. He never spoke much and was very shy and self-conscious. But the safe (changed) environment, the exercise, and now education were having a noticeable effect. He really liked what he read in my books, and began talking about Scientology with me. Finally, he originated, "I'm a real abbo, don't you think?" He was using his own slang for "aberree," a Dianetics term for any human with mental hang-ups (aberrations). "You and me both," I replied.

Bruce told me he wanted to go in and get some auditing. I couldn't have been happier. This was the first time he had proposed an endeavor of any significance on his own initiative, since early childhood.

Off to the mission we went. I was so proud to bring Bruce into the mission and introduce him to some of the folks I had come to know, like John the course supervisor. Bruce was escorted by the receptionist to get some interviews preparatory to signing up for auditing. As the interview extended past an hour, I went to a café next door to wait. I was reading the newspaper over coffee when I suddenly noticed a figure bolt past the window. It was Bruce, walking at a furious pace, hunched over, hands in his jacket pockets. His face hadn't looked so pallid since he was locked up at Dammasch. I dropped the paper and ran out the door after him. "Bruce!" I yelled at him from the sidewalk. He just kept walking up Salmon Street. I ran after him and slowed to his pace when I reached him. "Bruce, what happened, bro?"

He kept walking like I wasn't there. I grabbed his arm and tried to turn him toward me. He spun hard, flinging my arm off, and continued walking. I stood on the sidewalk with a cold winter wind whipping my face. I felt nauseous. I walked back to the mission and straight into the registrar area. Judy, the course supervisor John, and a tall, serious-looking guy were standing there talking.

"John, what happened with my brother?" I asked.

Judy directed all of us into her office and closed the door. John started, "Mark, Bruce apparently didn't like his program."

"What was the program?" I asked.

John continued, "Well, because of his history of institutionalization he does not qualify for auditing – so he was given a program of reading books."

I protested, "What do you mean? He's already reading books. You know my whole goal was to get him to receive auditing – and damn it, we moved mountains to make this happen."

He somberly said, "Well, we didn't know his psych history was so extensive – the ethics officer, Randy here, had to make the call."

"Psych history? So what? It's called the modern science of mental health, for crying out loud – that is what the fuck I'm doing here in the first place. This is a mental health problem, and he's willing to pay to get it fixed. So let's fix it!"

Randy calmly responded, "I'm sorry nobody explained this to you."

Randy then related how, because of problems the missions and organizations (larger intermediary churches of Scientology) had historically run into with former mental patients, there was a firm policy in place not to accept those with institutional histories for auditing. He said that behind every major attack on Scientology, from newspaper articles, to official government inquiries, to criminal prosecutions and civil lawsuits, there were psychiatrists. The American Psychiatric Association and the American Medical Association had declared war on Hubbard the moment he published *Dianetics* in 1950. They considered a handbook that any two folks could pick up and use – and straighten out their lives and cure psychosomatic ills to boot – was considered a threat to the great American health monopoly. Since then a great deal of the organizations' resources have been devoted to defending itself.

Randy tied Bruce's situation to the story by stating each of the most effective attacks on Scientology had used an easily-manipulated former psychiatric patient, holding the patient up as a victim of Scientology. For purely survival reasons, the policy of no institutional cases had been initiated and firmly adhered to for some time. For me, my personal experience with Dr. Stern and Dammasch lent a lot of credibility to the explanation. But, for all the sense it made, the explanation did not open any door to repairing the damage with Bruce. What was I to tell him? That he was so messed up that the only people I had told him could help him could *not* help him?

It turned out we never recovered to the level of communication where we could even discuss it. Bruce finally came stumbling down the wooden stairs to our cave at 2:00 the next morning. I had waited up the entire time. "Hi, bro," I greeted him.

"Huh" he mumbled, keeping his eyes to the floor as he headed to the one bedroom.

The smell of alcohol rushed at me in the air displaced as he slammed the bedroom door behind him. I quietly opened the door after him, and leaned down toward the bed. "Bruce", I said softly as I gently put a hand on his shoulder. Still dressed and wrapped in a blanket, he violently flipped onto his shoulder to face the wall. He tightly wound himself into the fetal position. As I predicted, Bruce went into a deep, dark hole. A place where no sounds, no light, no communication could penetrate. I sat on my couch bed in the common area. A weak remnant of a street light barely managed its way through our one window, dimly illuminating a spot on the floor. I sat watching it. I felt myself slipping into a dank, lifeless hole with my brother.

Verbal communication nearly ceased entirely between Bruce and I. Once in a while I could prompt him to take a hike with me. In a way, it was a strange reversal of our early childhood. Just as Bruce had once led expeditions through the woods, now I was leading Bruce. There was rarely any exchange of words. If I could get him to smile, I would enjoy a small victory. But whenever I tried to convert that into a conversation, he would shut me right out. A strapping mountaineering type on mission staff went out with us on a couple of Sundays. He did it as a favor to me. I thought expanding the company might help bring Bruce out of his shell. But my friend's attempts to talk with Bruce were more fruitless than my own. Somehow I could see in Bruce's expressions his sensing that my friend was putting up a front. Sure, the guy was buoyant and outgoing – but maybe it was forced, maybe it was saccharine and not pure sugar.

I became cynical. I was beginning to doubt my own sanity. I felt such a deep understanding of my brother's plight that I began to wonder whether I would come to live in that place myself. I don't know whether it was some sort of transference or a strong yearning to rationalize his psychosis. But I instinctively began to believe he saw the world clearly, in all its phoniness and pretense.

I reasoned that his distaste for relations was the inevitable result of the betrayals that human relations begat. Didn't our mother who vowed to raise us then suddenly disappear? Hadn't our father steered clear of us and to let us survive on our own? Hadn't Scott done everything in his power to put Bruce where he was? Weren't the psychiatrists out to control and subdue, rather than heal? Hadn't the only people who seemed to have workable answers to all this denied Bruce access to those answers? Maybe Bruce saw all this and was refusing to play the game, no matter how painful it might be for him personally.

I continued to attend evening courses at the mission. At the beginning of the Student Hat course I spent quite a few course periods struggling with the first reference in the course materials. Entitled "Keeping Scientology Working," it was the first item on every Scientology course, from the level of the Student Hat Course on up. It was designated as a "Policy Letter," and written by L. Ron Hubbard. Students and staff read this same policy over so many times, and used its contents to justify so much zealous behavior within the organizations, that the seven-page essay became known as "KSW" for short.

This particular policy (still in use today) was originally issued in 1965. It pronounces that Scientology had by that point achieved "uniformly workable technology." It states that the only troubles the organization ever encountered were because of incorrect application of that uniformly workable technology. Therefore, KSW called for zealous enforcement of the standard application of Scientology. By "standard" was meant precise, unquestioning adherence to all technical and administrative instructions from L. Ron Hubbard. No interpretations or alterations allowed. Only L. Ron Hubbard's words, followed to the letter. Quite a bit of attention was paid by the course supervisors to each student, on a one-to-one basis, seeking to elicit agreement that they would follow KSW to the letter.

My struggle was attempting to accept that level of certainty, and agreeing to that level of steadfast devotion to the idea that Scientology was *it*, to the utter exclusion of any other ideas or philosophies – all without the experience of finding out for myself whether Scientology was indeed *it*. I could not progress in my studies without first agreeing that the following ideas of L. Ron Hubbard were incontrovertibly true, and that I vowed to adopt and adhere to them:

- Any inability to agree to the tenets of KSW was due to the fact that "the not-too-bright have a bad point on the button 'self-importance," and that "the lower the IQ, the more the individual is shut off from the fruits of observation,"
- That "the [defense mechanisms] of people make them defend themselves against anything they confront, good or bad, and seek to make it wrong," and that "the bank [reactive mind] seeks to knock out the good and perpetuate the bad."
- The idea that "a group [of people] could evolve truth" is inherently false.
- That Hubbard relied on absolutely no major or basic ideas or suggestions from any other source in developing the world's only workable mental/spiritual technology, which he called Scientology.
- "Popular measures" and "democracy" have done nothing for humankind except "push him further into the mud."
- Humankind never before "evolved workable mental technology," but instead only "vicious technology." Scientology, therefore, must be "ruthlessly followed."
- The only common denominator among humans is the reactive mind. Therefore all agreements between humans who have not achieved the state of Clear can only be classified as "bank [reactive mind] agreement."
- "Bank agreement" can also be called "collective thought agreement." Collective thought agreement is responsible for "war, famine, disease" and the development of "the means of frying every man, woman, and child on the planet."
- "The decent, pleasant things on this planet come from *individual* actions and ideas that have somehow gotten by the Group Idea."
- "It's the bank that says the group is all and the individual nothing. It's the bank that says we must fail."
- "When somebody enrolls, consider he or she has joined up for the duration of the universe – never permit an 'open-minded' approach…If they enrolled, they're aboard; and if they're

aboard, they're here on the same terms as the rest of us – win or die in the attempt. Never let them be half-minded about being Scientologists."

- "The proper instruction attitude is, 'You're here so you're a Scientologist. Now we're going to make you into an expert auditor no matter what happens. We'd rather have you dead than incapable.'"
- "We're not playing some minor game in Scientology. It isn't cute or something to do for lack of something better. The whole agonized future of this planet, every man, woman and child on it, and your own destiny for the next trillions of years depend on what you do here and now with and in Scientology. This is a deadly serious activity. And if we miss getting out of the trap now, we may never again have another chance."

The tract dramatically drove home some conflicting ideas. On the one hand, Scientology is portrayed as the only technology for enhancing and preserving individuality. On the other hand, by the end of the policy Hubbard is demanding that no one be allowed past the *first* bulletin in Scientology training courses without assuming the identity of hard-core Scientologist, and agreeing to abide by the rules on the same terms as everyone else. The conflicting concepts between the group and the individual were finally resolved by me with the mental computation that the only way to truly realize true individuality is to forfeit individuality in favor of the purposes and goals of the group.

In retrospect, had it not been for the fact that my life seemed so bleak and hopeless, given the circumstances of my brother, I never would have agreed to this indoctrination. But the world and the state of mental health in my view were as bad as Hubbard described, and up to then I had not found anyone else who saw what I was seeing in such black-and-white terms. And so I decided to agree and to abide, even though deep inside I did not fully agree.

Only 30 years later did I fully appreciate how significant that moment of intellectual surrender would become. The realization occurred when I read Thomas Paine's *The Age of Reason,* which described precisely what I had done with my fresh, sharply-honed intentional abilities:

It is impossible to calculate the moral mischief, if I may so express it, that mental lying has produced in society. When a man has so far corrupted and prostituted the chastity of his mind, as to subscribe his professional belief to things he does not believe, he has prepared himself for the commission of every other crime.

It was difficult to see the future mischief such moral and mental compromise would bring, given the tremendous abilities I had attained. To transcend the body and communicate telepathically have been goals of spirituality from the dawn of humankind. That I could perform them after just a few weeks of study and practice was nothing short of a miracle.

Once I made it past the KSW policy, the Student Hat course was great. I was listening to Hubbard lectures from the early '60s, when he developed his study technology. I found the course room to be an island of sanity. No one was permitted to interrupt a student. For three to four hours a night, it was just me and Ron (as Hubbard was sometimes referred to within the church). While his lectures were on the subject of study, he had an engaging way of telling lengthy anecdotes from his life and observations of the world, all to drive home whatever point he was making. I found his view of Western civilization to be imbued with a healthy insouciance, meaning "a light-hearted unconcern." He commented on aspects of American society that I had been seeing, up to that time, as having a dark, depressing aspect. But he was discussing those areas of concern with a great deal of *un*concern, a sort of "don't let the pompous sons of bastards get you down." It gave me new perspectives and insights. Each night it pulled me out of the deep funk I'd manage to put myself into, trying to lift my brother out. Politicians, the military, educators, psychiatrists, priests, doctors – no lofty establishment institution or its members were out of bounds. It was not simply a tear-down, either. He was teaching what I considered the greatest lesson I learned in Scientology: the ability to disagree with what the society conditions you to believe.

I was particularly taken with Hubbard's description of the thetan (spirit), and the life force, or "theta," of which this spirit was composed. He described it as having no matter, energy, space, time or wavelength. It is the only true static in the universe – the mover unmoved. While I could not fully grasp the concept intellectually, what he described rang true, based upon my short subjective experiences with exteriorization.

Hubbard commented that authorities on the spirit, mind and

science called the entire concept hogwash. The problem with them, he claimed, was that they were just not observing the obvious. They were looking at the material world, while ignoring the *observer* of that material world. To try to describe the universe, while denying the existence of its observer, creator and mover – theta – was an exercise in futility. It was too simple for the priesthoods – academic, scientific, philosophic and otherwise – all shrouded and entrapped in complexities.

What I believed the medicos and scientists needed was a several-week session of TR 0 – that drill from the Communication Course in which one learns how to simply confront, and perhaps recognize theta or life force. And on that note, Ron proffered an axiom: "The degree of complexity is directly proportional to the degree of non-confront." This bit of wisdom would prove itself true and useful in my life, over and over again – even though it may ultimately have contributed to whole life chapters of stifling and destructive conformity.

Just as I was beginning to recoup a bit of my own sanity, my brother Scott came back into my life. He showed up to our cave and told me that a psychologist friend of his was an expert on Scientology, and that it was critical that I meet him. I agreed to meet Jim for lunch at a smorgasbord downtown the next day, mainly to get Scott away from our peaceful, if depressing, cave.

Jim was in his thirties, balding, wearing a thick turtleneck sweater. After the introductory pleasantries, Jim got down to business:

"Did you know that a woman recently sued Scientology for two million dollars, just two blocks from here in the Multnomah County Court House?"

"No, what happened to the woman?" I asked, surprised.

Jim got very serious, "She was systematically brainwashed; they made a zombie out of her. They turned her against her family so that she wouldn't even talk to them."

"Wow," I said, "how did they brainwash her?"

"She signed up for their Communication Course. When she went in, they had her sit in a chair staring at another cult member for hours on end. After weeks of this treatment, she lost all touch with reality. She had to receive professional psychiatric care to bring her back to her senses."

"Really?" I asked, "All she ever did was the Comm Course?"

He leaned closer for emphasis, "That's all it takes. Expert psychiatrists have testified that techniques used on the course are akin to Korean brainwashing tactics."

I looked him the eye and said, "It just goes to show how fucked up this country really is."

"What do you mean?" he asked, surprised at my response.

"Jim, I took that course, and it was the greatest thing that ever happened to me," I said, matter-of-factly. "I actually found out, subjectively and objectively, that I am a spiritual being, separate and apart from the flesh. It took Siddhartha Gautama an entire lifetime to attain that. It all makes perfect sense. Because I am sure that if the Buddha or Jesus Christ himself walked the streets today, they'd wind up in Dammasch State Hospital in a heartbeat."

Jim was flummoxed. He paused to gather himself, then took another tack. "Mark, you speak from subjectivity. Let me give you some objective facts."

Jim smugly announced that L. Ron Hubbard wasn't really a naval war hero.

I was slightly amused, "That makes sense. I wondered why they put that naval officer business in the promo in the first place. Had I seen it before I took a course, I probably would have walked on by. Military credentials are about the last thing that would appeal to somebody like me."

Jim then rattled off these bombshells excitedly: "Well, what if you knew that now he lives on a huge private yacht he bought with church funds, surrounded by young nymphs? That he sought psychiatric treatment while in the Navy? That he was convicted in absentia for fraud in France, and that he is on the lam from federal grand juries as we speak?"

I sincerely considered his question quietly for several seconds. I could see by Jim's expression that he was somewhat relieved to have put me on the defensive. I said, "Jim, let me tell you a little story. Last April a friend and I hitchhiked from Santa Cruz up to Eugene to attend the annual Ken Kesey Hoo- Haw Festival. We got there while they were still setting up, early on a Saturday morning. First thing we did was score some psilocybin mushrooms and eat them. Before I was even high, I spotted Ken Kesey himself, standing but 10 feet from us. I walk up to him and say, 'Mr. Kesey, your book *One Flew over the Cuckoo's Nest* kept me sane when I had to fish my brother out of the VA hospital in Oakland. Thank you, sir.' You know what Kesey's response was?"

Jim replied, "No, what was it?"

I continued, "He just stared blankly in my direction. He wasn't looking at me. He wasn't looking at anything. He was stuck so far inside his head that there was not even a hint of life in his eyes. You ever see a kid in high school who once was pretty normal, then he started taking acid and took so much that his brain literally got fried? I don't mean recreational use. I mean taking hundreds of trips, and winding up like a walking vegetable."

He looked dumbfounded, "Uh, no. No."

"How about a mental patient plowed under on Stelazine and Thorazine?"

"Uh…no."

"Well, it's a horrible sight; sort of like looking into the eyes of a cadaver in a morgue. It is not pretty. And that was Ken Kesey in the year 1977. Gone, checked out, nobody home. Are you getting the picture?"

"I think so," Jim replied.

I continued, "Well, I decided right then and there, I'll never take another hallucinogen. And I never did. Sure, I smoked some hash and weed, but I never touched hallucinogens again. It was that scary."

As I continued, Jim was beginning to look puzzled. "Four months later, I got to see my brother Bruce, who was locked up in Dammasch. He's got that Kesey look, only it's not acid that did it. Its Thorazine and Stelazine. Same effect – there's no one home. I didn't know the first thing about what to do. But I do remember fishing him out of the VA hospital in Oakland. And I remember putting on the Randall McMurphy act – right out of *Cuckoo's Nest* – just by hook or by crook, reach far-gone people with interest and enthusiasm. And I remember it lit a spark with my brother, and he got his ass out and back on his feet. Now, do you think that when I confronted the same situation – only worse – in Dammasch, that I gave a single flying fuck that Ken Kesey wound up in his own irreversible psychotic condition, when I considered I had better apply a little of the *Cuckoo's Nest* technique if I wanted to help my brother out of the personal hell he was suffering? Do you think because Ken Kesey had chosen to fry any last remnant of intelligence out of his once-brilliant mind, that that detracts from the insights he communicated in *Cuckoo's Nest*?

Does what happened to Kesey later in life make *Sometimes a Great Notion* any less the American classic it is?"*[To be fair to the late Mr. Kesey, it is entirely possible he was simply suffering from a bad batch of mushrooms that day. Several hours after our encounter, after ingesting mushrooms I purchased from a friend of Kesey's, I felt like Kesey had looked.]*

By then Jim was not even answering my questions.

"Finally, Jim, I am little more than offended that Scott and you have not lifted a finger to help Bruce, but instead have put all your effort into knee-capping *my* efforts to help him out."

Jim sat looking at me nervously. He looked around at other patrons who were looking at us. I realized this guy was not there to have a dialogue with me. He had an agenda. He was there to create certain effects in my mind, and when his script did not produce the desired results, he was at a loss for words.

I got up to leave. On the way out, I stopped and turned back to Jim and said, "And tell Scott that if he ever wants to attempt to derail this train again, don't send some representative to try it." Scott never did reach out to me after that, nor did I ever reach out to him.

CHAPTER EIGHT

A WORLD WITHOUT INSANITY

Scientologists are the people who are cleaning up the field of mental healing and effectively handling mental health on the planet. – *L. Ron Hubbard*

I felt somewhat liberated, having checkmated Scott's attempt to cripple my mission. However, this had not helped much in handling Bruce. He continued with his deep manic depression. The more he went out drinking, the worse it got. It seemed that any slight, mild gain would always be followed by a bigger, harsher setback.

After the mission had rejected him, Bruce had also stopped reading Scientology books; so the boost they seemed to have been giving him was now out of the picture. I felt I was in a race with time. I wanted to get my auditor training done and then – covertly, if necessary – audit Bruce, independent of the mission. But the longer I went on with my studies, the further back down the chute he drifted. I became so disheartened that I started becoming ill.

One night while on course, I had a stomach attack of some sort. It felt I'd had the wind knocked out of me. I was sent to see Randy, the Ethics Officer. Randy gave me a couple of Hubbard bulletins which stated that illness is always preceded by some form of suppression. Then he explained a procedure we would go through to determine the source of the suppression with the aid of an e-meter. As I read the material, I recognized that Scott was the source of the suppression preceding my illnesses. Suddenly feeling bright and alive, I told Randy about my realization. He acknowledged, but then tried to sign me up for some sessions on the meter to verify what I'd found. "Sorry, I can't afford it; and besides, I'm cool now."

Randy pressed the point, saying that we needed to put together a formal program, laying out how I would officially disconnect from Scott.

I told him I was not interested – the matter was resolved. Randy said he'd do the session for free, so onto the meter we went. It seemed Randy was trying to steer me toward a realization that Bruce was the real source of the suppression. I rejected this.

The issue dragged on for days. I became more distraught as I began to recognize Randy was doing much as the psychiatrists had done. In my view, he was trying to put the problem of a deeply troubled human being out of sight and out of mind. That is all that 'disconnection' would accomplish in my view.

Rightly or wrongly, I made a distinction then and there between how I interpreted Hubbard, and how anyone else did. I decided that no matter what anyone told me, I would hold to my own understandings when they conflicted with someone else's. This was consistent with the first thing I had read from Hubbard, on the first night I walked into the mission: "What is true is what is true for you. No one has any right to force data on you and command you to believe it or else. If it is not true for you, it isn't true. Think your own way through things, accept what is true for you, discard the rest. There is nothing unhappier than one who tries to live in a chaos of lies." Of course, all this was modified by my acceptance of KSW and the agreement that Hubbard and Scientology were *it.* Nonetheless, I would interpret "it" the way *I* saw it, and not necessarily the way the group did.

While it had initially seemed that the mission staff admired my persistence and ability to confront the evil of the Dammasch administration, the more I struggled with my brother's situation, the more they seemed to try to steer me away from my plans. I came to the conclusion that these people were so intent on protecting their organization by keeping any tough case like my brother off their lines, that I had to keep my plans to myself. I was going to complete that auditor training. And regardless of his institutional history, I was going to audit my brother in our own home and bring him back to full sanity.

About the time I'd resolved that once again it was me and my brother against the world, an unexpected bomb hit, throwing chaos into the mix and sinking my hopes.

It was a Saturday night, and I was going to stay up to tell Bruce my plans. When midnight had passed and Bruce still hadn't shown up at the cave, I became concerned. Had he gone on another drinking jag? I waited nervously. Around 3:00 a.m. I heard Bruce coming rapidly down the stairs. He threw open the door, then slammed it hard behind him. He looked hyped up. He had a gash on his forehead. I prepared myself for the hours-long, excruciating process of dragging half sentences out of him, trying to divine what had gone on.

Instead, Bruce immediately blurted out, "I think I might have killed a man."

"Oh, no, bro – what happened?"

"I'm at this club. Some fucker went after some girl that was high. I had to put him down."

"What do you mean, 'put him down'?"

"I grabbed him by the neck and put him against the wall and bounced him for a while; then he went limp and I dropped him."

"Fuck, where did this happen?"

"Forget it; fucker deserved it."

"Bruce, for God's sake, we gotta do something about this."

Silence. I walked right up to him. "Bruce, come on man, we gotta go back." Silence.

"Bruce, that's it, man. Listen to me," I demanded, grabbing him by the shoulder to make him look at me. "We're going back there right now."

Suddenly my neck was hit by what seemed like two iron arms. Bruce had my throat with both hands and was pushing me back into the common room.

"No!" he screamed.

Bam! My back hit the floor, and Bruce's body bounced on mine, knocking the wind out of me. He straddled me, lifted me off the concrete floor several inches and slammed me back down.

"No!" he yelled again. I was choking. He continued slamming me like a paint shaker. "No! No! No! No!" he yelled, slamming me against the floor with each repetition.

My head started bouncing off the hard, cold floor. Finally I blacked out and my body went limp.

Coming to, I opened my eyes slightly, only to hear the front door slam and then Bruce's feet sprinting up the stairs.

I felt warm blood oozing through my hair, off my head and onto the skin of my neck. It took several minutes of coughing before my breathing evened out. I lay there for another several minutes, staring at the ceiling in utter shock.

I finally got up and washed the blood out of my hair. Gingerly feeling the gash, I decided the bleeding was not severe enough to require treatment. I recognized that if Bruce had carried on a little longer, he may have put my lights out for good.

I went to see some people Bruce did drugs with, and determined the guy Bruce had beaten up was only shaken up, and not dead. I went to stay at a fellow student's apartment to try to get my thoughts straight, and avoid being offed in the night by my brother.

I felt like an utter failure. I fought off flu symptoms, walked a great deal, and contemplated the future. I concluded that for the sake of my ultimate plan, I'd have to get away from Bruce for the moment.

I got back into communication with my dad, and we agreed to get Bruce to come back to his home. Dad would do it only on the condition that Bruce voluntarily checked in with the VA hospital in Long Beach and get onto some medication. I would stay in Portland and complete my studies.

With Bruce back home, I went back to my training. Instead of becoming closer to the staff and students at the mission, I could feel us beginning to draw apart. They were good enough people, but they seemed more interested in their personal advancements than in the weightier problems that consumed my mind: How to salvage my brother, or perhaps even tackle the causes of his troubles.

Mission staff, rather than assisting with any advice about my brother, seemed more intent on convincing me that Bruce was only pulling me down, and that my only chance for personal salvation was to disconnect from him. Their running refrain had an effect.

As I grew more distant from both the mission staff and my brother, I grew closer to L. Ron Hubbard through study of his writings and lectures. At first I had embraced Scientology as a subject that offered tools that increased my ability to deal with tough situations in my life. More and more as listened to more Hubbard lectures, I saw it as a philosophical practice, closely aligned with my broader spiritual goals and purposes.

A series of lectures Hubbard had recorded in 1954 in Phoenix, Arizona, resonated strongly. During this phase of his journey he was experimenting with direct exteriorization techniques. He claimed that from one third to one half of all humans could cleanly exteriorize from their bodies, when given one single command: "Be three feet back of your head." Later he advised *against* attempting this, because further research showed it was not necessarily healthy to exteriorize a person who still carried a burden of aberrations in the reactive mind. Instead, Hubbard prescribed the person be audited up through the steps of the grade chart he had developed (the series of steps spelled out in Chapter Five of this book) before direct exteriorization techniques were attempted. However, just the idea that one could simply decide to exteriorize struck a chord with me, in light of the facile, rapid exteriorizations I had experienced.

One thing in particular which sold me on Scientology was Hubbard's lecture embracing the Tao Te Ching and Buddhism, and drawing parallels between those philosophies and Scientology. He said the Tao *"is a very civilized piece of work. It would be the kind of civilized work which you would expect maybe to appear from a very, very educated, extremely compassionate, pleasant people, of a higher intellectual order than we are accustomed to read."*

He drew parallels between the Tao and the place Scientology attempts to take people spiritually: *"Who knows but what if we took the Tao, just as written, and knowing what we know already about Scientology, we simply set out to practice the Tao – I don't know but what we wouldn't get a Theta Clear [highest spiritual state then envisioned for Scientology]."* He also claimed that Scientology processes were directed toward realization of the Tao. He noted in several lectures that Scientology was an inevitable discovery, whether by himself or by someone else:

> *"And so we can look back across a certain span of time, across a great many minds and into a great many places where man has been able to sit still long enough to think through this oldest record and find where it joins up with the present and to what we in Scientology are rightly indebted. For to say that out of whole cloth, and with no background, that a Westerner such as myself should suddenly develop all you need to know to do the thing they were trying to do is an incredible and an unbelievable and an untrue statement. Had the information of the Veda not been available to me, if I had not had a very sharp cognizance of earlier information on this whole track and if at the same*

time I had never been trained in an American university which gave me a background of science, there could not have been enough understanding of the Western world to apply anything Eastern to, and we would have simply had the Eastern world again…So we combined the collective wisdom of all those ages with a sufficient impatience and urgency, a sufficiency of scientific methodology. (And I think, by the way, that Gautama Sakyamuni [the Buddha] probably had a better command of scientific methodology than any of your chairs of science in Western universities.) We have to depend though, upon this scientific methodology and mathematics and so forth, to catalyze and bring to a head the ambition of ten thousand years of thinking men. And if I have added anything to this at all, it has simply been the urgency necessary to arrive, which was fairly well lacking in the Eastern world."

Given my background with the Tao, Buddhism, and Krishnamurti and given the more rapid and more certain gains I had attained in relatively short order with Scientology, I could think of no more rational or purposeful direction to go than to pursue Scientology with heart and soul.

About the time I was forming this certainty that Scientology was the way, an intriguing fellow showed up in the mission, to give a presentation to staff and public. He was short and portly, had a close-cut beard and curly hair. He had intense, clear eyes and an engaging personality. He wore a clean, blue naval-like suit, with a golden lanyard. Billy Kahn told the audience that Ron's organization, the Sea Organization, was looking for people who were serious about bringing sanity to the entire planet. While this organization had originally been so named because it had been based aboard a ship at sea, it was now expanding onto land throughout the world. The Sea Org was composed of Scientologists who were willing to dedicate their present lives, *and* many future lifetimes, to delivering the highest-level services of Scientology to the most advanced of Scientologists. Further, they pledged to manage the organizations of Scientology, and also to tackle the societal ills that keep the populace under suppression and in a degraded state.

Kahn explained that the Sea Org's discipline was tough, but the rewards were immeasurable in terms of the personal, spiritual satisfaction of genuinely serving mankind. Billy presented a slide show featuring shots of the Sea Organization's original ship. It also highlighted the Flag Land Base (or "Flag"), the massive advanced service center in a beautifully renovated twelve-story hotel in

Clearwater, Florida. There were images of the advanced service organizations and management centers in Copenhagen, Denmark and in the United Kingdom. He then showed an aerial shot of the Cedars of Lebanon Hospital complex, covering a block and a half in Los Angeles. He explained that Sea Org members were busy renovating the entire complex so that it could house major intermediate and advanced service centers, in the heart of an area that was home to the greatest concentration of Scientologists in the world.

Billy said that he represented the Publications Organization, or "Pubs," which was responsible for printing and distributing Hubbard's books on a massive scale, and for broad-based promotional campaigns. He told the crowd how many new recruits were needed for the renovation efforts, and then to man the exciting new center. I signed up for a personal interview with Kahn for the next day. I wasn't sold, but certainly wanted to learn more.

When I met Kahn he said he had checked up on me and was impressed with what I had accomplished with my brother. I told him that quite frankly helping my brother was the only reason I had gotten involved in Scientology, and I was disappointed that I couldn't get more cooperation in delivering that help.

Billy empathized with me. He drew a distinction between the mission staff and Sea Organization staff like himself. The former he positioned as something of a group of dilettantes – good folk who use Scientology to make life nicer for themselves and their communities, but who lack the drive and dedication to humankind that Sea Org members had. The latter he positioned as the professionals, the dedicated few on a mission to tackle the causes of human misery.

Kahn was a very competent, smooth recruiter. He convinced me that I was dead right about being dedicated to salvaging my brother. He said the Sea Org worked directly on reforming the kinds of societal ills that led to tragic situations like my brother's. He said that once Scientology was better established in society, it would set up its own hospitals for recovering psychotics. He referred me to several of Hubbard's writings on handling a person in a full-blown psychotic break, such as my brother had suffered. He also told me about a church program called Narconon, which was already actively rehabilitating drug addicts. He provided me with some literature that boasted of Narconon's great successes. He tied several of the Sea

Org's activities back to the aims of Scientology: *A civilization without insanity, without criminals, and without war, where the able can prosper and honest beings can have rights and where man is free to rise to greater heights.*

When I balked, Kahn delivered the *coup de grace.* It was something Hubbard had written in 1969, in which he claimed: "SCIENTOLOGISTS ARE THE PEOPLE WHO ARE CLEANING UP THE FIELD OF MENTAL HEALING AND EFFECTIVELY HANDLING MENTAL HEALTH ON THE PLANET." Kahn told me that this was the number-one target of the Sea Org, and that a person with my first-hand experience in dealing with the existing mental health system would be a most valued asset.

Now that he had a thoroughly captive audience, he leaned over and asked me, "How would you like to head the project to start up the first psychotic-handling facility in Scientology history?"

"Are you kidding me? I'd love to," I said, "but I don't see it in the cards in the near future, from all you've briefed me on."

"Oh, no – once you come down, get your basic training, work in the Pubs organization for a while, you'll be eligible for assignment to Sea Org special projects. We are expanding at such an incredible rate, I think it will be a lot sooner than you can even imagine."

Now that Kahn had my agreement, he handed me the Sea Org contract: a single-page promise that I would serve mankind for the next one billion years; a commitment to stay with it, lifetime after lifetime, until the aims of Scientology for the world were achieved. I told Kahn I'd have to think about that one.

I did think about it for several days.

A spirited debate broke out between my ears. On the one side, the assertion was that it's best to continue with your simple plan, stay with the mission in Portland and learn to be an auditor, and heal Bruce yourself. On the other hand, there was this: the plan isn't working – you can't even live with your brother, let alone cure him; the only way you can handle him is to take responsibility for creating facilities that *can* do it, and in that way help mankind too.

Ultimately, a mixture of my greatest weaknesses and fears (my failures to handle insanity within my own family, and my apathy over ever winning at it) and my greatest strength (my ability to put bodily comfort aside and sacrifice for the betterment of all) led me to sign that billion-year contract. In the back of my mind I still held doubts about Kahn's representations. I also realized that I would always have a safety valve, in the event he'd been outright conning me. I could do what I had always done in the past when I believed I was entrapped: hit the road.

I walked out of the mission that night with a light step, my head teeming with ideas of helping my brother and a whole lot of other folks who are similarly situated. A few weeks later I hopped onto an airplane to Los Angeles, the beginning of a new billion-year adventure.

CHAPTER NINE

SCIENTOLOGY'S PETER PRINCIPLE

Peter Principle: The ***Peter Principle*** *states that "in a hierarchy every employee tends to rise to his level of incompetence," meaning that employees tend to be promoted until they reach a position in which they cannot work competently.*

The Cedars of Lebanon Hospital complex covered one and one half blocks on Hollywood's eastern border, where it meets the City of Los Angeles. It was built in the 1930s and abandoned sometime earlier in the '70s. Its seven-story main hospital building had been a Hollywood landmark for years. The church had bought it for a song, and was in the early stages of a massive renovation project. The plan was for the complex to house several different organizations. First, the Los Angeles Church of Scientology Organization, delivering introductory and lower-level services. Next, the American Saint Hill Organization (named after a similar organization located at Saint Hill Manor, in England) which would deliver intermediate services. Next, the Advanced Organization of Los Angeles (delivering upper-level Scientology services), the Publications Organization, and the church's Western United States (WUS) management headquarters.

Apparently, quite a few Billy Kahns had been ranging out across the US, promising the fulfillment of whatever dreams potential recruits held dearest. I met dozens of young men and woman who had only recently come on board, just as I had, from cities all over the country. First order of business for each of us was to enter the

Estates Project Force (EPF). In the EPF one goes through a number of basic training courses, orienting and indoctrinating one in the ways of the Sea Org. You start with a batch of lectures Hubbard recorded in the late '60s and early '70s. In these talks he sounds quite a bit more serious than in the taped lectures I had been listening to at the Portland Mission, most of which were recorded in the early '60s.

In these lectures, Hubbard tells how in the late '60s, attacks on Scientology by establishment vested interests had become so numerous and so intense that a Fabian organization was the only answer. He explained "Fabian" as meaning "on the move" or "elusive" – thus never gratifying the enemy with an easy target.

An organization was created that was to be to the world what the thetan is to the body, ideally: three feet in back of it, invisible, and able to control it. The Sea Org was born in 1967. Hubbard purchased a ship and had the Sea Org refit it. He christened the vessel the *Apollo*. Ron lived aboard, and relocated Scientology's international management headquarters there, too. The *Apollo* frequented many Mediterranean and Caribbean ports until 1975, when it was retired. Hubbard and the Sea Org returned to land in Florida. The strict sea-faring discipline mutually enforced amongst its members, and their shared sense of deep dedication, spurred the group to many almost super-human exploits – mostly having to do with expanding the Scientology network across the world, despite the best efforts of such august groups as the American Psychiatric Association (APA), American Medical Association (AMA), and CIA to squash it.

Because shared dedication toward common goals and the discipline of life at sea had created such an effective organization, the Sea Org maintained a nautical, naval tradition. Many staff wore navy-like uniforms. Naval ranks and ratings were bestowed for outstanding achievements. Meals were taken communally, with diners grouped in military-style messes. Sleeping quarters were referred to as berthing, floors were called decks, and Scientology's founder, Hubbard, was known as the Commodore.

It all was a bit too regimented for me, coming from an untamed childhood and free-wheeling teenage upbringing. But there was also something refreshing about the simple order and the high ethical standards. I had experienced something similar in playing high school and college basketball. This new strict environment I'd entered was even better, in that it was all directed toward a worthwhile common purpose: to bring peace to Earth and sanity to all its people.

The EPF studied for five hours in the evenings, and worked the rest of the day on renovation projects. Hubbard explained that one hallmark of a Sea Org member was that from the outset, he or she learned to confront and handle MEST (the physical world – matter, energy, space and time). This had a very healthy effect on the individual's later capabilities as an administrator or technical staff member (delivering auditing and training services).

In his recorded lectures to Sea Org members, Hubbard's tone and mood ranged between cheerful, confident insouciance, and conspiratorial tones regarding what Scientology was doing to bring about a sane, crime- and war-free world – and how the establishment was working to crush those efforts.

Hubbard talked as if you, the listener, were in with a tight-knit group; a trusted few who had the fate of the world in their hands. I found it all rather adventurous and heady. Given my experience with institutional psychiatry, and having been exposed to the best of Scientology with my exterior-to-the-body experiences, Hubbard's Sea Org lectures carried a lot of weight and credibility with me.

New recruits lived in converted hospital rooms, two double bunks to a small room. Men and women berthed on separate floors. Casual, promiscuous, or extra-marital sexual relations were strictly forbidden. Dining was communal in the Sea Org. At the complex, hundreds of members ate at two sittings in the old hospital cafeteria. The food was wholesome, we got eight hours of sleep time, and received $17.20 a week as pocket money.

I had no complaints. I did initially bristle at the lack of free time – one day off every other week, provided your work statistics were up for the week. I found the experience, on the whole, a rather successful socialist experiment. Morale was high among hundreds of people, all working along a good purpose line.

After several days of manual labor, I was summoned to the seventh floor of one of the buildings. I reported to the Mission Ops, or mission operator. (Some types of Sea Org projects were referred to as "missions," similar to the term used for some military operations. This usage was different to its use to refer to a small Scientology organization, such as the one I'd studied in, in Portland.)

The woman looked sharp in her naval-style uniform, complete

with gold lanyard and colorful campaign bars. She informed me that I had been chosen to go on a mission which was critical to the success of the overall renovations program. My mission was to serve, along with two others, in the purchasing office for all the renovations. I was put through Mission School, a several-day course which taught me a lot of administrative rules and protocol; then I was sworn in as a missionaire.

I studied with another fellow who had arrived in the Sea Org on just about the same day I did. He was also my age, and we shared similar backgrounds and interests. Marc Pesch was almost a six-foot-four, east-coast version of me. We both had had interesting, action-filled youth years, and found hitchhiking, hiking and adventure after high school. We both brought with us a strong work ethic.

When we completed our briefing, Marc and I reported to the I/C (in-charge) of our mission. We were pleasantly surprised to find our In-Charge was a laid-back, friendly woman named Vicki. Vicki was happy to get a couple of competent gamers who knew how to work hard, and enjoyed it. Marc and I were a team. Marc would call suppliers (lumber, paint, hardware, motors, electrical, you name it), find the best deal in Los Angeles, and I'd pay for, pick up and deliver the material back to the renovation sites.

Most often I delivered to the Rehabilitation Project Force (RPF). The RPF was a strictly-controlled group of Sea Org staff who had been "busted" from their posts for severe sabotage of projects, treasonous activity, or for being found to have evil, destructive tendencies, evidenced by a particular phenomenon that sometimes occurred in auditing sessions using an e-meter. In auditing, the e-meter was used to detect areas of travail, conflict or upset just below the awareness of the person being audited. When such areas were approached, the needle on the meter's dial would move; auditors were trained to recognize the various different patterns of needle motion, to understand what each meant, and then to apply the appropriate auditing technique to relieve the trouble. One rare but distinctly recognizable needle action was called a "rock slam." It looked like the needle had "gone crazy," violently slashing and slamming back and forth across the dial. A rock slam indicated that the preclear (the person being audited) harbored an evil purpose or destructive intention. If the intention expressed or area addressed had to do with Scientology, L. Ron Hubbard, or anything to do with the subject of the mind or spirit, such an individual was labeled a suppressive person - roughly equivalent to a sociopath or psychopath.

One of the purposes of the Rehabilitation Project Force program was to "de-psychopath" such people. According to strict organizational policy, the RPF's schedule was to include five hours of every day devoted to study and auditing, addressing these and other mental or spiritual troubles. The intention was to fully rehabilitate the person – to help him or her return to being a contributing staff member.

Despite the policy's requirements, the RPF in Los Angeles was doing nothing but manual labor, eighteen hours a day, all in the rush to finish the big renovations project. The RPF – about 300 people in all – made up the bulk of the work force for the whole enterprise.

As part of their rehabilitation (penance for the misdeeds that landed them in the RPF) members dressed in beat-up boiler suits (similar to jump suits). They were not allowed to walk, but instead had to run anywhere they went. They were not permitted to speak to any person not in the RPF unless first addressed by that person. I probably would have bolted at the sight of this slave-labor force, had it not been for the great morale, efficiency and *esprit de corps* they demonstrated.

Marc and I worked like a professional ball team. We were fast and competent, and we had fun along the way. Since we worked in an isolated unit and wore regular civilian clothes to interact with outside vendors, Marc and I were pretty much spared the regimented lifestyle of most Sea Org members. We were irreverent about the pomp and formality. We became good negotiators and saved the church hundreds of thousands of dollars over the several months we were on the project, so the powers-that-be were not much concerned how we conducted ourselves personally. Despite the urgency of the project, I even managed to get a few Sundays off that year, and visited my dad and brother, living less than two hours away from Los Angeles.

Some of the most memorable events of my initial months in the Sea Org were all-staff briefings periodically given by Heber Jenztsch, the church's spokesperson. Heber was a hearty fellow in his 40s. He had been a professional stage and screen actor, and was a fine singer, with a deep, pleasant voice – and he could really work a crowd with his humor and wit.

On a couple of occasions during 1977, he gathered all the local staff to brief them, after the news media had reported on FBI raids on the Los Angeles and Washington, D.C. church headquarters – the biggest coordinated raid in FBI history. As Heber told it, the FBI and IRS had targeted the church for decades, at the behest of the American Psychiatric Association and the American Medical Association. It seems the AMA considered Hubbard and Scientology threats to the "Great Health Monopoly," since they offered inexpensive, effective methods for curing insanity, neurosis and psychosomatic illness.

For years, the church had been making extensive use of the Freedom of Information Act, seeking to uncover evidence of illegal and unconstitutional government attacks on L. Ron Hubbard and Scientology. After a number of years of cross-referencing documents, the church learned that the FBI, the Department of Justice and IRS were systematically hiding information which, under law, ought to have been disclosed. A couple of overzealous staff members of the church's public relations and legal unit, the Guardian's Office, had a plan. They got jobs at the Department of Justice and IRS, and made photo copies of the information being unlawfully withheld. This, according to Heber, was why the FBI reacted so violently with the massive raids.

Heber contended that the "D.C. 9" – nine indicted high-ranking members of the Guardian's Office, including Hubbard's wife Mary Sue – were being pursued by the Department of Justice for stealing Xerox paper, since there was no law precluding the transfer of information from government files. Heber told amusing anecdotes about the raid, like how tough it was for FBI agents to work up the courage to get around the complex's guard dog (a very friendly German Shepherd all staff were familiar with). Heber's stage presence and insouciance were much like that demonstrated by Hubbard in his lectures.

After one of Heber's briefings, the Guardian's Office had every single one of the hundreds of staff at the complex dress up in "civies" (civilian clothes) to be bused to the United States District Courthouse in Los Angeles. Upon arrival we were given signs condemning the US government for "raiding a church." We marched around the courthouse for hours, while Heber worked the curious media who showed up.

In mid-summer 1978 Marc and I wrapped up our mission. After a huge completion party, Marc went off to the sub-organization that had recruited him, and I went off to Kahn's Publication Organization (referred to as "Pubs"). Pubs was located about five miles from the Cedars complex, closer to downtown LA.

Pubs was a bit too regimented for my liking. Most of the 50-some staff wore dark slacks and white shirts, and the executives also wore naval rank epaulets on their shoulders. I was assigned to be an expeditor. My job was to help out with menial tasks in whatever division had a heavy workload and needed some grunts. I worked shipping books, stuffing envelopes, delivering books to the Scientology organizations around LA, sweeping, cleaning – whatever Billy Kahn decided to assign me on any given day. I was also to be on training courses five hour a day, in the staff course room. There I met the head of staff training and auditing, John Colletto.

Colletto was a Class VIII auditor – a very advanced level of auditor training and, presumably, skill. Attaining this level included the right for Colletto to use the title "Dean of Technology." The fact that Pubs staff were under the care of such a highly trained Scientologist was a big part of Billy Kahn's recruitment pitch. Despite the hype and his lofty title, John turned out to be a dull, serious, bored, overweight, bespectacled man in his late twenties. For someone who was supposed to have attained the higher levels of training and spirituality in Scientology, he struck me as a pretty troubled individual.

My assigned study period meant I'd be alone for five hours each day under Colletto's supervision. He showed me no warmth – in fact, what I often got instead was disdain.

The texts for my courses consisted of organizational policy letters and directives, written over a span of many years. They were full of Scientology organizational jargon, which made study a grinding task. Adding to the difficulty was the fact that the jargon itself had evolved over time, so that writings from different periods had different terminology. Sometimes my only hope for making sense of what I read was to ask Colletto for clarifications. But it seemed whenever I asked his help, he would take the opportunity to leave me feeling stupid. I began to withdraw into myself and just try to grind it out alone.

During study time one day, I began dozing off. "Wake up," snapped Colletto.

"I must have gone by a word I didn't get," I said, referring to the principle from Hubbard's study technology that when someone passes a misunderstood word, they can become foggy or dope off.

Instead of helping me find what word I didn't understand (as course supervisors are trained to do), Colletto pulled out the *Scientology Technical Dictionary*. Opening the book, he showed me the definition of "implant" – a technical term from auditing technology, meaning *"a painful and forceful means of overwhelming a being with artificial purposes or false concepts, in a malicious attempt to control and suppress him."*

I thought I understood Colletto's point. In Scientology auditing, one recalls moments of pain and unconsciousness from his past, reviewing them until they are discharged of the mental energy they contain, and their destructive mental and spiritual effects. By reviewing and relieving enough such incidents, the state of Clear can eventually be reached.

"Yeah, I get it. I suppose these implants can come up during one's auditing."

"They do come up. Everybody has them. How many do you think you might have?"

"I don't know. I haven't had any auditing. So I suppose I'll find out I have a few."

Leaning across the table and fixing me with an icy stare, just inches from my face, Colletto said, "Try a few *million*." At that he got up, went back to his desk, picked up some papers and started reading.

I sat there, stunned and more confused than ever. What was the point of *that*? I thought to myself, "This highly-trained guy got in my face just like that Dr. Stern, the psychiatrist. Same intent, emanating the same wavelength." The effect was the same, too – Colletto had left me feeling as small, dumb and confused as I had when speaking with the doctor.

During a break, I asked Colletto's superior if I could speak with him outside. His name was Mike Sutter. He was my age, but he was trained in the technology. I told Sutter I was real uncomfortable studying with this Colletto character, and that Colletto was the polar opposite of what I thought Scientology was about. He was the complete antithesis of the high-energy, friendly course supervisors I'd known in Portland. I had the idea Colletto was trying to make me feel smaller and more confused. Sutter sighed and told me he knew Colletto had some issues, but I needed to concentrate on my material and not get sidetracked by Colletto's personality.

This was just the first of many encounters with Sea Org bureaucracy. Sutter was apt at sidestepping issues and convincing me to grin and bear it, a quality I would later find common among Sea Org executives. In fact, Mike Sutter was a good example of what I came to think of as the Scientology "Peter Principle" bureaucracy.

In Scientology organizations, rather than rising to the level of their incompetence (as described in the book *The Peter Principle*), executives tended to rise to the degree they were respectful and subservient to others' ranks, training levels, and organizational positions. An executive was considered competent to the degree he could navigate the politics of those three factors, irrespective of the facts and equities of the matters they encountered. People who were particularly wary of poking their noses into any trouble, were competent at making a convincing case against a scapegoat, and were unquestioningly loyal to their superiors were the "cream" that tended to rise to the top in Scientology management.

Back in the course room with Colletto, I felt sort of imprisoned – trapped in a place I did not want to be, with a person I had no desire to be around. I began to daydream about heading back out on the road. I weighed the pluses and minuses of going back to pursuing my dreams of traveling and writing.

A couple weeks later, while on the verge of bolting from the Sea Org altogether, I was informed by a new course supervisor that Colletto had been sent to the Rehabilitation Project Force (RPF). Apparently (and through no connection with my complaint about the fellow) some auditor had run into a Rock Slam read on the e-meter while auditing Colletto. As described earlier, this indicated the presence of a hidden, powerfully motivating evil purpose. I did not fully understand the technicalities, but in this particular instance I felt somewhat vindicated. I also gave a pass to the bureaucracy, thinking that if they could isolate an anti-social person – and better yet, cure him – then this system might have something going for it, regardless of how crazy it may have looked.

Relieved, I felt matters now might regularize. Maybe I'd be able to complete my basic staff studies in peace and carry on with some measure of equilibrium in my Sea Org life.

Instead, my world was again turned suddenly, violently upside down.

CHAPTER TEN

A MATTER OF LIFE AND DEATH

If you stay in the center and embrace death with your whole heart, you will endure forever. – Tao Te Ching

Billy Kahn approached me one late August evening right about quitting time. "Mark, I was wondering whether you could help me with something; it's sort of personal. You know Diane Colletto is my cousin?"

"No," I replied. I only knew her as the small, quiet, mature, dark, curly-headed woman who was responsible for marketing Dianetics and Scientology books. It was her job to see that the books sold in large numbers, both in Scientology orgs and missions and in commercial bookstores. It always struck me as odd that such a seemingly mousy woman could command an undertaking one would expect a gangbuster to head.

"Recently her husband John suddenly picked up and left from the RPF. He made a call to her that she considers threatening," Billy said, rolling his eyes a bit.

"He threatened her?" I asked.

Billy smiled, "She thinks he did. I doubt it, but look, Diane is a delicate girl and she's a bit shaken with the whole notion of John leaving and all. However much she has this mocked up in her head, it doesn't really matter. She leaves later than anyone else and I thought she'd just feel more comfortable if someone rode along with her. Would you stay late and do that?"

"Sure. Whatever you need, man."

He added, "There really is nothing to it. It is really just…well, she's my cousin, and I want to do it just so she doesn't have any attention on it, okay?"

"All right," I replied. "What do you expect this guy might do?"

"Nothing, absolutely nothing," Bill said. "John has always been a blowhard. But for God's sakes, he's a Class VIII auditor. No, just ride with her to make her feel better."

"No problem, Billy, I'll get ahead on letter stuffing while I wait," I assured him.

Billy said, "Great, thanks," got up from his chair, threw his jacket over his shoulder, smiled and walked out. Most of the other staff filtered out by 10:30. Diane stayed till some time past 11:00. She quietly walked into the room where I was stuffing envelopes and said, "Hello. Do you want to go now?" "Sure," I replied. We locked up behind us, got into her compact car and headed west on Rampart Boulevard. It was an unseasonably cold weekday night. There was very little traffic, even on the large boulevards. Diane didn't say a thing as we drove to the Complex. Oddly, rather than turn right on a main boulevard which would take us one short block from the Complex, she took a number of smaller streets, winding us up a block to the west of the Complex. We pulled to a stop at Catalina St. and Fountain Avenue, a two-lane road that served as the back border of the complex. We had just a block to go to get to the staff entrance. There was not a soul or a moving vehicle in sight.

Just before Diane turned right onto Fountain, a car parked half a block west and facing our direction turned on its headlights. As we pulled onto Fountain, the distant car sped up behind us and tailgated for a couple seconds, then flipped on its bright lights. Diane looked up at the rearview mirror. Almost instantly the other car, an old, cream-colored Volvo, accelerated and pulled up to our driver's side, straddling the broken white line in the middle of the road. I felt a violent slam as the Volvo veered sharply into our side, jolting the vehicle to the right. Inexplicably, Diane just let go of the steering wheel and let up on the gas. The Volvo overtook us, and drove our car into the curb.

John Colletto leaped out of the Volvo and approached Diane's side of the car. I quickly opened the passenger-side door, and just as I was half-way out, I heard the driver side window crash. Through the windshield I saw a brilliant flash near Diane's left leg, and heard a loud, sharp pop. I continued running around the car's hood toward Colletto.

My first thought was that Colletto was terrorizing his wife with a cap or blank gun. As I rounded the left front headlight and rushed toward Colletto, I saw blood oozing out of Diane's left leg. Colletto grabbed her black hair with his left hand, yanked her head up and put the gun to her head with his right.

"You fucking bitch!" he screamed at her, as I smacked my forearm into the side of his head. I was off balance, but managed to get a grip on Colletto's collar and swing him into the street.

"Run! Run, Diane!" I yelled, as John and I spun hard out into the middle of the road. I caught a glimpse of her opening her door and climbing out. We continued to spin, Colletto desperately attempting to point the gun at Diane while I struggled to get a lock on his neck and take him down. I wrestled myself in closer and forced my left forearm into the front of his neck. I began to squeeze with everything I had. As we grappled across the road, I suddenly felt and heard a crushing blow across the back of my neck. The more I applied pressure on John's neck the harder he slammed the gun barrel into the back of my head and neck. I could not see Diane anymore, and hoped she had gotten away.

Suddenly, the gun hit a soft spot and I went blank, like a black hood coming down over my eyes. My body went limp and splayed across the asphalt. My face hit the gutter on the far side of the road, but my vision had returned enough to see that Colletto had landed on his back in the center of the street. He rose to his feet and ran toward the sidewalk where Diane's car had been pinned. On the other side of the sidewalk, a three-foot-high picket fence framed a little bungalow's half-dirt, half-lawn front yard.

As I rose to my feet, I saw John approaching Diane, who was lying face down on the sidewalk, a large pool of blood forming around her wounded leg. I sprinted toward the two. John pulled her up by the hair and was bringing the gun up with his other hand. Before he could put the muzzle to her head, I hit him with a flying tackle. We landed in a tangle up against the picket fence. Diane looked up and our eyes met for a fraction of second. "Run, Diane!" I yelled again, grabbing John's right arm as he attempted to take aim at her.

The wrestling got tricky as I tried to maneuver this 250-pound body holding a loaded weapon. With one arm I had to keep the gun pointed away from both Diane and me, while using the rest of my body to bring Colletto down. I tried kneeing him in the groin, but it was well protected by his massive paunch. I twisted the weapon into the air above Colletto's head and we spun again.

Gaining a foothold, I used my legs to shove both of us over the picket fence and onto the dirt lawn. As we hit, Colletto's gun hand was freed and I saw the barrel coming for my face. I thrust my hand out to deflect it. Blam! A shot fired inches from my face. I put both my hands on John's to force the gun away from my face. As we struggled to our feet, another bullet narrowly missed my head. Gaining a good position at last, I threw Colletto to the ground, hard. Landing on top of him, I pinned the gun barrel to the ground with one hand. John squeezed off another round, and on reflex my hand jerked back. Rolling over on top of me, John grabbed the gun with both hands.

I had but one hand free to force his arms back from pointing it straight at me. He rolled again, and I had to use both hands to unpin myself from the ground. I felt the muzzle go straight into the base of my skull.

CLICK! My entire body went limp, and instantly I was watching the scene from ten feet above our bodies. I was sure I was dead. Then I spotted that John was sprinting back to the picket fence; the gun had misfired.

By the time I'd scrambled to my feet and jumped the fence, he had the gun pressed to Diane's throat.

Once again I grabbed him by the neck and we swung back around into the middle of the road. He crouched low and swung me off him. As I got up, he again was kneeling over Diane's body. He stuck the gun muzzle into her mouth. I sprinted at him and as I took off into a flying kick, the gun fired. Diane's body went limp. John dropped the gun as my foot sent him rolling westward into the street. He got up and sprinted away. I picked up the gun, aimed it at him and pulled the trigger. CLICK! It was empty.

I turned and ran eastward on Fountain, then left down Catalina toward the staff entrance to the complex. As I rounded the corner, the staff security guard spotted me running toward him, waving a gun above my head and yelling "Help!" at the top of my lungs. Terrified, the guard ran in the other direction. As I turned to run back to Diane, I saw Colletto speed off in his Volvo. I threw the pistol at the back window, but without enough velocity to catch the speeding car.

I was surprised to see no one on the street. It seemed like we had been fighting for an hour. When I got to Diane's body, she was on her back, bloody bubbles gurgling from her mouth. I knelt down and propped her upper body against my thigh, hoping to open her breathing passage. I took off my shirt, bunched into a makeshift pillow and cradled her head against my stomach. There was more gurgling, and blood was spraying all over my chest and face. In a few seconds there were no more bubbles – only blood, pouring from the side of her mouth. We were both covered in blood and sitting in a pool of it.

Just then an LAPD squad car came screaming around the corner. It spun, bounced off our curb only a few yards away and came to rest in the middle of Fountain Ave. Two officers jumped out, kneeled behind their doors and aimed their pistols at me.

"Face down, fucker!" one of them screamed.

"No!" I protested. "I'm helping her!"

"Face down NOW, or we'll put you down. NOW!"

I gently laid Diane down on the concrete, and lay down on the sidewalk, my face in a pool of her blood.

One of the cops ran to me, pulled my arms behind my back and cuffed me. The other ran to Diane, felt for a pulse, looked up at his partner and said, "She's gone." As I was being hauled over to the black-and-white, two more police cars roared up to the scene. I explained to the cop assigned to guard me what had happened. I pointed with my head to where the gun lay, several yards down the street. He asked another officer to retrieve the weapon. I scanned the area, searching for any witnesses. There was not a single civilian in sight. By then, two more police cars and an ambulance had arrived. With six sets of orange, red and blue lights spinning, the block had a surrealistic look.

Just as I had about convinced the first officer of my innocence, two more cops showed up and started interrogating me all over again – antagonistically, as if I were the perpetrator. Two more cops gathered round. As I sat defenseless in the back of the squad car, my hands cuffed behind my back, blood covering my shirtless body, with not a witness in sight, it dawned on me that I might be tried for murder.

Just as the police were about to slam the door and haul me into the station, I heard a Mexican-sounding voice approaching the vehicle. "Hey, hey! I seen the whole thing!" A thin, thirty-something Latino came right for my door. Addressing me, he said, "Man, I seen the whole thing from up there!" pointing to a second-story apartment window directly across the street. "I seen the whole thing. Man, you were great!"

The cops looked at one another, bewildered. The Latino fellow took off his white tank-top t-shirt and approached me. When he got too close, a cop grabbed his shoulder. The man tossed me the shirt as he was pulled away. "You must be freezing. Take it, man." As they pulled the Latino man away, he told the officers "You got the wrong man, man. He was great, man."

The first cop who originally cuffed me helped me out of the car. He unlocked my cuffs and let me put the t-shirt on. It didn't do a lot to cover my body, but I suddenly felt a whole lot warmer. A sergeant arrived on the scene and spoke to several of the officers, out of my earshot. When they broke up, two officers approached me, put me into the back of the squad car and sped from the scene.

When I arrived at Rampart Station I had no idea that I would be put through the gauntlet. I was afforded one small styrofoam cup of stale, black coffee. It would be the last sign of civility I would see until dawn. I sat in a bleak holding room for an hour. Then I was lead out to an interview room, to meet the detective assigned to the case. He had black hair, a thick mustache, and a pock-marked complexion. He carried a no-nonsense attitude, like "Don't even waste my time with stories; I've heard them all."

He certainly wasn't interested in my story. Instead, he wanted to know what Diane Colletto and I had going on that we were out past 11:30 on a weekday night.

"Nothing. I didn't even know the woman until an hour before."

"Oh, so it was some quick pick-up, huh?" he grinned.

I explained exactly what occurred before the fateful car trip. He told me wasn't buying any of it, and more importantly, neither would a jury. He told me I could rot in the California penal system for the rest of my life, or I could be a good boy, cooperate, maybe get twenty years, be out in ten on parole and live a relatively normal life.

I asked about the witness that arrived on the scene. He called out the door to another officer, "Anybody make a statement in this case, Phil?"

Phil replied with a bored "No."

"Sorry pal, no witnesses."

"But, what happened to the guy who showed up and said he saw the whole thing?" I protested.

The detective smirked, "Who knows? If he existed, maybe he had his own dirty laundry and headed for the hills."

The detective left and then returned to the room several times, each time confronting me with another piece of condemning evidence. "You know your prints are all over that gun, don't you?" he said at one point.

I replied, "Of course they are, and I was the one who pointed out where the gun was, to one of your officers. I've got nothing to hide."

About 4:00 a.m., the detective informed me there was a phone call for me. "You can play roulette, take the call and something good happens. If not, you used up the one call that you could have used to arrange counsel and bail."

I elected to take the call. "Heber Jentzsch here."

I was in awe to be talking directly to a man of such stature. He told me to listen well, then proceeded to lay out in detail John Colletto's psychiatric and criminal history. August 1966, arrested for illegal amphetamine distribution, incarcerated. July 1967, committed to Camarillo State Hospital for the Criminally Insane after pummeling a girlfriend. He was administered electroshock treatment during that visit. Heber went on for about three minutes with a non-stop rap sheet on John Colletto. He finally advised, "Just tell him all that."

When Heber had finished, I told him earnestly, "Thank you."

"No problem", he replied. "Keep your head up."

After I related all I had learned about Colletto's past, the detective told me he would get back to me and left the room. I sat alone for another hour. Then another officer came in, handed me my wallet and my belt and told me I was free to leave.

It was just before sunrise when I walked out onto Rampart Boulevard. I took a deep breath of cool, early morning air. I lit a Camel as I walked slowly up the street. My perceptions were as sharp as they had ever been, yet I was in a strange sort of reverie. I wondered how that final bullet had misfired when the muzzle was pressed against my skull – but then fired when it was shoved down Diane's throat. I thought about the man who had come to my defense, and then mysteriously disappeared. Perhaps he was in the country without the proper paperwork, and the police had intimidated him into disappearing when it came time to make a statement.

Years later, that very Rampart Division of the LAPD would become subject of a Los Angeles Times series about its engaging in widespread corruption involving misuse and abuse of informants. I didn't know about any such abuses at the time of the incident, but I knew very well they'd done everything in their power to get me to confess to a crime I had not committed.

In reviewing the night's events, I recognized that with no witnesses, the police could easily have pinned the crime on me. I felt a deep sense of gratitude toward the witness who had stepped forward, probably against his own best interests. He might have saved me from a life in prison. I felt remorse for having failed to save Diane, and grief over the loss of her life. I concluded that had I been given the opportunity to re-live the incident, the only thing I'd have done differently would have been to first locate a blunt object and knock out the assailant before he could fire a fatal shot.

As all these musings settled, my final thought gave me a measure of peace. It was the recognition that at a moment when I faced death very directly indeed, I had most definitely departed from my body. It was as clean a break between the material and the spiritual as I had experienced in 1973 in the Fallbrook gym, and in 1977 at the Portland Mission. I would never again question that my true personal identity was quite separate and distinct from my body. I would never again fear death.

CHAPTER ELEVEN

OVER THE RAINBOW

Somewhere, over the rainbow,
Skies are blue.
And the dreams that you dare to dream
Really do come true.
– *Somewhere Over the Rainbow*, E.Y. Harburg

When I returned to the Complex, Kahn and the Pubs executives treated me like a returning war veteran. They seemed impressed that I had fought the armed Colletto to the last shot. I thought their reaction was a bit odd. I myself was more disappointed that I'd allowed him to kill Diane.

The Commanding Officer (the person in charge, in any Sea Org outfit) at Pubs was a woman named Vicki. She had holed up in her berthing room at the Complex for fear that Colletto might return to off her next. She apparently got this idea in talking it over with big-wigs in the church's legal arm, called the Guardian's Office. The reasoning went that since Vicki had ordered Colletto to the RPF in the first place, he might return, seeking revenge.

Kahn told me that Vicki would feel a whole lot safer if I was posted in the room across the hall from hers until Colletto was found. He asked if there was anything I needed. I told him, "A baseball bat." Kahn went out and found a Louisville Slugger and deposited it with me in an old hospital room across the hall from

Vicki's. I sat by the window for a couple days reading books and keeping an eye on the entrance to the complex.

The assignment ended when the LA Police Department reported that they had found Colletto in a semi-rural area, with a pistol in his hand and a bullet through his head. The coroner ruled it a suicide.

The Scientology funeral ceremony for Diane was a memorable affair. A minister read off the church's funeral service, authored by Hubbard. It is quite a piece of poetry and treats the spirit with dignity. The service is addressed to both the audience and to the deceased. In this case, the minister addressed the audience with:

Our suff'ring is self-centered here, for we have lost, in truth,
the smile, the touch, the skill and happiness we gained from Diane
who gave to us from her past ability to live and fare against the tides and storms of fate.
It's true we've lost Diane's shoulder up against the wheel and lost as well her counsel and her strength
But lost them only for a while.

After several similar stanzas it addressed Diane directly:

Goodbye, Diane.
Your people thank you for having lived
Earth is better for your having lived
Men, women and children are alive today
because you lived.
We thank you for coming to us.
We do not contest your
right to go away.
Your debts are paid.
This chapter of thy life is shut.
Go now, dear Diane, and live once more
in happier time and place.
Thank you, Diane.

And then, back to the audience:

All now here lift up
Your eyes and say to Diane
Goodbye.

Everyone complied. When we all had said goodbye, a super-light energy accompanied by a cool breeze shot through my hair and over the top of the others gathered there, lasting just a brief moment. Afterward, several others commented on having experienced the same afterward. Diane had connected with me and I felt I received a "thank you" from her. It was not verbal, but more real to me than words. And then I perceived Diane leaving through a window overlooking a courtyard. To this day that moment stands out as one of the most spiritual experiences of my life. It was an objective perception of exteriorization and continuance of the soul beyond the body.

Life at Pubs seemed pretty mundane once I was back into the grind. But that did not last for long. I was called into an office by a couple of Commodore's Messenger Organization missionaires. The CMO, as the organization was commonly called, was composed of younger people. At the time ages ranged from about seventeen to the early twenties. The older members had served as message runners for Hubbard when they were kids, aboard the *Apollo*. As they grew, Hubbard gave them more complicated duties, saw to their training and took them under his wing. By the time some of the original messengers were in their late teens, they had formed up an organization. Now the CMO was beginning to set up remote units connected to larger Sea Org installations, to serve as eyes and ears for Hubbard around the world. The CMO was also beginning to recruit new members who had never served near Hubbard, nor even met him.

One of the missionaires informed me that I had been chosen to go "over the rainbow." This meant I was to go to the secret base where Hubbard was living. I asked why me, since I was green, had little Scientology training and no auditing. I was told that Hubbard had been briefed on the Colletto incident and commented positively on whoever it had been who stood up to the gunman. One of the messengers on duty at the time passed that comment along to the recruitment mission. The mission looked up my files, interviewed my superiors and decided I could make the grade. I was told that virtually nobody – including the highest-ranking people in LA – knew the location of Hubbard's base, or what I was being recruited for. So I had to keep my mouth shut, not mentioning a word of this to anyone. I was then told to fill out a life history form.

The life history form was quite an undertaking. Its various

sections asked for details about nearly every aspect of my life. Such things as every drug I'd ever taken, when and where; every sexual encounter I'd ever had, with whom, when and where; every unethical act I'd ever committed, when and where; every friend I ever had, when and where. It went on and on. I hesitated at confessing my entire life to who knows who. But I reconciled that they needed to be careful who they let near Hubbard, given the efforts to drag him down over the years. When I'd completed the lengthy form I was told to be sessionable the next day. "Sessionable" means that one is prepared for an auditing session – well rested, well fed and having had no alcohol for at least a full day before the session's start.

I arrived for my session the next day and met my auditor, Ellen. She was a good-looking, twenty-something woman with a professional bearing. She explained that my sessions were going to consist of security checking – a form of confessional auditing. In security checking, and all auditing that employs the e-meter, the preclear and auditor are seated across from each other at a table or desk. The meter faces the auditor, positioned so its dial can be easily seen and its controls worked. The preclear holds the meter's electrodes (metal cylinders similar to cans), one in each hand. A tiny, imperceptible electrical current (about that of a double-A battery) flows from the meter, though the preclear's body and back to the meter. The meter is designed and calibrated such that it will register extremely minute changes in the body's electrical state, caused by mental changes and reactions. Such reactions are reflected in motions of a slim, light needle on the meter's main dial. Auditors are extensively trained and drilled to recognize the various needle motions, to understand what they mean, and how to appropriately proceed based on what the meter does and what the preclear says and does. Since the meter is sensitive enough to detect mental reactions and changes that are slightly *below* the preclear's level of conscious awareness, the auditor can use it to assist the preclear to uncover thoughts, reactions, concerns and mental barriers that wouldn't otherwise be detectable. By locating and addressing such hidden troubles, they can be relieved – which is the entire purpose of auditing.

In security checking, the auditor reads questions to the preclear from a list prepared before the session. As a question is read, the auditor notes whether it produces a reaction on the meter. Such a reaction indicates that there is "charge" (unwanted mental energy) in the preclear's mind, in connection with what the question asks. The auditor then works with the preclear to discover the thoughts or incidents underlying the charge, and uses the appropriate auditing techniques to alleviate it. A question that produces a reaction on the meter is said to be "charged" or "reading." The meter needles reaction is called a "read."

It is called security checking because it was developed for use in detecting security risks – people who intended to harm or interfere with the organization in some way (even if such intentions were unknown even to the person being checked, such as unwanted intentions stemming from mental troubles). A security check's questions concern past harmful actions one has committed, and kept hidden.

So I was to receive a security check, to ensure that I wasn't a risk. Ellen pointed out, though, that I ought to relax and enjoy the process – since airing one's past transgressions and misdeeds, particularly those that one has tried hardest to keep secret, is one of the most mentally and spiritually therapeutic activities there is.

Despite Ellen's advice to relax and enjoy it, the security check began about like pulling teeth without Novocaine. Revealing your closely-held secrets to a woman you hardly know isn't easy. This was particularly so because she dutifully kept handwritten notes of everything I told her. But soon I found that there was a tremendous relief attained in venting transgressions.

Hubbard's theory behind confessional type auditing is that every time one transgresses against what he considers is right, and then withholds that wrongdoing, a certain percentage of his or her available attention is locked up – pinned back in time with the decision to keep a secret. I found this to be true for me. The more I progressed through the security check, the more attention I had free in the present. I felt fresher and more alive. I also began to see the real utility of the e-meter. Hubbard noted that as one stacks up a vault of guilty secrets, another byproduct of locking away attention out of the present is that amnesia sets in. Since the meter registers just below the level of awareness, the auditor can guide the person toward recovering memory that has been blotted out.

As I went about my daily activities after each session, I began noticing I could recall whole segments of my life which before had seemed erased from memory. I also starting noticing a lot more detail in my surroundings – as if my perceptions had sharpened. All of my senses – taste, touch, sight, smell, hearing, and intuition – were noticeably improving. This made me feel fresh and interested. Most startling was the increase in visual perception. I noticed my peripheral vision markedly increasing, session by session.

Finally, right in the middle of a day's session, I went exterior again, very clearly rising above my head and viewing the session from above my body and that of the auditor. When the session ended, all I could think to do was take a long walk, to get oriented to operating the body from a position a few feet above and back of the head. I walked for several blocks, marveling at the city, the cars, the people, the lights. Everything looked brand new, as though I'd never seen it before. After an hour or so, I sort of slid back into a position closer to my head. However, over the next several days I noticed that, unlike previous exteriorizations, I continued to have several separate moments during any given day where I would notice myself above the head.

My fear of the unknown, going to an undisclosed location and cutting virtually all ties with the life and people I had known, began to dissipate. I reasoned that if this technology could produce a state of spiritual awareness of the kind I'd experienced in such short order, then dedicating my life wholeheartedly to making that technology more available and accessible was the most honorable thing I could do.

The journey over the rainbow was like something out of a spy novel. I left my clothes in a box in an empty room off an unused corridor of the complex. I made sure nobody saw me enter the corridor. The next morning I was instructed to walk to the parking lot of a grocery store several blocks from the complex. I was told to "tail shake" – that is, to take a long, circuitous route and keep an eye over my shoulder to ensure nobody was following me. I was given a description of a fellow who worked in the unit called LRH (Hubbard) External Communications (LEC). I was to meet this person in the designated parking lot. After conscientiously carrying out all these instructions, I saw my man sitting behind the wheel of a compact car. He nodded me over.

When I got into the passenger seat, the driver introduced himself as simply "Chuck." He promptly took off and went into his own tail-shaking mode. He drove randomly through the streets of LA's Silver Lake District, through winding residential sections, down dead-end streets and back. He constantly flicked his eyes to his side-view and rearview mirrors, checking for tails. Then we went over the hills and into the San Fernando Valley. Once there, the entire tail-shaking drill began anew.

After another ten minutes of driving as if trying to get out of maze, Chuck pulled into a supermarket parking lot. He pulled up next to another compact car, with a low-key looking man in his late twenties sitting in the driver's seat. Chuck and his contact simultaneously opened their doors, walked to the back of their respective cars and opened their trunks. The two drivers exchanged banker's boxes full of written communications (usually called "dispatches" in Scientology policies), tucked them into their trunks, then returned to their driver's seats. Motioning at the other car with his head, Chuck looked at me and smiled. "There's your ride," he said. "Good luck."

"Hi Mark; I'm Sarge," said the second car's driver, as I settled into the front passenger seat. He was a skinny man wearing a cowboy shirt and jeans, which seemed to fit perfectly with his laid-back personality. Sarge sort of looked like the working man's version of Jack Nicholson. With a country-western radio station on at a pleasant, background volume, he handled the driving chore like an old pro. Sarge did the tail-shake routine, but he drove more slowly. He was more casual but more thorough than Chuck had been. Once Sarge was assured no one was following us, he relaxed even more.

"Actually my name is Steve. Steve Pfauth. Sarge is my 'a-k-a,' – my 'also known as.' We all have aka's for security purposes. We keep real tight security for the Old Man. You know – with all the FBI and media nonsense and all. You should start thinking of an aka for yourself. The idea goes like this. Suppose you're out in the local town on a liberty (a day off, in Sea Org lingo). If someone recognizes you, but they hear the person you're with calling you by an unfamiliar name, they might just convince themselves you're just a look-alike. It ought to be something close to your name so it's easy to remember, and will stick with the people at the base."

As Sarge spoke, the radio played the song *El Paso* by Marty Robbins. "How does 'Marty' sound?" I asked. Sarge hesitated, grinned, looked at the radio to acknowledge where I got the idea, and said "Perfect."

We had a couple-hour drive east on Interstate 10. Sarge spent the time briefing me on security. According to Sarge, we were headed toward a place called WHQ (Winter Headquarters), a several-acre property in La Quinta, near Indio, California. LRH's home was there; people called it "Rifle." Hubbard's main priority was producing a series of instructional and promotional films for Scientology. Hubbard considered this vitally important for raising the quality and quantity of auditors across the world. His wife Mary Sue and some high-level Guardian's Office staff had been at WHQ at its inception, a couple years earlier. However, they hadn't been around much since the July, 1977 FBI raids on their LA and Washington, DC offices. The Guardian's Office (GO) was still involved in supervision of overall security for the WHQ base.

When we finally arrived to WHQ, it seemed as though I really had arrived "over the rainbow." The place had a spiritual air about it, perceptible from the moment we drove onto the property. The staff were very friendly, but not in a syrupy, cultish way. They were very much engaged and worked long hours, but at meals and during the course of the work day, their communication level was very high – infectiously so.

Some old date packing sheds on the property had been converted into storage for landscaping gear and for film-making equipment and lights. There was a dining hall, a study room for staff training, and some smaller residential units where people slept. At the time, there were about 150 staff at WHQ.

I learned that the Commodore's Messenger Org (CMO) was getting more and more involved with management of the church. They were trying to take the job of management off of LRH's plate, so he could concentrate on his films, and developing new technology. I would later learn there was a necessity for that withdrawal from direct control because of the complications of the FBI raids connected with his wife's GO operations.

About the time I arrived, LRH had begun to isolate himself from direct contact with any senior management personnel of the church – both the administrators of the Guardian's Office, which handled all external-facing affairs (legal, public relations, etc.) and the administrators of the Sea Organization who managed all other aspects of church operations. I would later learn that Hubbard had recently recovered from an illness that had nearly taken his life earlier that year.

When I first arrived at WHQ, my job was pulling weeds in a several-acre date palm grove, which separated Hubbard's home and the rest of the WHQ buildings. I also served as garbage man (today it would be "waste management engineer"), keeping the grounds clean and the trash cans around the property empty. After doing all this for about a week, I was put into briefing for another mission. I was to join twenty-five other new recruits, forming up a team to renovate a newly acquired property. It was referred to as SHQ (Summer Headquarters). The idea was that Hubbard would have two bases of operations. SHQ was located about forty minutes from WHQ. It was a 500-acre former resort property near Hemet, California. I would serve as purchaser for the renovations crew.

Within a couple of weeks I joined the new SHQ crew in renovating Hubbard's quarters at WHQ. Hubbard ordered that the small house be stripped of fiberglass insulation, since breathing in loose fibers was considered a serious health hazard. Hubbard moved to a hotel in Palm Springs until the job was done. We worked around the clock for a couple of weeks, stripping the insulation out of the walls and attic, vacuuming every last microscopic fiber out of the home, filling the walls with pulp insulation, sealing everything up and finally cleaning every square inch to white-glove standards.

From time to time during the wind-down of the job, the Commodore's Messenger in charge of the project came to inspect. Eighteen-year-old, five-foot five-inch David Miscavige was Action Chief, in charge of firing and running all missions out of WHQ. He hadn't spent much time on watch with Hubbard himself, but by virtue of his CMO Action Chief post, he had his hands in a lot of the action being ordered by Hubbard. Miscavige had intense blue eyes, dirty blonde long hair and mustache. When he came into the house to inspect, he'd be trailed by the executives in charge of operations on the ground. The latter were nervous and quick to answer any of Miscavige's questions, their answers always punctuated with a sharp "Sir."

I never had any direct contact with Miscavige during that project. But his importance had been made clear. Some high-level Sea Org executives I had come to respect acted like boot-camp privates around him, bending over backward to stay in his good graces.

Any time Hubbard was staying at Rifle, the male WHQ staff all took turns doing night security watch duty. On one occasion, I drew night watch duty, just after we had finished a couple of all-nighters readying Hubbard's home for his return. I sat in a beach chair on Hubbard's front lawn, with a flashlight and a walkie-talkie. I was positioned a few yards away from Hubbard's office window. He worked in the office until about 3:00 in the morning, visiting with staff he called in from around the base. I was thrilled to hear the muffled boom of Hubbard's voice as he joked, hollered, and spoke in more direct tones with his Messengers and the staff who visited.

That was as close as I would ever come to meeting Hubbard. After he went to sleep, I had a very difficult time keeping my eyes open, not having slept the entire night before – and having had very little sleep the entire week leading up to my watch duty. I finally dozed off, only to be awakened by automatic sprinklers coming on, just before dawn.

CHAPTER TWELVE

THE ECHO CHAMBER

A "No" uttered from the deepest conviction is better than a "Yes" merely uttered to please, or worse, to avoid trouble. – Mahatma Gandhi

Most of those in the twenty-five-member crew that fired to renovate SHQ were as green as I. We were a fairly motley crew. Most were in their early twenties and had long hair and/or beards. Our Commanding Officer was Captain Bill Robertson. He was a heavy-set, blonde, middle-aged man with much the same powerful bearing as Hubbard. In fact, Robertson had once been the Deputy Commodore, answering to no one but Hubbard himself. But Robertson – like all other veteran Sea Org Officers – was now apparently losing direct access to Hubbard. It seems the Commodore's Messenger Org was being organized and groomed to take over international management of Scientology. Increasingly, veteran Sea Org officers were being stripped of command status.

Robertson's fear was evident when I received my first written dispatch from Ron. It was a short memo asking me to consider liaising with the purchaser of the Los Angeles Complex renovations. Ron wanted me to work with the LA purchaser to make a deal with the same paint company that had been used for the LA renovations, since the paint quality was great and the price we'd finagled was even better.

I responded that that would not be a problem since I was the LA purchaser who had made that very paint purchase deal. Robertson was anxious for me to write all this up and give it to him for forwarding to Ron. Two days later, Robertson came into my office with Ron's reply. Oddly, it was addressed to Robertson, not me. I asked to see what had been sent to Ron. Robertson produced a dispatch he had written himself and sent in lieu of mine. He had stolen all of the technical detail I had provided, and passed off the expertise as his own. The dispatch was larded with repeated references to the brilliance of Ron's original order. I found it unsettling that this huge man, a Sea Org legend, would stoop to such dishonest, obsequious conduct, just to curry favor with Ron. I was to learn, though, that Robertson's example of echoing back to Hubbard with praise for the genius of his ideas was a requirement for any communication to be forwarded to him.

Within days of arriving to SHQ, Miscavige came storming into the small group of administrative offices that once had served the resort. They were now occupied by Robertson, a couple other veteran officers in charge of our crew, and me as the purchaser. Miscavige and another messenger stomped into Robertson's office, which was right across from my desk, slammed the door behind him and started giving Robertson a tongue-lashing, liberally laced with obscenities. After less than a minute, Miscavige ripped the door open and stomped out of the office and then the building, presumably to make the forty-minute return drive to WHQ.

I turned to the second-in-charge of our crew, the veteran Gary Wiese. "Who the fuck does he think he is?" I asked. Wiese said that he was a Commodore's Messenger. I told Wiese that I didn't think he was serving Hubbard very well by being such a prick. Wiese told me I ought to hold my criticism. He showed me a Sea Org directive from Hubbard, issued less than two months earlier. Entitled *Commodore's Messengers*, it included this injunction: "A Commodore's Messenger carrying an order or running a project or otherwise on duty is an emissary of the Commodore. What is said or done to that Messenger by the staff or person receiving the Messenger's orders is being said or done to the Commodore." Wiese told me that I had better keep any observations I had about Messengers to myself, or I could wind up in a heap of trouble.

I heeded the warning. But the irrationality of Hubbard's order was not lost on me – and it became more obvious as time went on.

Many of the messengers I dealt with over the next couple of years demonstrated immaturity, lack of education, lack of judgment, and arrogance. This was particularly so as the top Messenger organization, known as CMO International, began to form up. It took on a lot of young people who had never met Hubbard, let alone been trained by him on how to conduct themselves and do business. Further, for the most part the messengers had not had the benefit of much auditing, nor were they trained in the auditing technology or even the basics of Scientology philosophy. On the plus side, they had a no-nonsense attitude about getting tasks efficiently performed to a high-standard result, and a clear loyalty to one person alone: Hubbard himself.

I was soon put into a position where I could intimately observe the messengers' interaction with Hubbard on the one side and international church managers on the other. After a few months of doing touch-up renovations on the several blocks of old motel rooms on the SHQ property, the entire crew from WHQ moved to SHQ. The WHQ location had been compromised by some staff who had departed, so it was decided to shut the place down entirely. Hubbard took off with a couple of messengers to parts unknown while the new base was readied.

SHQ became the international headquarters of Scientology management, and remains so to this day. I was promoted to a small unit called LRH External Communications (LEC). LEC was an adjunct to and served the CMO, but its members were not messengers. The unit consisted of an in-charge, two telex operators and a couple of staff to handle mail and serve as couriers. Our job was to relay communications from the SHQ base to Hubbard and vice versa. Since Ron was sending orders and directives to Sea Organization management, which was then located in Clearwater Florida, we also relayed communications from SHQ to another small unit in Los Angeles, which would forward it on to Florida and other locations.

I was posted as a courier. My direct supervisor was the fellow who had brought me to WHQ originally, Sarge. His job was now Mail Director in LEC. After a while Sarge went off to a new secret unit with Hubbard, in an apartment complex in nearby Hemet. This new, tiny base of operations was referred to as X. Sarge and I worked out a number of drop locations in San Bernardino and Riverside, where he and I would meet to exchange boxes of communications, as well as people going to and from Hubbard's Hemet locale.

Every day I collected internal communications from the CMO offices, logged them and packaged them. In addition to the X runs, I would drive mail packages to Los Angeles, taking along any staff who were leaving SHQ, usually to go on a mission of one kind or another. I had to learn the art of tail-shaking and all aspects of security. It was intended that SHQ would remain secure (its location kept secret). Further, once whatever heat had made Hubbard decide to go on the road had blown over, he would return to SHQ to complete production of his technical training films.

There were a couple dozen messengers posted at SHQ. They had formed up into a formal organization called CMO Int (Commodore's Messenger Organization International). At Hubbard's direction they were organized around picking up the management duties he had been performing, with a view toward taking management off his plate entirely. Hubbard advised that the most senior and competent of the messenger's form up a "watch dog committee" (WDC) to serve as the highest management oversight body within the growing Scientology bureaucracy.

Hubbard had written nine encyclopedic volumes on organizational principles and procedures, which we referred to as administrative technology. This body of work was based on the philosophy of Scientology and its technologies of mental and spiritual betterment. When applied intelligently and ethically, it made for a very efficient operation.

Unfortunately, Hubbard's instructions to set up a whole new echelon of super-management contradicted a great deal of his nine-volume body of work on administrative theory and practice. Most notably they set up a bypass of entire echelons of existing management, which per Ron's own administrative technology would result in the demise of those bypassed. Since I had only trained in this work on the fly and wasn't considered proficient in the administrative technology, I simply noted the incongruity conditionally and carried on.

I also doubled as the physical education instructor for the CMO. Hubbard had written a dispatch ordering the post be created – that someone who knows something about physical conditioning be put in charge of the messengers' daily exercise. He included the injunction that anyone who did not show up for exercise would lose their pay for that week. Although the messengers were all senior to me, they had to treat me with some respect for two reasons. One, if I did not make an exception, and they missed a day of exercise (which was common, given the long working hours in the Sea Org), they could lose their pay on my order. Two, they were prohibited from doing anything to delay LRH's communication lines, yet were continually asking me the favor of holding the mail run for them.

The messengers had their own section in the crew dining hall. They were treated to higher-quality food than the rest of the crew. Regular (non-messenger) crew members were posted as stewards, to wait on them at meals. The crew at large (mainly the technical films crew, known as Golden Era Productions, and the estates maintenance staff) were served from a communal buffet set-up.

The messengers often took off for paid group outings, such as going to the movies, a play, bowling or the like – a luxury the regular crew rarely experienced. At the same time, for the most part the standards of competence and discipline were higher in the CMO. For the dozen or so main messengers who were responsible for handling international management and obtaining compliance to Hubbard's orders, life was not easy.

As Action Chief and an original watchdog committee member, Miscavige came to know me fairly well. Action sent and received far more communications to and from the base than any other unit, so he was continually asking me to delay the communication run's departure, so important items could be included rather than waiting for the next run. He and the rest of the messengers learned to count on me to buy them time, knowing I was willing and able to make up the time on the road.

Miscavige was obsessive about winning sports contests; it was a by-any-means-necessary proposition for him. Since he was one of the alpha messengers, he repeatedly chose me to play on his team when the messengers split up for team sports like basketball, football or volleyball. And since he had me on his team, and the rest of the messengers were lame at sports, we generally won. Since I was generally a pretty easy-going person, most of the messengers got along with me. I also wasn't under the same continual pressure as the messengers, with steady streams of orders from Hubbard.

Running Hubbard's super-secret lines of communication was

adventurous and fun for a while. But after several months I'd mastered the job, so the next couple years were fairly uneventful. Working at the highest levels of the Sea Organization, and continually training on Hubbard's administrative methods, I became fully indoctrinated into the mindset of a veteran Sea Org member. That ethic and frame of mind could be summed up as follows.

First, one of the most fundamental principles of Scientology philosophy – one that is learned and used from the outset – gives one a brand-new view of the universe. This is the principle of the dynamics of existence. Hubbard postulated that life could be arbitrarily broken down into eight separate drives or urges toward survival. These drives he called the dynamics (summarized from writings of Ron):

> ***1st dynamic****, the urge toward existence as one's self. Here we have individuality expressed fully. Also called the self dynamic.*
> ***2nd dynamic****, the urge toward existence as a sexual activity. The second dynamic has two divisions, (a) the sexual act itself, and (b) the family unit, including the rearing of children. Also called the sex dynamic.*
> ***3rd dynamic****, the urge toward existence in groups of individuals. Any group or part of an entire class could be considered to be a part of the third dynamic. The school, the society, the town, the nation, are each part of the third dynamic and each one is a third dynamic. Also known as the group dynamic.*
> ***4th dynamic****, the urge toward existence as mankind. Whereas a race could be considered a third dynamic, all races would be considered the fourth dynamic. Also called the mankind dynamic.*
> ***5th dynamic****, the urge toward existence of the animal kingdom. This includes all living things whether vegetable or animal, anything motivated by life. Also called the animal dynamic.*
> ***6th dynamic****, the urge toward existence as the physical universe. The physical universe is defined as Matter, Energy, Space, and Time, or MEST for short in Scientology. Also known as the universe dynamic.*
> ***7th dynamic****, the urge toward existence as or of spirits. Anything spiritual, with or without identity, would come under the heading of the seventh dynamic. Also called the spiritual dynamic.*
> ***8th dynamic****, the urge toward existence as infinity. This is also identified as the Supreme Being. Scientology professes not to intrude into the dynamic of the Supreme Being in keeping with its considering itself a science. Also*

called the infinity or God dynamic.

The concept of the dynamics can be used to great effect in determining the course of action one will take in any given situation – in other words, one's personal ethics. The ethics system of Scientology can be easily summed up by the following equation. Right or good actions consist of those which result in the greatest good for the greatest number of dynamics, and the least harm to the greatest number. Wrong or bad actions would be the converse. Over the years, I was able to help others sort out many personal difficulties more than satisfactorily, just by educating them on this formula and encouraging them to apply it.

The method works quite well when you heed Hubbard's advice that no dynamic has seniority over any other dynamic – they are all of equal importance and value. Herein lay one of the first major paradoxes I was to encounter in Scientology. It could well be the basic point in the dichotomy that exists between Scientology the philosophy or technology and Scientology the culture and organization. The first and most distinctive point of a Sea Org member or staff Scientologist's ethos is adoption of the idea that the third dynamic – the group – trumps all other dynamics. More specifically, the third dynamic of the Scientology society, the Scientology organization, and most notably the Sea Organization takes precedence over any other dynamic or even combination of dynamics.

This was firmly held as true, notwithstanding Hubbard writings stating that an attitude of "the group is everything and the individual is nothing" is about as anathema to spiritual freedom as one could imagine. While there is no specific Scientology writing that says the group trumps all a person's other dynamics, the concept has become so thoroughly agreed upon as to be palpable. It goes something like this: "because Scientology is the *only* technology that can free an individual along all dynamics, it and the organizations that propagate it are more important than the dynamics themselves." This is so well agreed upon amongst Scientologists that it has lead to a corollary truth: amongst Scientologists, the ends of the organization always justify the means used to attain them.

That is lesson number one for the Sea Organization member. It is a point of pride amongst Sea Org members, considered the main factor distinguishing them from non-members. It is such a firmly-held belief that Sea Organization members consider regular Scientology staff and public Scientologists (lay parishioners) a lower class of being – all because of that single distinction.

The second lesson of the Sea Org member is that one develops a can-do attitude. Grousing or wasting time discussing how things might not get done will get you shot (figuratively) fast. So one adopts and applies Hubbard's motto for the Sea Org: "Make it go right." One learns to turn off negative thought when given a program to execute or an instruction to accomplish something. That has its advantages in terms of execution of projects and orders; but, over time it can have catastrophic consequences.

Lesson three is that one never present a problem to a senior. You solve any problem that arises by making it go right. If you require authorization from above to act, you present your senior with a written proposal which includes: (a) the specific situation you are confronting, clearly defined (b) all relevant data concerning the matter, and (c) your proposed solution to the problem. One is trained to compile these petitions, called "completed staff work" or "CSW," in such a thorough fashion that the senior person can digest it and sign it off as either okay or not okay, with no further questioning or discussion required.

Fourth, you learn to never accept a problem from someone junior to you. You only accept thorough and honest completed staff work (in proper form, as described) with an acceptable solution proposed. One also learns to override others' concerns or considerations – with anything from strongly expressed intention all the way up to physical force if necessary - that might interfere with one's own programs.

Fifth – and really part and parcel of numbers three and four above – you learn to respect the chain of command. The closer one is to L. Ron Hubbard (referred to as the Commodore in the Sea Org) the less one asks questions and the more one puts his life on the line to get done whatever is demanded.

Sixth, you learn loyalty to the Commodore and his organization, the Sea Org. If you follow Hubbard's policy and technology and effectively execute a lot of the planning and programming Hubbard himself has instituted, you are considered "on source." "Source" in this context means Hubbard, the source of Scientology. If you eschew Hubbard's advice, fail to follow his teachings and directives exactly, or advise action that does not align with Hubbard's intentions and policy, you are considered "off source," one of the most damning labels a Sea Org member can receive.

When you've got hundreds of people operating as per one through six above, and you become aware of the results in terms of more and more people leading better lives using Scientology technologies, it can be a very rewarding experience. And that reinforces the lessons, day in and day out. Soon the first lesson – the group taking precedence over all other dynamics – is so solidly fixed that it is never given another thought.

The seventh lesson was explained and memorialized by L. Ron Hubbard in a thirteen-page policy letter entitled "The Responsibilities of Leaders." It begins with a several-page essay summarizing the rise and fall of nineteenth-century South American liberator Simon Bolivar. Hubbard speaks of Bolivar in glowing terms: brave, dashing, and cunning. He recounts how one of Bolivar's many mistresses, Manuela Saenz, stood above all the rest. Hubbard then analyzes Bolivar's failure to empower Saenz to use any means she deemed necessary to keep his enemies at bay, and how Saenz failed to demand or utilize such power. That, per Hubbard, was the reason that Bolivar and Saenz wound up dying in a ditch, penniless.

Among other things, Hubbard criticizes Saenz for the following faults:

> *...she never collected or forged or stole any document to bring down enemies...*
> *...she never used a penny to buy a quick knife or even a solid piece of evidence...*
> *...she was not ruthless enough to make up for his lack of ruthlessness...*
> *...she never handed over any daughter of a family clamoring against her to Negro troops and then said, "Which over-verbal family is next?"*

And so Bolivar and Saenz became victims of the petty jealousies and shortcomings of the mere mortals who surrounded the romantic couple. The policy letter concludes with three pages of Hubbard's seven points about power to be learned from Bolivar's life. They are offered as points one can only fully grasp if one has already learned well the six lessons of a veteran Sea Organization member, described earlier. Those seven points about power deserve some attention here, for three reasons.

One is that Hubbard and his wife wound up living the Bolivar story Ron recounted as we shall see. Second, while adherence to the policy contributed to great strides for Scientology expansion, in Hubbard's waning years the policy's lessons had a backfire effect. Third, this one single writing would become the bible of his successors. It would take precedence over all other of the thousands of pages of policy letters Hubbard had issued.

Here are Hubbard's seven points concerning power:

> One: *…if you lead, you must either let them (those you lead) get on with it or lead them on with it actively.*
> Two: *When the game or show is over, there must be a new game or a new show. And if there isn't, somebody else is jolly well going to start one, and if you won't let anyone do it, the game will become getting you.*
> Three: *If you have power, use it or delegate it or you sure won't have it long.*
> Four: *When you have people, use them or they will soon become most unhappy and you won't have them anymore.*

All very rational and sage so far. But the final three points are a bit more complicated:

> Five: *When you move off a point of power, pay all your obligations on the nail, empower all your friends completely and move off with your pockets full of artillery, potential blackmail on every erstwhile rival, unlimited funds in your private account and the addresses of experienced assassins and go live in Bulgravia and bribe the police…Abandoning power utterly is dangerous indeed.*

Then we graduate up to intrigue and believing that the ends must necessarily justify the means in dealing with any attempt to lessen a power:

> Six: *When you're close to power get some delegated to you, enough to do your job and protect yourself and your interests, for you can be shot, fellow, shot, as the position near power is delicious but dangerous, dangerous always, open to the taunts of any enemy of the power who dare not boot the power but can boot you. So to live at all in the shadow or employ of a power, you must yourself gather and USE enough power to hold your own – without just nattering (carpingly criticize) to the power to "kill Pete," in straightforward*

> *or more suppressive veiled ways to him, as these wreck the power that supports yours. He doesn't have to know all the bad news, and if he's a power really, he won't ask all the time, "What are all those dead bodies doing at the door?" And if you are clever, you never let it be thought* HE *killed them – that weakens you and also hurts the power source. "Well, boss, about those dead bodies, nobody will suppose you did it.* ***She*** *over there, those pink legs sticking out, didn't like me." "Well," he'll say if he really is a power, "why are you bothering me with it if it's done and you did it. Where's my blue ink?" Or "Skipper, three shore patrolmen will be along soon with your cook, Dober, and they'll want to tell you he beat up Simson?" "Who's Simson?" "He's a clerk in the enemy office downtown." "Good. When they've done it, take Dober down to the dispensary for any treatment he needs. Oh yes. Raise his pay." Or "Sir, could I have the power to sign divisional orders?" "Sure."*

And when one can develop that attitude and park one's conscience when it comes to dealing with the "enemy" of the power one serves and from whom one derives his own power, the final point can be performed without a second thought.

> Seven: *And lastly and most important, for we all aren't on the stage with our names in lights, always push power in the direction of anyone on whose power you depend. It may be more money for the power or more ease or a snarling defense of the power to a critic or even the dull thud of one of his enemies in the dark or the glorious blaze of the whole enemy camp as a birthday surprise.*

During my two years handling Hubbard's communications to and from his messengers at the international Scientology headquarters, Hubbard withdrew further and further from the church. I would soon learn the reason why, and play a central role in attempting to combat that reason. As competing factions within the by-then sprawling international Scientology network vied for power in the larger-than-life vacuum left by Ron, he who adhered most exclusively and closely to the seven points of power from *The Responsibilities of Leaders* would emerge with *all* the power.

CHAPTER THIRTEEN

COINTELPRO

Cointelpro: (an acronym for ***Co****unter* ***Intel****ligence* ***Pro****gram) was a series of covert, and often illegal, projects conducted by the United States Federal Bureau of Investigation (FBI) aimed at surveiling, infiltrating, discrediting, and disrupting domestic political organizations.* – Wikipedia

By the efforts of a number of dedicated Sea Org members and thousands of staff members around the world applying the seven fundamental tenets of a staff member, Scientology had reached its apex of breadth and membership by mid-1981. The new international management echelon had fully formed up at the Int Headquarters base (formerly known as Summer Headquarters). Known as the Commodore's Messenger Organization International (CMO Int), it was lead by the Watch Dog Committee (WDC), made up of Hubbard's most trusted senior messengers. At the top were Dede Reisdorf Voegeding, the Commanding Officer (CO CMO INT and WDC Chairman) and her sister Gale Reisdorf Irwin (Deputy Commanding Officer) – early-twenty-something women who were virtually raised from their young teens by L. Ron Hubbard and his wife Mary Sue. Hubbard's accolades to Dede and Gale had been legion over the previous two years. He had credited them with having reformed management and taken the task of directly handling international management off of his plate.

Scientology had missions that introduced people to Scientology and delivered the first several levels of its Bridge to Freedom in most cities across the Western world with a population over 500,000 people. In most cases those missions were bustling, productive affairs, much like the one in Portland, Oregon through which I had been introduced to Scientology.

There were Scientology "churches" or "organizations" in most major cities with a population of more than one million people. The organizations (or "orgs" in Scientology speak) were the next level mission parishioners visited to carry on with their auditing (counseling) and training.

Then there were Sea Org service organizations. These were larger Advanced Organizations, located in Los Angeles, at Saint Hill Manor in Sussex, England (Hubbard's home in the sixties), and in Copenhagen, Denmark. Auditing and training above the level of Clear (called "Operating Thetan" or "OT" levels) were delivered in the advanced orgs.

Finally, there was the Flag Land Base in Clearwater, Florida. It was referred to amongst Scientologists as Flag. Here the highest-level spiritual services were delivered. Advanced Scientologists would travel to Flag from around the world for auditing and training retreats, lasting from a week to several months.

Just as I was being bolstered by the idea that Scientology was on the verge of reaching levels of expansion that would make its aim of a sane planet something more than a pipe dream, I received a couple of alarming wake-up calls.

The first was from my father. My brother Bruce had died. He had picked one too many bar-room fights. After one of them he had been followed home and knifed to death, his body left to rot in a Southern California field. My father was as devastated as I was. I was given some auditing that addressed the loss, and many similar losses that had occurred over this and previous lifetimes. It pulled me out of the worst of my grieving and gave me the strength to go home for a couple of days, to help lift my dad out of his depression.

In my brief time away from the Int base, I had some time to contemplate. I resolved that I had done what I could, with the tools I had, to help raise my brother out of his madness, but had failed. Now I would re-dedicate myself to the goals that had prompted me to choose a mission much larger than my brother's salvation. It would be the mission to handle the causes of insanity on the planet. I would do the best I was capable of doing to forward the aims of the Sea Org and L. Ron Hubbard, live or die in the attempt.

The second wake-up call occurred in early July, 1981. I was summoned to the offices on the Int base where the senior-most messengers ran projects. I reported to the mission In-Charge, a senior messenger named Terri Gamboa. Terri, in her mid-twenties, was older than most of the other messengers. Like Dede and Gale, she had been raised by Hubbard through her teens, aboard the Sea Org ship *Apollo*. She was sharp as a laser and no-nonsense. If you too were sharp as a laser and no-nonsense, she could be exceptionally friendly. If you strayed from whatever the task at hand might be, she could come down on you like a storm. Terri was taught personally by Ron not to think in complex terms. Instead, she was programmed to use all of her natural personality and talents to obtain compliance to Ron's intentions.

Terri was accompanied by her mission second, Norman Starkey. Norman was not a messenger, but was a veteran Sea Org executive who had once captained the Sea Org's flagship, the *Apollo*. He was a Sea Org legend, having been trained in seamanship by L. Ron Hubbard himself, during the late sixties and early seventies.

I was briefed that I had been chosen to join the team of what was called the "Special Project." The operator of the project – that is, the executive one step above and directing it – was David Miscavige. His title was Special Project Ops (short for Operator). The Special Project was of such importance that nobody in the Commodores Messenger's Organization was permitted to interrupt or cross what we were doing. There was a special line of command that went directly from Hubbard himself, through Miscavige, to us.

At that time Hubbard's whereabouts were unknown and he had just two people accompanying him. The first was Annie Broeker, a twenty-four-year-old who had served as a messenger to Hubbard since she was a child. Annie handled virtually all of Hubbard's domestic and office needs. Annie's husband Pat also went along to serve as the liaison – the point of communication relay to and from Miscavige. Because of the nature of the Special Project, we were to take no orders from the top level of church management, CMO International – Dede and Gale included.

The briefing for the project was shocking. L. Ron Hubbard was in danger. It was because of a terrible betrayal by the group responsible for protecting Hubbard and the church from external attacks, the Guardian's Office (GO). Mary Sue Hubbard, as Scientology's Controller, was senior to and ultimately responsible for the Guardian's Office. The GO was formed in 1966 to serve as the buffer between the vested interests who wanted to destroy Scientology, and L. Ron Hubbard, the Sea Org, and all Scientology organizations. It was set up by Mary Sue to act autonomously – separate from Hubbard and the Sea Org – so that they could concentrate completely on the task of managing the organizations and the delivery of Scientology itself. It was the shock squad network that Hubbard had criticized Manuela Saenz for failing to set up to protect Simon Bolivar.

By 1981 the Guardian's Office had become a huge bureaucracy. First there was Controller's Committee – the GO's oversight group, based in Los Angeles and headed by Mary Sue. Guardian's Office Worldwide (GO WW), with its more than 200 staff, managed an international network of Guardian's Office units from its headquarters at Saint Hill Manor in Sussex, England. It had formed continental offices in the United States, England, Europe, Canada, South Africa, and Australia. Each of these offices had from 50 to 200 staff of their own. The Continental Offices supervised smaller local offices in all major cities across the world. Each of these local offices was housed on the premises of a Scientology church (org), but was not under that church's control. All told, the GO network consisted of nearly 3,000 staff. It had massive intelligence files both at worldwide headquarters in England, and at the largest continental office, located in Los Angeles (GO US).

Since joining up with the Sea Org, I had already learned that the GO was to be respected and feared. I would occasionally see GO staff walking around the Complex in Los Angeles. They wore regular business attire, and had a serious, secretive air about them, very much in keeping with their reputation for toughness. They had to be tough – they were the ones who dealt directly with the enemies of Scientology. They were not to be fooled around with. In addition to being immune to discipline from Sea Org members, they were accomplished at the darker arts of espionage and intelligence.

According to the secret briefing I received, the GO had been infiltrated by FBI operatives, who had encouraged the GO to participate in illegal acts. The FBI conducted a raid on the church and GO in 1977; they followed this up with indictments and convictions of Mary Sue Hubbard and ten other top GO executives on charges of obstruction of justice. The indictment spelled out the GO's activities in infiltrating government offices, seeking to obtain files on Scientology. Tens of thousands of pages of internal GO documents seized in the raid had briefly gone on the public record, during court proceedings in Washington, D.C. Taking advantage of that window of opportunity, several enemies of the church had photocopied thousands of pages. Now, exposés detailing the GO's underhanded tactics were being published in mainstream media (the *Los Angeles Times*, the *St. Petersburg Times*, the *Washington Post*, the *Boston Globe*, even national magazines).

Exacerbating matters was the fact that in 1978 an unrelated, Christian cult had made international headlines when its leader Jim Jones led 900 of his followers in a mass suicide in Jonestown, Guyana. Anti-cult groups were springing up around the country, and with the news of the FBI raids and the hijinks of the GO, they began targeting Scientology as well as Jones' People's Temple, the Hare Krishnas, and the Unification Church (Moonies). A network of such anti-cult groups had formed up, concentrating more and more on Scientology. It recruited lawyers who had filed more than three dozen lawsuits across the nation. Most of the suits named the corporation housing the highest levels of GO and Sea Org management, the Church of Scientology of California. That was where the money was. But they also named L. Ron Hubbard as a defendant. As a result, process servers, government operatives and investigative reporters were hot on Hubbard's trail.

Hubbard had ordered the Special Project be formed, with the purpose of getting to the bottom of the attempts to target him personally. He felt the GO could no longer be trusted. Via Mary Sue, they were giving him more and more bad news about how the mounting lawsuits could not be easily and swiftly handled. The Special Project's objective was to bypass the GO, get to the truth of the matter, form up a defense for Hubbard and attain an "all clear." This meant all legal threats to Hubbard were to be ended, so that he could return to the Int Base and finally turn over the reins of management, and complete production of his technical training films. These two objectives were his major life goals at the time – the most important things to be accomplished in his final years. Only the attainment of an All Clear would allow them to go forward. By that summer Hubbard was seventy years old.

Gamboa and Starkey, under Miscavige's direction, had hired counsel to represent Hubbard's interests. We would refer to them as "the X attorneys" for security purposes. They were to be consulted in directing the GO toward termination of all outstanding lawsuits, by the fastest means.

Miscavige was also running another series of missions into the Controller's Committee, Guardian's Office Worldwide in England, and Guardian's Office US in Los Angeles. These missions were supposed to be ferreting out FBI operatives and removing staff and executives who remained loyal to Mary Sue Hubbard. I was briefed that in the final analysis, Mary Sue had been found to be L. Ron Hubbard's chief nemesis – the person most responsible for bringing about the unprecedented and dangerous state of affairs. She had allegedly run the entire international GO network, supervising its criminal activities, all while living with Ron and keeping him in the dark about the GO's unethical and unlawful practices. The missions being run by Miscavige were meant to secure the Guardian's Office, so that the Special Project would be able to work with reliable people – people who would not get us in further trouble and who would listen to us, rather than to Mary Sue and the old Guardian's Office crew.

My initial job was to gain access to the hundreds of file cabinets full of GO files in Los Angeles, become familiar with the details of the litigation, and organize the information so that Gamboa and Starkey could assimilate it, with the aim of forming and executing a strategy to extract Hubbard from the various suits. One of my duties was to marry up information from the files with information obtained from the missions Miscavige had sent out to root out FBI infiltrators. The idea was to come up with conclusive, prosecutable evidence that the GO had been put up to committing crimes by the FBI in the first place. I took this objective seriously for a couple of reasons. I had studied up on the FBI's history, which included its having followed precisely that pattern against civil rights and peace groups of the 1960s. This was done under the program called Cointelpro (Counter Intelligence Program). The groups targeted under Cointelpro overlapped with President Richard Nixon's infamous White House Enemy List. L. Ron Hubbard and the church of Scientology were named on Nixon's Enemy List. Given the fact that the list of GO crimes seemed so antithetical to all I knew and had been exposed to about Scientology, I found the possibility of government infiltration was very credible. It took on even greater credibility when I was shown a Hubbard dispatch of recent vintage, stating that he knew the GO had been infiltrated and had informed Mary Sue of the fact years ago. The dispatch lamented that unfortunately Mary Sue could never muster reliable resources to ferret out the infiltrators, because of the internal chaos these FBI "plants" had created and because her GO was so "off Source" (slang for ignorant or disdainful the organizational methodology Hubbard had set forth in his thousands of Policy Letters).

The U.S. offices of the GO were located in the converted hospital complex the church had purchased in Los Angeles. The offices occupied three full floors, covering tens of thousands of square feet of space. The organization consisted of an intelligence (intel) bureau, a legal bureau, a public relations bureau and a number of internal administrative bureaus. The largest bureau by far was Intel. It was manned by more than 100 staff, who ran secretive operatives into government agencies, hostile law offices, press outlets, psychological associations, anti-cult groups, wildcat Scientology groups and even individuals who were critical of Scientology.

For legal purposes I concentrated first on reviewing and summarizing what were known as the "seized documents," tens of thousands of pages of FBI-seized GO memoranda outlining their covert operations. These were the documents that the adverse litigants had in their arsenal, and were the basis of a number of exposés in major newspapers across the world. Since these documents were being used in pending lawsuits to influence judges to hate Scientology, a complete assessment of them and how deep they reached was of vital importance.

As part of the initial run-through I also kept charts of information, seeking to run back the source of the idea that the GO should commit illegal acts. First priority was finding links that would show that the government's star witness, former GO operative Michael Meisner, was the long-term FBI mole. Over the four years since the 1977 raids, the GO had asserted so heavily and so repeatedly that Meisner had been a mole all along, and an FBI *agent provocateur* long before the raid, that it was considered almost a certainty that Meisner was *the* plant. Starkey continually nudged me to come up with the proof that Meisner a) originated the idea of committing illegal acts in the GO, and b) was on the government payroll long before the raid.

After a few weeks, my work proved quite the opposite. The documents made it clear that Meisner was neither a plant to begin with, nor the guy behind the notion the GO should commit wholesale crimes. By the time Meisner had gotten involved in GO intelligence work, the GO had already been breaking and entering, stealing and running illegal operations for years. Further, the documents detailed how, over time, Meisner transformed from being a loyal Scientology operative into a doubting man, uncertain of his own worth and ethics, to a virtual GO prisoner and ultimately to a government witness.

It turned out that the least important of the documents were those outlining the infiltration efforts into the FBI, U.S. and many State Attorney Generals' offices, the Internal Revenue Service, the Central Intelligence Agency, etc. The fact that a group of people would have the chutzpah to take on mammoth agencies like these could be positioned as more of a point of pride than of infamy, in the eyes of the public at large. It could be well documented that the infiltration program had been resorted to in response to several federal agencies illegally concealing files and documents in dozens of Freedom of Information Act lawsuits which the GO had been litigating for a decade.

Far more damning – and far less possible to rationalize to courts, the media and the public – were the tens of thousands of pages of documents outlining operations against private citizens, former members (heretics and apostates alike), journalists, and critics of Scientology.

When the GO briefed Scientology staff and parishioners, they concentrated on the government's operations. Such briefings were purely along the lines of "Look what these massive, suppressive agencies are doing to stop man's only hope for spiritual freedom!" They never mentioned the darker ops they'd run against the little guys who'd questioned Scientology. The latter acts were those that would bring on the enmity of the courts, the media and general public for decades to come.

Paulette Cooper, New York author of the book *Scandal of*

Scientology, took the worst of it. The seized documents detailed how the GO had framed Cooper for making a bomb threat against the New York church of Scientology. They had sent an operative into her home to steal stationery with her fingerprints on it, and to lift handwriting samples. The GO then created a note threatening to bomb the church, forged Cooper's signature and mailed it to the church on her own fingerprint-laden stationery. So sophisticated was the op (as the GO called operations, for short) that an indictment was returned against Cooper for the threat.

There were also reports from a GO operative who became such a trusted friend of Cooper that he lived in her apartment. The operative detailed how Cooper was falling apart emotionally and mentally under the stress of developments in the manufactured case against her. The only thing that saved Cooper from conviction and prison was the July, 1977 FBI raids on Scientology organizations that uncovered the operation in the GO's own documents. That was not the bottom of the GO's rotten barrel. The GO posted Cooper's phone number in subways and bathroom stalls across New York City, soliciting for lewd sexual acts. The GO broke into Cooper's psychotherapist's office and made copies of all of his files on her. They even infiltrated her law firm and copied all of their Cooper files. The most infamous of the many secret operations against Cooper was called "Operation Freakout," intended literally to drive her insane and have her institutionalized.

Perhaps number two on the all-time sick ops list of GO targets was Gabriel Cazares. He was the Mayor of Clearwater, Florida in 1976, when the church had quietly moved there under a false cover, purchasing the landmark Fort Harrison Hotel. The hotel had been the center of the town's civic life for the preceding 40 years, and the church was quietly converting it into its new "Mecca," called Flag – the ultimate Scientology religious retreat. Cazares was suspicious and worked with the largest newspaper in Florida, the nearby *St. Petersburg Times,* to investigate and expose the real owners. The seized documents detailed programs to silence and ruin Cazares with such titles as "Operation Taco-less" and "Operation Italian Fog."

The GO attempted to seed the Immigration and Naturalization Service with manufactured documents about Cazares (a US citizen), aiming to bring about his deportation to Mexico. Another operation documented the GO's efforts to ruin Cazares through a created love interest, a young, good-looking Scientologist. Once Cazares took the bait, the GO had their *femme fatal* arrange an afternoon hotel tryst. When Cazares left the hotel with his mistress in his car, the GO had a pedestrian slam the side of his car and fall to the ground as if struck by Cazares. The operative in the car encouraged Cazares to put the pedal to the metal and leave the scene, so no one would learn of their affair. The GO then attempted to blackmail Cazares. GO operatives held the arranged affair and the created "hit-and-run" over Cazares's head to attempt to leverage his silence. When Cazares sued the church for libel, the church manipulated Cazares into hiring as his counsel an undercover Scientologist with an attorney license. Cazares's own lawyer in a suit against the church of Scientology was a Scientology operative.

These are only two of the hundreds of people who were targeted for similar treatment, all meticulously documented in the files that had just recently been made public. The documents raised my hair. Had they been alone in a vacuum, I might have bolted from the Sea Org right then and there, in the summer of 1981. But there were other fruits of investigation that made matters seem not so black and white. The GO had compiled pretty convincing dossiers on a vast US government and private agency conspiracy to destroy L. Ron Hubbard and Dianetics and Scientology. They had also obtained documents that indicated Paulette Cooper was a long-standing operative of the American Medical Association, part of its three-decade mission to discredit Hubbard and take down Scientology. The GO also had uncovered documentation that Cazares, for all his heroic lone-ranger publicity, had been a numbered FBI informant, possibly run in to disrupt church operations.

Additionally, except for Cooper and Cazares and one other similarly-situated individual named McLean, all of the three to four dozen lawsuits pending against the church and L. Ron Hubbard were brought by individuals who had not received similar treatment. For the most part, the rest of the plaintiffs were former members who were claiming that the church had emotionally destroyed them through their participation in Scientology religious services. They were also suing for fraud, claiming that promises made by the organization about the benefits to be had from Scientology were false, and that the church misrepresented the biography of Hubbard to the public at large. They all seemed to be attempting to capitalize on the church's rampant bad publicity, and the fact that a woman in Portland, Oregon had been awarded two million dollars in a judgment against the church, after she had simply participated in the same Communication Course that I felt had changed my life so much for the better.

Complicating matters further were the then-recently-unearthed connections of those coordinating the lawsuits against the church and Hubbard. GO Intel had fished some documents out of the dumpster of the main coordinating attorney for the plaintiffs against the church. His name was Michael Flynn, from Boston Massachusetts. The documents outlined a far-reaching conspiracy to use the lawsuits to bring down Scientology, with less-than-altruistic motivation.

Flynn had set up a corporation, Flynn Associates Management Corporation (FAMCO), for the purposes of soliciting and filing lawsuits against Scientology and Hubbard across the country. FAMCO was attempting to raise funds by selling shares in the litigation scheme. FAMCO outlined a strategy of filing "turn-key" (or "cookie cutter") lawsuits in numerous, inconvenient venues, seeking to bury the Church of Scientology in litigation. FAMCO projected filing more than a thousand lawsuits. The plan called for holding a coordination conference with private lawyers from around the country, representatives from the US Department of Justice, Internal Revenue Service and American Medical Association, and friendly journalists from *Reader's Digest*, CBS *60 Minutes* and others. Flynn's documents indicated he was already serving as the main coordination point between private attorneys, government agencies and the media. FAMCO's planning documents stated that it was intent on closing Scientology organizations, creating widespread hostile publicity, and causing government agency attacks.

The threat was formidable. The stakes were enormous. The total being asked for in the existing lawsuits alone was more than one billion dollars. That billion-dollar potential liability constituted five to ten times the total net worth of the church, all assets real and liquid. To make matters worse, the IRS, which was part and parcel of the FAMCO plan, had tax bills outstanding against churches of Scientology that totaled another billion dollars. All told, what faced us at the start of our mission was a potential decimation of the church of Scientology, ten times over.

Complicating matters was the state of church financial records.

Over the decades, the Guardian's Office had been in control of finance from the local organization level to international management, to L. Ron Hubbard. Hubbard had received many millions of dollars from the church over the years. All of it probably could have been justified under IRS non-profit standards. That is, if the payments were received for clear, defensible reasons. But they were not. Money flowed to Hubbard continuously, and the Guardian's Office continually had to provide justifications and reasons for the flows, after the fact. So, instead of two decades of sound, defensible records, we had two decades of what appeared to be fraudulent, after-the-fact attempts to justify a virtual collapse between church coffers and Hubbard's personal accounts.

The Special Project learned that while we were busy getting up to speed on the litigation and the complexity of the whole FAMCO matter, and while Miscavige was busy purging the GO of misfits, Mary Sue was secretly undermining our efforts. She was directing GO staff to get the FAMCO litigation settled directly with Michael Flynn. The "smoking gun" on the alleged sabotage was a letter from GO attorney Jay Roth to Michael Flynn, agreeing in principle to settle all outstanding litigation for the sum of $1.6 million. Miscavige's immediate claim of sabotage was readily validated by Hubbard's lawyers, the X attorneys.

The X attorneys were the three-man firm of Lenske, Lenske, and Heller, of Canoga Park, California. They were an obscure, low-profile group. Hubbard wanted it that way. He had instructed Special Project to hire some competent lawyers who were "hungry." He did not want seasoned veterans who would lecture him on his liabilities and downsides. He wanted some attack dogs that *would* attack. In Lenske, Lenske and Heller he got the "hungry," but instead of the "attack" he got "echo chamber." They proved extremely competent at the Sea Org art of feeding back to Hubbard what he wanted to hear. Sherman Lenske was a bookish fellow who handled Hubbard's corporate and tax issues. Larry Heller and Sherman's brother, the equally-bookish Steve, were the litigation attorneys. Steve and Larry apparently agreed with Miscavige's assessment that settling for $1.6 million was out of the question. The litigation was not worth that kind of payment. Worse, it would encourage others to follow suit and lead to a never-ending series of expensive buy-outs of future litigation brought against the church.

Mary Sue, her existing GO management structure, and the attorneys they retained thought that the X attorneys were unqualified to make such an assessment for two reasons. First, they were the new kids on the block, while the situation they were advising on had a three-decade history. Second, the lawyers the GO retained were some of the most experienced and aggressive litigators in America. The X attorneys, by contrast, had handled nothing more complex or exciting than a couple of small businesses bickering over chump's change. The GO attorneys' view was that considering the breadth of the litigation and its potential cost and liability, $1.6 million was the bargain of the century.

The GO and Mary Sue's assessment of the X attorneys applied equally to Miscavige, as far as they were concerned. There were no gray areas between the two camps. But since Miscavige controlled the only line of communication to Hubbard, his view was "white" and that of Mary Sue was pure "black." In Miscavige's view, since he was the Commodore's Messenger serving as Hubbard's emissary in matters legal, and Mary Sue found Miscavige to be at best naïve, Mary Sue Hubbard was evil – and she would be treated as such by the church until the day she died.

Complicating matters, according to Gamboa and Starkey, Dede Voegeding – the church's highest ecclesiastical officer at the time, was sympathetic toward Mary Sue. She had argued with Miscavige that Mary Sue ought to be shown some respect and dignity for having served her husband faithfully for thirty years, including having pled guilty to criminal charges and so shielding Ron from any criminal liability he might have. Gamboa and Starkey told me that Miscavige had also learned that Dede had betrayed Hubbard by disclosing his whereabouts to GO-hired Hubbard biographer Omar Garrison; a claim Voegeding would later claim was ludicrous, given that she had no idea where Hubbard was living at the time.

According to Gamboa and Starkey, and later asserted to me by Miscavige himself, since communication runs to and from Hubbard were infrequent and unpredictable, Miscavige had to make some monumentally brave decisions, all on his lonesome. First, he snuck a report to Pat Broeker, his relay to Hubbard, disclosing "crimes" he'd discovered, supposedly committed by Dede. In addition to having allegedly sided with Mary Sue against L. Ron Hubbard, Dede had committed a dark financial sin. A couple years earlier, Hubbard had issued a directive to catch Scientology service prices up with inflation. He ordered that prices for Scientology services be increased by 5% per month, indefinitely. Having presided as the church's most senior management executive (Watchdog Committee Chairman) for a couple of years, Dede saw that adherence to the automatic price increase directive was putting Scientology services out of the price range of most common working folk. This was the demographic for which services were supposed to be made affordable, per long-standing church policy. Hubbard reacted to Miscavige's report by ordering Dede from her post, to be replaced by her sister Gale Reisdorf Irwin. This paved the way for Miscavige's next bold move.

Miscavige reported to Hubbard that his own attorneys, Lenske and Heller, advised that Mary Sue Hubbard was not only sabotaging the civil litigation against Hubbard, but that her involvement in the GO crime network was so well spelled out in the by-then-public seized documents, that the church and Hubbard would need to distance themselves from her. The strategy would call for a dismissal of Mary Sue and the ten other senior GO executives who had been convicted, a mass purge of GO staff who had any inkling of ongoing criminal activity, and a public relations strategy of characterizing the GO as a handful of "rogue" staff who had been rounded up and expelled when their actions were discovered. This, of course, was completely consistent with what Hubbard had suggested in a number of his written dispatches to the Special Project. It was the echo chamber in full force.

This was apparently not as difficult for Hubbard as one might reckon. Since late 1978, when I first arrived at Hubbard's secret desert headquarters, Hubbard had not lived in the same location as his wife. They had already taken measures to create distance between Hubbard and the GO criminal case, in which Mary Sue was the lead defendant. The Hubbards had only met in person a few times since then.

Ron bought a home for Mary Sue in Los Angeles, where she had lived since 1978. While there was regular and lengthy letter correspondence between the two, all of their letters were screened and forwarded by messengers. Many times the messengers would delay Mary Sue's letters to Hubbard in order not to try his nerves. If he was in a particularly bad mood, the letters would sit until he was more upbeat and able to handle them emotionally.

Hubbard approved Miscavige's plan and expanded on the theme. Writing that he had not the slightest inkling of what Mary Sue and her aides had been up to with their intelligence ops, he advised that any GO staff who had done or knew of anything illegal being done could never again be on staff, closing with this emphasis: "…and I don't care if they grow wings." Hubbard referred to the idea of settlement as reflecting "defeatist GO mentality." By late summer 1981, a number of dispatches arrived from Hubbard advising on how to attack the pending litigation aggressively.

I was then treated to Miscavige's version of his carrying out Mary Sue's dismissal. They met at a pre-arranged neutral location, a hotel room in Hollywood. Miscavige had the room wired for recording. John Brousseau – formerly Hubbard's driver and car mechanic – sat in a van outside the hotel, recording the conversation between Mary Sue and Miscavige on a reel-to-reel recording device. According to Miscavige, Mary Sue defiantly refused to step down, not caring one bit how it would adversely affect her husband and the future of Scientology. Mary Sue had even raised a heavy glass ashtray in her hand threatening to crash it into Miscavige's skull. Miscavige would only win her compliance by virtue of his ace-in-the-hole. An ace that Miscavige would never, to this day, acknowledge publicly. That is, Mary Sue demanded to speak to her husband so that she could truthfully inform him of her side of the story. Miscavige smugly replied, "No." And that was the end of Mary Sue, because no one could reach Hubbard except through Miscavige.

Mary Sue would never communicate to her husband again. A couple of letters from Hubbard made it to her just before and just after her federal jail sentence was served. But the line of communication would, from the Miscavige confrontation forward, be virtually one-way.

Over the next several months of immersion in the files, it became more and more clear that my superiors – Miscavige, Gamboa and Starkey – were rather naïve about the outside world, the legal system, and how the courts, government and media operated. They were accustomed to ramrodding through compliance to Hubbard orders, in an insular environment where nobody dared counter Hubbard's intentions. They plied Ron with unreal assessments of the situation facing him. They communicated a black-and-white, good-versus-evil world, when in fact it was not. It was the outside world and it was filled with every shade of gray in between.

They characterized all the suits as frivolous, while in fact several of them (notably those brought by Cazares, Cooper and McLean) were about as strong and well backed by devastating evidence as any multi-million dollar suit brought against the most abusive of corporate America. Gamboa and Starkey represented that the X attorneys they had hired had studied the scene thoroughly, and agreed upon an All Clear date. A date by which all legal threats to Hubbard would be extinguished, and by which Hubbard could return to the 500-acre international headquarters compound near Hemet, without fear of process servers or government agents seeking him out.

They did not relay to Hubbard what I had reported to them, because they were apparently well trained in keeping upsetting information off Hubbard's plate. It was information that may have had Hubbard looking at the situation a tad more realistically. Specifically, the fact that the United States Department of Justice was still attempting to make a criminal case against Hubbard himself for the acts of the Guardian's Office. GO attorneys were actively dealing with two separate grand juries, seated in New York and Tampa and led by prosecutors whose main aim was to link L. Ron Hubbard to criminal acts carried out by the Guardian's Office against author Paulette Cooper and Mayor Gabriel Cazares.

Hubbard's responses to the Special Project's reports were as unreal as the reports themselves. In late July, 1981, he authorized the proposed October, 1981 All Clear date, and began flooding the base near Hemet with orders to prepare for his arrival.

Had Hubbard listened to his wife Mary Sue, he would have learned something a lot closer to the truth. Having dealt with the outside world and attacks against Scientology for the preceding three decades, she understood the silliness of proposing the dismissal of three dozen lawsuits (and two federal grand juries) in less than three months. She understood one would be lucky to schedule a single motion for hearing in that period. She understood the cases were in no procedural posture for dismissal and would not be, under the best of circumstances, for years to come.

But Hubbard would not hear from his wife.

CHAPTER FOURTEEN

THOUGHT STOPPING

Thought Stopping: The most far-reaching and complex of human problems are compressed into brief, highly reductive, definitive-sounding phrases, easily memorized and easily expressed. These become the start and finish of any ideological analysis. – Robert Lifton, *Thought Reform and the Psychology of Totalism*

In late 1981, the Int base became a beehive of activity, readying the property for Hubbard's return. Ninety miles west, back in Los Angeles where the Special Project had permanently relocated, the pressure was even more intense. The three dozen lawsuits were spread across Los Angeles, San Francisco, Portland, Las Vegas, Tampa, Boston, New York City, Washington, D.C. and several smaller venues in between. The defense of the lawsuits was poorly managed. Several of them were about to go into default for unanswered motions. Few of the attorneys defending the nearly identical suits were in communication or coordination with any of the other defense attorneys. Inconsistent responses were being filed on identical legal and factual issues, and the better-coordinated FAMCO team was exploiting those inconsistencies.

There were motions pending to obtain substituted service on Hubbard. This is a vehicle for inclusion of a party in a suit when that party cannot be located so that summons can physically be served. Upon showing that normal efforts to locate a party for service were fruitless, a party can, with court approval, publish notification of the lawsuit in the legal ads section of a newspaper in the area where the missing person is believed to be. The court will then consider the missing person on notice and served. This was Flynn and company's vehicle of choice, because he knew something that we also knew: under no circumstances would Hubbard appear in court or for a deposition.

Hubbard outlined our strategy for All Clear as follows. First, we were to get Hubbard extracted from the suits. We were to make a case, by affidavits and documentation, that Hubbard did not run the church and was by no means its managing agent. We were to established firm judicial precedent that Scientology is a religion, entitled to the protections of the First Amendment to the US Constitution. This tied into defeating the charges of fraud. We could not possibly maintain the church's mission into the future if the principle claims of Scientology were found to be false. First Amendment protection seemed the only iron-fortified wall against such claims plaguing us for years to come.

We called a general coordination conference. In a large conference room at the downtown Los Angeles Bonaventure Hotel we assembled about three dozen attorneys from around the country. We briefed them on the FAMCO plan and the identical nature of the issues. We had lawyers specializing in issues such as the First Amendment give talks to the rest. We had a list of all counsel compiled, and emphasized that coordination was of the essence – as the entire FAMCO plan banked on overwhelming the church in far-flung jurisdictions.

We settled on a plan: we would engage in discovery in most of the cases, while we had Boston civil rights lawyer Harvey Silverglate attack Flynn's flagship case in his home town with a constitutional challenge to establish our First Amendment religious precedent. Silverglate, along with seven or eight other Boston lawyers who accompanied him, was also to compile a bar complaint against Michael Flynn for his illicit FAMCO plan. Finally, we set out to hire separate counsel in a number of jurisdictions, to represent Hubbard in special appearances challenging the attempts to have him included through substituted service. A special appearance for such a limited purpose does not constitute accepting service and becoming a served party to the litigation. It is a one-shot, ultra-technical challenge to the sufficiency of the means of service.

I accompanied Starkey to weekly conferences with GO legal, PR and intel executives, where we would review the progress of each case. Starkey commanded a lot of respect initially, what with his history of working with Hubbard and being Miscavige's go-to missionaire. However, as much as Starkey had a command presence and engaging personality, he lacked patience for detail and intelligence. Starkey was the epitome of what I earlier referred to as Scientology's Peter Principle: to the extent someone could override his own better judgment, logic, and simple compassion for the well-being of others in order to force, by any means necessary, compliance to orders and intentions from the top, well, to that degree a person was eminently promotable in corporate Scientology. Starkey was Miscavige's favorite; in the same way that, I suppose, under the desperate circumstances he found himself, Hubbard favored the likes of Miscavige.

While I was aware of the incongruity of an ill-briefed, unsophisticated man lording over the micromanagement of dozens of lawyers across the country, I began engaging in thought-stopping in order to carry on. The term "thought-stopping" was first introduced by Robert Jay Lifton in his 1961 book, *Thought Reform and Psychological Totalism.* He described how totalitarian environments could force one to stop his own rational thoughts, by adopting black-and-white labels to stand for good or evil. Once so labeled, an idea is easily rejected and given no further thought. Lifton outlined how communists' minds were controlled by being led to adopt the idea that everything emanating from a "bourgeois attitude" could be dismissed as propaganda. In that way, huge bodies of data or truth could be simply dismissed by doctrinal labeling. Thus one stops entire sectors of thought from generating in one's own mind.

Ironically, the same was (and still is) being run on the American populace, with such devices as labeling anything liberal as constituting "socialist attitudes" or "communist attitudes," and anything conservative as constituting "fascist attitudes." Jefferson Hawkins, a former high-level Scientologist whom I would later come to know and work with, wrote an insightful essay on his blog (leavingscientology.wordpress.com) relating Lifton's theories to the corporate Scientology experience.

In any event, from mid 1981 forward my own thought-stopping

process intensified – that is, labeling any idea contrary to that coming from command as "disaffected," "enemy" and "anti-Scientology." Ironically, my duties over the next several years would include debunking those very theories of Lifton, and Lifton himself, as they were used by psychiatrists testifying on behalf of plaintiffs in the damages lawsuits I was assigned to terminate.

Thought stopping in this psychological sense should not be confused with the virtue of ending the influence of random thoughts, as practiced in Zen, Taoism, and in – ironically – Dianetics and Scientology spiritual practice. Since the time of the Buddha (Siddhartha Gautama) and Lao Tzu (in his book, *Tao Te Ching*) the East understood the salutary effects of making troubling thoughts disappear by simply confronting them, rather than reacting to them or complying with them. Thought stopping in the Lifton scenario meant precisely the opposite – rather than facing and thus depowering stray thought from within, he referred to rejecting whole bodies of thought and information from without, by labeling them.

Starkey had zero ability to tell Miscavige anything other than what Miscavige wanted to hear. He consistently relayed unreal orders from Miscavige to the GO staff. He would assign a GO case manager to get a particular plaintiff into deposition within, say, two weeks. Civil litigation practice did not afford a party the ability to compel attendance that fast; but given the fact Miscavige was Hubbard's ramrod, controlled the only line of communication to Ron, and was known to have busted the Founder's wife personally, nobody dared respond with anything but "Yes, sir." Then, two weeks later, under intense pressure from Miscavige, Starkey would dress down the staff member for failure to comply. He could be brutal – and Miscavige validated and rewarded brutality.

By the time October rolled around, Silverglate had not yet managed to have his constitutional challenge scheduled for hearing in the Boston federal district court. The bar complaint on Flynn for his illicit FAMCO scheme had been filed – but it would be years before we would hear of a determination. Several attorneys were on the verge of quitting, having received a barrage of Miscavige-originated demands that they perform some task in a time frame that would result in a loss, and probably provoke sanctions from a court. Increasingly, I had to quietly intervene to patch up beat-up, defeated staff and attorneys and by power of persuasion rehabilitate their willingness to carry on. The development of that skill would begin my transformation from files clerk to executive.

Toward the end of October, Miscavige was visiting Special Project offices daily – going straight into the office shared by Starkey and Gamboa, not even acknowledging the existence of anyone else present (me or the several other administrative staff we had accumulated). We could hear Miscavige's voice vibrating through the walls and down the hall, raining down insults on Starkey and Gamboa. When Miscavige would leave, I would be hauled in by Starkey to explain details about where various things stood in the litigation. Starkey said they needed to get a report on All Clear up to the Old Man (as many veteran Sea Org members referred to Hubbard). The report had to be detailed and complete, because he was not happy that the All Clear date had not been met.

Over the course of dozens of heated Miscavige visits, followed by lengthy meetings where Starkey picked my brain for details, it became crystal clear that the reports being prepared for Hubbard were as unreal as Starkey was about the litigation. For example, Starkey was reporting that the first motion for substituted service on Hubbard would be heard by a Boston Federal District Court Judge in November, and that the X attorneys fully anticipated a precedent-setting win – one which would serve to prevent Hubbard from being injected into any of the couple dozen lawsuits in which he had been named. Technically it was true that the X attorneys had said as much. They would not dare counter anything Miscavige, Gamboa or Starkey demanded, because these were the people who delivered their checks. Starkey just omitted from the report anything the GO attorneys (the ones who would actually have to go into court and litigate) had to say. In this case he omitted the view of the man handling the opposition to the application for substituted service, Leonard Boudin of New York City.

Leonard was considered one of the deans of litigation in all of America. Among his credentials was the successful defense of Daniel Ellsberg in the Pentagon Papers case. "Sir, I don't think Leonard is that optimistic," I said. Norman snapped, "He's a goddamn GO loser, boy. Don't forget who you are working for: L. Ron Hubbard!" Through such upbraidings I learned to simply answer the questions I was asked, when it came to contributing to any communications to L. Ron Hubbard.

It wasn't that Starkey and Miscavige were presenting Hubbard with outright lies. It was that they were very skillfully presenting a picture littered with half-truths and omissions. Inconvenient truths did not make it into their reports. In fact, the reported weakness of the cases against L. Ron Hubbard himself was true. The enemy had a dearth of credible witnesses to tie Hubbard to the day-to-day management of the church, something they would need to do in order to drag him into the litigation. It would not become clear to me until many years later – well after the dust and smoke of the war had settled – that David Miscavige had begun providing the enemy with the sort of credible witnesses they needed, all in the course of loyally carrying out Hubbard's defense and wishes.

Starkey's report contained no reference to the outstanding grand juries, because the X attorneys agreed with Miscavige and Starkey's assessment: "They've got nothing because LRH did not know a thing; they'll go away." Of course, eventually they did go away. But only after several GO executives, including Mary Sue Hubbard, fell on their swords and went to jail rather than cooperate with the Department of Justice. And after a few GO line staff went to jail for several months for refusing to answer questions under oath before grand juries. I learned all about that when I became the liaison to the eleven who were on their way to jail, and even wound up exerting a bit of influence in that outcome. Landing in that position was necessary because Miscavige and Starkey had burnt all bridges with the GO.

It started in late 1981 – a few months after Mary Sue's removal from post. Miscavige and Starkey plied me with questions about the eleven convicts that only one or more of them could have answered. So I established communication with Duke Snider, who was considered the coordinator for the defense of the eleven. Snider was suspicious and guarded, but with a lot of friendliness, understanding and patience I was always able to get the information I needed, or the cooperation the church needed.

One night after I had established that line of communication, I was called into Gamboa and Starkey's office. They told me that they needed to establish a line of communication directly with Mary Sue. She was so upset at her removal that she refused to speak to Miscavige or anyone who worked with him directly, including any Commodore's Messenger. Gamboa and Starkey said that Miscavige was worried that Mary Sue was going off the reservation, and would do something in her own criminal case that would sabotage the Special Project and All Clear. Miscavige suggested that "maybe Marty ought to call her; he seems to get along with everybody." And so I was given Mary Sue's number and made the call.

"Hello," she answered tentatively.

"Hi, Mary Sue, it's Marty Rathbun here. I've been the Special Project liaison to Duke Snider and rest of the defendants and wanted to open up a line of communication with you."

"You tell that son of a bitch Miscavige that I don't want to hear from him, and that means any Messenger Org flunky of his." She was vehement, but not loud. Her voice was hoarse and soft, from smoking I would learn, but with a sweet Texas lilt.

"No problem. I am not a messenger. They wouldn't have a guy like me. I'm just really a staff member trying to establish some kind of line of coordination of information. I understand you're going to need access to GO files for your defense, and I can take care of all that for you."

"Yeah, but you are with Terri and Miscavige. If Ron really knew what was going on, they'd find themselves on the outside looking in."

"Wow. Unfortunately, I am at their mercy on that score. I have no communication line to Ron. I'm just doing whatever I can to help him out of the mess he's in. And I'm sure he wants you helped out of the mess you are in."

With that, Mary Sue calmed down and started telling me about the help she needed. She rattled off a number of facts relating to her pending appeal, which she needed documents to back up. I dutifully noted them and promised a rapid turn-around. I stayed up late that night compiling what she needed, and made sure everything was delivered the next day. From then on out, Mary Sue stayed in pretty close touch with me. This would turn out to be invaluable, from Special Project's perspective. In the coming years I would be the liaison to her civil attorney, Barry Litt of Los Angeles, and would serve as point person to enlist her and Barry's help with the civil litigation.

While that potential liability to All Clear – created in large part by Miscavige - was averted just in the nick of time, Miscavige was busily converting other equally important friends into foes. I did not know all this at the time; I was too busy with the insanity of juggling nearly forty lawsuits. But I subsequently learned the seeds of Hubbard's demise were being sown by the very fellow he'd entrusted with ensuring his survival.

Miscavige apparently detected a lack of full-out, unequivocal loyalty to himself on the part of the new CO CMO International, Gale Reisdorf Irwin – sister of the erstwhile CO, Dede Reisdorf Voegeding. Gale was becoming overwhelmed by the pressure Hubbard was exerting on the CMO, to take complete control and responsibility for all of Scientology management. But what bothered her most was that Miscavige was becoming increasingly bossy, meddlesome, and personally derisive toward her and other CMO staff. Finally, late in 1981, Gale was driven to a pre-arranged phone booth to set up a meeting with Pat Broeker, the man on Hubbard's side of the rainbow who received and delivered all communication to and from Hubbard. She intended to report that Miscavige had lost his mind, and that his abusiveness toward her and the staff had become intolerable. Miscavige caught wind of the rendezvous, gathered some loyal staff, piled into a van and intercepted Irwin in downtown Hemet, physically preventing her from making the call to Broeker.

Miscavige then contacted Broeker himself and unloaded about Gale. Broeker was an old pal and former bunkmate of Miscavige, and chose to listen only to Miscavige's version of the story. As was his wont with those who defied him, Miscavige then proceeded to put Irwin out of commission for good. He put together a report stating that Gale remained loyal to her sister, the pro-Mary Sue and thus pro-GO Dede, and presented a convincing (although doctored, as I learned later) case that Gale had been sending cooked international Scientology statistics to Hubbard for months.

Hubbard's response would supply Miscavige with ammunition that would assist him to wipe out virtually all of L. Ron Hubbard's most loyal friends and aides over the next two years; friends and allies that Hubbard had earned over three decades. Hubbard wrote that what Miscavige had missed was that "when you take out a suppressive person, you must take out every one of his or her connections."

A suppressive person, in Scientology vernacular, is roughly equivalent to a sociopath – a conscienceless individual who could put on a convincing front of wanting others to thrive, while harboring the secret goal of destroying everyone in his or her vicinity. Hubbard had written and lectured on the subject rather extensively in the sixties. Ironically, thirty years later the very mental health profession that condemned Hubbard during his life would describe the sociopath or psychopath in very much the same terms Hubbard had in the fifties and sixties. A comparison between Hubbard's writings and lectures, and current leading mental health texts on the subject bears this out. (See *The Sociopath Next Door* by Martha Stout, and *Snakes in Suits* by Robert Hare, and compare them to Hubbard's 1951 book, *Science of Survival.* Also see *What is Wrong With Scientology?*, 2012, Amazon Books).

Hubbard ordered that his erstwhile closest and most trusted messengers, Dede Reisdorf Voegeding and Gale Reisdorf Irwin, along with their closest associate Lois Jory Reisdorf, be stripped of messenger status, shipped to the largest Sea Org installation – the Flag Mecca in Clearwater Florida – be forced to confess to Flag's several hundred rank and file crew about their supposed plots to do Hubbard in, and then be posted as maids, branded as never again eligible for promotion. The sentence violated quite a bit that Hubbard had established as firm justice policy within Scientology organizations, most notably the idea that errant staff, no matter how far astray, could always make good somehow.

Miscavige made the lives of Dede and Gale as bad as Hubbard had ordered. He added in his own vengeful punishments, such as enforcing a work schedule that put their health at risk, and repeated public hazings that left them but one escape route: leaving the Sea Organization.

To complicate matters, a curious phenomenon arose when word began to get out to the Scientology world that the Guardian's Office had been tamed. For years the GO had been notorious for having stomped on the rights of executives and staff of Scientology organizations. That included a history of treating mission holders roughly. Mission holders were the front line of Scientology. They operated much like a franchise system. Missions were the introductory service organizations, just like the one in Portland through which I became involved in Scientology. A mission holder was granted the right to open and operate a mission, and to make as much money as he saw fit, provided he passed along 5% of his mission's weekly income to the Guardian's Office Worldwide. The idea was the 5% would be used for broad public promotional campaigns to get the word out to the world about Scientology – something that theoretically would redound to the missions' benefit. Several big-time mission holders ran two, three or more separate missions. Throughout the seventies, mission holders had done more to expand Scientology than just about any other network or group of people. Missions had sprung up everywhere, and many were healthy, bustling with new people being introduced to Scientology studies and counseling.

At this same time, a veteran Sea Org member named Bill Franks was appointed as the church's Executive Director International. Hubbard appointed Franks in hopes of having a strong central figure to start taking on responsibility for church management – a job Hubbard was desperately attempting to turn over to others, through the CMO. It would also, he hoped, serve to insulate him more from charges he micro managed church affairs himself. Franks had big visions for making Scientology a household word. For support, he went straight to the most effective and influential of all Scientologists: the mission holders. In late 1981, Franks appeared at an annual Mission Holders Conference at the Clearwater Mecca. He ingratiated himself with the mission holders by telling tales of having conquered the once-feared and hated GO. The tales were grossly embellished; Franks had played only a minor, figurehead role in that saga.

Much to Franks' chagrin, the mission holders demanded a truth commission be convened on the spot, calling for a full, public confession of the crimes of the GO – not only against the public at large, but against mission holders and staffs of Scientology organizations. Franks had inadvertently sparked a rebellion. To save face, Franks told the mission holders he agreed with them about the need for a truth commission, but that he was being held back from doing so by the folks at CMO International, and their management oversight group the Watch Dog Committee. In fact, he was being held back by legal advice: an indiscriminate disclosure of GO crimes could have catastrophic effects in the pending litigation and with grand juries.

When Miscavige caught wind of the debacle, he ordered Franks back to the Int base and had him put under security watch, accusing him of leading a power push to undermine the CMO and Hubbard.

Ultimately, Franks reacted to the deprivation of his speech, privacy and liberty by leaving the church. He departed, like Dede and Gale, with a large chip on his shoulder, courtesy of Miscavige.

In 1981 Miscavige planted the final seeds that would guarantee Hubbard's continued seclusion until his death. Miscavige was directly running Sea Org member Laurel Sullivan on a mission known as Mission Corporate Category Sort Out. Sullivan's job was to work with GO higher-ups to explore a whole new corporate structure for the church. To that date, all roads had led to the "mother church," the corporation housing virtually all of management and holding virtually all church property and financial reserves; this mother church was officially titled the Church of Scientology of California (CSC). Because of the huge sums of money being funneled to Hubbard by CSC, the paper trail led straight to Ron. Laurel's job was to figure out how to reorganize so that Hubbard's affairs and assets would be separated out from CSC's, and so that new corporations could be created to keep the church's wealth out of the hands of the three dozen litigants suing CSC and L. Ron Hubbard. The idea was also to set things up so that in the future no single corporation would serve as an easy, deep-pocket target for litigants.

During her many months in Los Angeles working closely with Mary Sue and GO executives, Laurel found herself in a moral conflict. Miscavige was systematically removing (and branding as evil) each of the people she had been directed to work with. Miscavige learned that Laurel – like Dede and Gale – was particularly disgusted by the treatment he had inflicted upon Mary Sue Hubbard. Laurel had worked closely with the Hubbards for many years, as Ron's personal public relations officer. So while on mission to sort out the corporations, Laurel naturally continued to work on a long-term project of hers, on the side: a biography of L. Ron Hubbard. Earlier she had helped retain the official biographer, non-Scientologist author Omar Garrison. One of her staff, Gerry Armstrong, worked full time as LRH Archivist, researching and collecting documents on Hubbard's life and supplying them to the biographer.

After several months of working in Los Angeles and interfacing with the GO, Armstrong became aware that the enemies of Scientology were targeting L. Ron Hubbard. He also became aware that one of the major issues in the lawsuits and with hostile media was the claim that Hubbard and the church defrauded prospective church members by publishing false claims about Hubbard's life accomplishments. Armstrong had been approached on many occasions by Laurel and the GO people to provide documentation in support of certain church claims about Hubbard, which had been challenged. On several occasions Armstrong had been stumped. He not only couldn't find documentation in support of the claims, he instead found documentation that undermined some of the more frequent public representations about Hubbard.

After Miscavige busted Gerry's direct superior, Laurel, Armstrong formally brought the matter of the potentially false representations to the attention of authorities in CMO International. Armstrong respectfully recommended that the church cease issuing any representations that it could not back up with documentation. The matter was referred to Miscavige, since he was responsible for L. Ron Hubbard's defense. Rather than investigate Armstrong's concerns, Miscavige sent Starkey to intimidate Armstrong into line, treating him as if he was imagining his concerns because his mind had been "infected" by the GO.

Ultimately, by the end of 1981, Sullivan and Armstrong left the church, in protest at being treated as criminals.

I did not know a lot of the details of the stories of Dede, Gale, Franks, Armstrong and Sullivan at the time they were occurring. From July, 1981 through January, 1982, I was busy working eighteen- to twenty-hour days, seven days a week, on L. Ron Hubbard's defense. It ultimately took decades to put all the pieces into place – some of which are shared above for continuity's sake. Other details will unfold as we proceed. At that time, however, I was briefed in detail by Miscavige, Starkey and Gamboa as follows: Ron Hubbard considered Mary Sue Hubbard to be a traitor of the lowest order. She had, for the past fifteen years, carefully concealed from her husband the creation and operation of an international crime syndicate called the GO. She and her network were so arrogant and criminal they had set themselves up for the biggest raid in FBI history, and subsequently the most damning event in Scientology's history: the convictions of Mary Sue and ten other high-level members of the GO.

The briefing continued by characterizing Dede, Gale, Laurel and

Gerry as dupes of Mary Sue and the GO. All had been caught red-handed in acts of disloyalty and sabotage against L. Ron Hubbard, all unduly influenced by Mary Sue and the GO. It was all very thick and complex. It was made more so by Hubbard's own memo to the Special Project, stating as fact that the GO had been infiltrated by the FBI many years earlier, and that any illegal acts the GO had committed were done at the behest of the very agency that convicted Mary Sue and the others of those same acts. Hubbard wrote that Mary Sue and the GO were susceptible to infiltration because they were "off source" – meaning they did not recognize Hubbard technology and policy and thus did not apply it.

Ironically, regardless of how "off source" Mary Sue and the GO might have been, and no matter how much they were treated as traitorous pariahs because of their indictment, not one of the former high-level GO officers ever turned to testify against Scientology and Ron. Rather, the ranks of enemy witnesses would soon swell with former higher-level Sea Org veterans and Commodore's Messengers.

Since LRH's wife and senior messengers had betrayed him, there were only a small handful of people he could trust. I was now one of that small handful. I was told not to trust anyone from the GO; I was not to trust anyone from the CMO. I was not to trust anyone but my superiors in Special Project, Gamboa, Starkey and Miscavige. They backed up this admonition with a memo from Hubbard to the Special Project, expressing his thanks to us, "the desperate few upon whose shoulders the world rests."

CHAPTER FIFTEEN

PREPARING FOR WAR

In these days of "cold war" when actual warfare is impossible due to atomic weapons, the warfare is waged in the press and public in the form of ideas.
– L. Ron Hubbard, *Battle Tactics*

Many of those who have made it this far in the narrative may well be wondering why on earth this story does not end by New Year's 1982. By late 1981, I certainly harbored my doubts about the wisdom of carrying on. It was not a neat, easy-to-understand scenario. As demands increased that my thoughts and allegiances become more black-and-white, the world unfolding before me was becoming ever more shadowy, with every possible shade unfolding.

Two things kept me on board. First, there were the gains that I had experienced with the use of Scientology. More than once I had experienced exteriorization of the spirit from the body, with full perception. To me, that alone was proof that Hubbard had hit upon something wise men had sought since Siddhartha Gautama (the Buddha). If Hubbard was acting in a fashion that was not particularly rational – at the age of seventy in the face of the pressure he was under, that did not change the fact of what his philosophy could and did produce spiritually. Second, when I learned that since 1950 Hubbard had been facing situations like this, but of even greater gravity and magnitude, my respect for his life's work was reinforced.

Being the first outsider to breach the secret GO files, and having had six months to study them initially, I developed a perspective that I do not believe was shared by anyone – with the possible exception of L. Ron Hubbard himself. The GO executives' convictions stemmed from their efforts to get at what government agencies were unlawfully withholding from the church in Freedom of Information Act (FOIA) proceedings. The "secret" GO files were known, within the GO itself, as the "non-FOIA" files. These were government and private agency/association documents obtained by means other than the FOIA. In other words, these were the documents that were unlawfully obtained, by infiltration and unauthorized copying. They amounted to tens of thousands of pages. By order of Miscavige, they would never see the light of day, because to utilize them would open the door to discrediting Ron's public relations strategy: telling the world that the GO were rogue, low-level hoodlums whose activities church leadership was shocked to learn of, after the fact. To use the files as ammo would be to benefit from fruits of a poison tree, which Miscavige and Hubbard had decided must be disowned.

I was to learn that Mary Sue Hubbard and the Guardians Office had already made that same determination, some time earlier. In working with several GO counsel who had been through the criminal case, I learned a history known to only a few. Those counsel were some of the most radical, activist lawyers of the sixties and seventies. They included the aforementioned Boudin, as well as Philip Hirschkop and Chicago Seven lawyer William Kuntsler.

According to other less famous members of that team, the defense lawyers were intent on taking the U.S. v Mary Sue Hubbard case to jury trial. They advised a justification defense that would put several United States government agencies on trial for their two-decade conspiracy with private organizations, such as the American Medical Association and the American Psychiatric Association, to destroy L. Ron Hubbard and the revolutionary ideas he was promulgating. Years were spent putting that case together. Within the secret, non-FOIA documents was a plethora of evidence which could be used in mounting a very credible defense along the lines that the church of Scientology was well justified in fighting fire with fire.

Months and months of back-and-forth between the activist lawyers on the one side, and the labyrinthine bureaucracy that was the GO on the other, resulted in abandonment of the idea of conducting what could potentially have been the most spectacular trial in United States history. That bureaucracy wended its way up through Mary Sue Hubbard and ended with L. Ron Hubbard as final arbiter. Hubbard even once had the august Leonard Boudin summoned to Winter Headquarters in La Quinta, California so that, as Ron put it, he could "straighten him out with a yank." Concerns over the possibility of L. Ron Hubbard being pulled into the battle royal, as well as fears about fallout if the government were to bring out a mountain of evidence of vicious GO operations against private citizens, were at the root of the prolonged indecision. Ultimately the justification defense would be nixed. Instead, the defendants would be tried and convicted on an agreed upon record of evidence of their acts against government agencies.

The secret, non-FOIA files are fascinating. They consist of file cabinets full of documents purloined from the Department of Justice, the FBI, the CIA, the IRS, military intelligence branches, and similar agencies in the United Kingdom, South Africa, Canada, and a number of European nations. There were also stacks of records taken from the files of the American Medical Association, the American Psychiatric Association, the American Psychological Association, and similar associations in all of the above-mentioned countries.

The documents told an incredible saga. And the story was told in the words of those conducting the crusade against Hubbard, not by Hubbard himself, nor by the church. Within weeks of the May 9, 1950 publication of *Dianetics: The Modern Science of Mental Health*, vested pharmaceutical and medical interests declared war on L. Ron Hubbard. On June 1, 1950, the editor of the Journal of the American Medical Association (AMA), one Austin Smith, shot missives to doctors and medical societies across America, asking for authoritative statements condemning Hubbard and his work. There was no indication Smith had done the slightest study of Dianetics himself before judging it, beyond noting the book's general contention that mental therapy did not need to be brutal, nor did it need to be expensive.

Smith's correspondence betrayed fear of the initial, overwhelmingly positive public response to the book, which asserted that common folk could handle many of their own psychosomatic ills and neuroses for the dirt-cheap price of a simple book. To the great health monopoly of America, this was heresy, blasphemy and worse. Smith corresponded directly with then-Director of the Food and Drug Administration, Erwin E. Nelson. Nelson, once head of the Pharmacology Department of Tulane University, had for years served as the FDA's point man for new drug approvals. During his reign he had green-lighted more than 7,000 applications from pharmaceutical manufacturers.

Smith's devotion to drugs, and vested interest in opposing non-drug alternatives, would later be made clear when he traded on his authoritative AMA position to head the Pharmaceutical Manufacturing Association, and then parlayed both positions to make a fortune the rest of his life, serving as President and Chairman of Parke, Davis and Co. Pharmaceuticals, and later as Vice Chair of its parent company, Warner-Lambert and Co.

For the next 20 years, the AMA's then-mighty Department of Investigation would take clandestine action against Hubbard and his organizations. Two successive heads of investigation for the AMA, Oliver Field (1950s) and Thomas Spinelli (1960s and 1970s), would work hand-in-glove with several governmental agencies to infiltrate Hubbard's lectures and organizations.

Another early, active participant in Hubbard hunting was J. Edgar Hoover, the sociopath who lorded over the entire federal government (including Congress) during his decades as Director of the Federal Bureau of Investigation. One operation Hoover's boys ran on early-fifties Dianetics groups would cripple them for years to come. The FBI infiltrated the groups using its broader Operation Cominfil (Communist Infiltration) as pretext to find out who were the most devoted and experienced members holding the Dianetics groups together. Then the FBI overtly requested membership lists from the organizations, under the pretext they would compare them to their files and alert the groups to any members who were also secret members of the Communist Party (and thus, presumably, Soviet agents). When the lists came back from the FBI, nearly a third of all of the names had been labeled (in most cases falsely) as communists. Hubbard, being a tad on the communist-paranoid side, as was common at the time, and believing the government he paid taxes to was acting in good faith, dismissed those identified as communists. This act set the fledgling movement back by years.

The documents showed that the AMA and FDA worked closely

with the US Department of Justice up through the early sixties, infiltrating Hubbard lectures and organizations at every opportunity. Memos spanning twelve years document desperate attempts to make a case for medical fraud (or quackery) against Hubbard personally. The memos also showed informant after informant reporting back that Hubbard was not making scientific guarantees of cures for specific diseases, as the AMA was accusing him of doing.

AMA and FDA informants began approaching Hubbard after public lectures, trying to directly entrap him into making such statements. In the late fifties, one informant even attempted to elicit from Hubbard a recommendation of an illegal abortion doctor. If these investigators, who spent twelve years attempting to entrap Hubbard, had bothered to read his books, they would have understood why that particular operation failed so miserably; Hubbard was an outspoken, harsh critic of abortion.

In the early 1960s, the FDA sent an agent to Hubbard's home at St. Hill Manor near East Grinstead, Sussex, England, posing as a reporter for one of America's then-leading magazines, the *Saturday Evening Post.* The reporter spent days at St. Hill as Hubbard's guest. The reporter gained Ron's trust by swearing he would clear up some of the more outlandish accusations the mainstream media had used to sully his reputation over more than a decade. Documents taken from Food and Drug Administration (FDA) files by the GO included daily cables from this reporter/agent, reporting Hubbard's every move and utterance to the FDA. To add insult to injury, the reporter wrote a damning indictment of Hubbard, which was published in the *Post.* According to a once-prominent Scientology promoter, Alan Walters, who was studying under Hubbard in England at the time, Hubbard's disposition notably – and permanently – changed for the worse after this betrayal.

Though it is not difficult to make the connection between the attacks instigated and sustained by the likes of the AMA, the FDA and the fellows running them – all beholden to drug manufacturing interests – such connection does not wholly account for the viciousness, persistence and magnitude of the attacks on Hubbard and Scientology. The documents demonstrated there must be a stronger motivation inspiring the force by which Hubbard was being opposed.

Perhaps L. Ron Hubbard's most vehement antagonist and long-term enemy was the American Psychiatric Association. For two decades the APA served as the authoritative hub for disinformation ammunition against Hubbard, to be used by government agencies and media outlets. The man who was most rabidly anti-Hubbard and anti-Scientology from the start was head of the APA in the critical, fledgling years 1952 and 1953, Dr. Ewen Cameron. Cameron had far more to lose by reason of Hubbard's continued success than the AMA and FDA boys. Cameron had been involved in – and continued to be, throughout the fifties – the most barbaric human torture experiments imaginable. He headed up CIA mind control projects, which sought means to wipe out a person's entire living memory, then mentally programming them to unwittingly carry out espionage objectives, including assassination. Among Cameron's practices carried out on illegally imprisoned "patients" was the daily use of multiple, debilitating electric shocks and drugging, which kept subjects unconscious for weeks on end. The full array of Cameron's serial crimes has been accurately and painstakingly detailed in Naomi Klein's *The Shock Doctrine: The Rise of Disaster Capitalism* (Knopf Canada, 2007).

Why would Cameron, and dozens of the most elite psychiatrists of the early fifties, care about L. Ron Hubbard and the proliferation of his non-violent, inexpensive techniques for helping people do precisely the opposite of what those psychiatrists were purportedly attempting to produce? Consider this. Cameron became president of the APA the year after Hubbard published this passage in his 1951 book, *Science of Survival*:

> *"There is another form of hypnotism which falls between the surgical operation and straight hypnotism without physical pain. This form of hypnotism has been a carefully guarded secret of certain military and intelligence organizations. It is a vicious war weapon and may be of considerably more use in conquering a society than the atom bomb. This is no exaggeration. The extensiveness of the use of this form of hypnotism in espionage work is so wide today that it is long past the time when people should have become alarmed about it. It required Dianetic processing to uncover "pain-drug-hypnosis." Otherwise, pain-drug-hypnosis was out of sight, unsuspected and unknown."*

Hubbard went on for several pages describing in detail the

techniques government agencies and their leading psychiatric "researchers" were using to create Manchurian candidates, and amnesia-for-life cases out of those who carried secrets the government wanted forgotten. Ewen Cameron and the rest of the very best psychiatrists, who had been paid a pretty penny by the Central Intelligence Agency in the late forties and throughout the fifties, may have breathed a collective sigh of relief that Hubbard's second book did not top the New York Times bestseller list for a year, as his first book *Dianetics* had. The AMA, FBI and friendly media had done a decent job of chasing Hubbard from the national spotlight and pushing him into the refuge of Dianetics and Scientology groups. That Hubbard had hit so close to the quick with his disclosures of what Dianetics and Scientology processes had uncovered about the dirty work of the CIA and the very best psychiatrists, it is a wonder he was not physically assassinated.

Perhaps because of his high profile, and the growing ranks of dedicated religionists surrounding him, the APA, AMA, CIA, FBI, FDA and friendly media alliances would have to settle for old-fashioned (albeit of unprecedented intensity) character assassination. The documents demonstrated that the ranks of the massive government and private agencies arrayed against Hubbard and Scientology were swelled by other military and intelligence groups also involved in mind control experiments, including Naval Intelligence, Air Force Intelligence and Army Intelligence.

The truth of Hubbard's 1951 pronouncements about our government's dirty activities would not be corroborated publicly until the mid to late seventies, with the advent of the Freedom of Information Act and the U.S. Congress Church Committee Hearings into unlawful CIA domestic intelligence operations. That Ron was twenty years ahead of his time in recognizing what the CIA and psychiatrists were up to was acknowledged by author Walter Bowart in one of the first popular exposures of that activity, *Operation Mind Control* (Dell, 1978). By then, Hubbard had been so discredited by establishment campaigns, and his church subjected to such intense fire for scandals of its own manufacture, that nary a person would listen to the longer history, the bigger picture.

By the early eighties, the mainstream media were so full of the FBI raid and convictions of Mary Sue Hubbard and other GO people that the church of Scientology was on the verge of extinction.

Ironically, the church of Scientology was by then becoming infamous, in the public mind, for the very type of activity L. Ron Hubbard had once been subjected to: domestic intelligence operations. But, given his reaction to early criticism, Ron was not a blameless victim. He had been a trained intelligence man in the U.S. Navy during World War II. He preached fighting fire with greater fire.

As early as 1955, Hubbard had the following advice for Scientologists who found themselves under attack:

> *"The DEFENSE of anything is UNTENABLE. The only way to defend anything is to ATTACK, and if you ever forget that then you will lose every battle you are ever engaged in, whether it is in terms of personal conversation, public debate, or a court of law. NEVER BE INTERESTED IN CHARGES. DO, yourself, much MORE CHARGING and you will WIN. And the public, seeing that you won, will then have a communication line to the effect that Scientologists WIN. Don't ever let them have any other thought than that Scientology takes all of its objectives…*
>
> *… The purpose of the suit is to harass and discourage rather than to win. The law can be used very easily to harass, and enough harassment on somebody who is simply on the thin edge anyway, well knowing that he is not authorized, will generally be sufficient to cause his professional decease. If possible, of course, ruin him utterly."*

Adoption of that attitude assured Scientology's survival through the fifties and well into the sixties. In fact, that one passage would be my motto for the next ten years, in preventing the imminent death of Scientology in the eighties.

However, by the mid sixties, when the cumulative attacks on Hubbard and Scientology reached their apex, Hubbard took the "fight fire with fire" philosophy to a level that would wind up virtually imprisoning him during the final five years of his life. That conclusion is easy to arrive at now, decades later, when the dust has been settled for many years. I am sure it was not so easy for L. Ron Hubbard to predict, considering the pressure he was facing in the mid sixties.

Hubbard's perspective by the mid sixties was that he had been unjustly persecuted. After fifteen years of devoting every single day to helping others through the development of Scientology, the establishment's payback was ruthless. Hubbard had established his home, research center, and worldwide headquarters for Scientology training and management at St. Hill Manor in England. It was the first time in his entire adult life that he had remained in a stable location for more than five years. He raised his four children there, and clearly enjoyed the pastoral peace of English country living.

Meanwhile, the powers that be had not been so peaceful. In the U.S., the FDA, frustrated after a decade of failed attempts to catch or even frame Hubbard, launched an attack against the lone physical device integral to the practice of Scientology: the e-meter. In 1962, the FDA raided the Founding Church in Washington, D.C., and began proceedings to ban the use of the meter.

Prompted mainly by inflammatory reports from the AMA, FDA, and APA, a parliamentary inquiry in Australia banned the practice of Scientology. Similar movements were afoot in South Africa and the United Kingdom. The four countries where Hubbard had visited, lectured and established Scientology the most were on the verge of running Scientology and Hubbard out, lock, stock and barrel. The final indignity came when the United Kingdom's Home Office revoked Hubbard's visa, essentially telling him he was no longer welcome even in his adopted home.

It was during this period, at the height of the Cold War, while being pursued viciously by Cold War agencies using Cold War tactics, that Hubbard drew upon his own Cold War training from the United States Navy.

Hubbard formed the Sea Organization – the elite Scientology few who would manage Scientology internationally and assist Ron with his further researches. They would take to the sea, starting with a single ship and expanding into a flotilla of several.

Ron introduced harsh policies, meant to deal with the fallout from the many government and private-agency infiltrations of Scientology communities. Among these harsh policies was the practice of excommunication. The excommunicated would be labeled "suppressive persons." Policy would direct that suppressive persons could be treated as "fair game" – that they "may be tricked, lied to, sued, destroyed without any recourse to justice." This policy was later cancelled; the directive in which Hubbard did so stated that the public labeling of enemies as "fair game" had caused bad public relations and should therefore cease. Still, it noted that policies for the handling of suppressive persons remained intact.

Hubbard established the Guardian's Office to work autonomously to the rest of Scientology to fight the war with the establishment. He appointed Jane Kember, a South African with government intelligence experience, to head the GO as a lifetime appointment. He then appointed the one person he could trust above all others – his wife Mary Sue – to serve as Controller, the sole point of GO oversight, and liaison between the GO and himself.

Hubbard began instructing the GO, through Mary Sue, that the intelligence tactics of the enemy agencies attempting to destroy Scientology ought to be used in dealing with those same agencies.

Now Hubbard's writings took on a markedly different tone than most of what he had written before. Rather than speak of turning the other cheek and dealing with establishment attacks with a healthy insouciance, Hubbard prepared the GO to do what the enemy was doing, but to do it better.

On February 16, 1969, he noted, in a confidential policy letter entitled Battle Tactics:

> *"In these days of "cold war" when actual warfare is impossible due to atomic weapons, the warfare is waged in the press and public in the form of ideas. If you uniformly apply the tactics and strategy of battle to the rows we get into, press or legal or public confrontation, you will win. Wars are composed of many battles. Never treat a war like a skirmish. Treat all skirmishes like wars."*

Later that year he followed up with more explicit instructions to the GO, in a confidential Guardian's Order entitled *Intelligence Actions*, dated 2 December, 1969:

> *"<u>COVERT OPERATION</u>*
>
> *A covert operation can be arranged by a Case Officer, using agents but is normally on another set of lines so as to expose nothing of covert data collection by engaging on a covert operation. Essentially a covert operation is intended to embarrass, discredit or overthrow or remove an actual or possible opponent.*
>
> *It is a small war carried on without its true source being disclosed. Generally the operation is preceded by data collection to establish the*

target validity and to plan the operation.

It follows all the rules of war but uses propaganda, psychological effect, surprise, shock, etc., to achieve its ends."

Hubbard later issued a confidential Guardian's Order titled *Counter Attack Tactics* on 28 March, 1972, more explicitly directing how to fight fire with fire:

"(a) Wherever an attack is in progress (and even when being held off by counter-propaganda from PR or actions from Legal) at once swiftly draw up a precise program using Intelligence principles and cross filing to isolate the attacker.
(b) Identify the instigator.
(c) When identified or even suspected as the instigator, draw up a project which includes at least three channels to cost him his job.
(d) Draw up a second project at once to survey and discover what the person really is defending and threaten it effectively.
(e) Execute the projects rapidly.
(f) On achieving success inform PR so that PR can call off the PR counterattack and capitalize on any information gained if it does not expose Intelligence.
(g) Inform legal so Legal can re-plan and utilize the information also gained to mop up."

Having been electrified by the rush of Scientology-induced out-of-body experiences, and having learned the details of the enormous cross L. Ron Hubbard had had to bear through the decades, my indoctrination into Hubbard's war directives was viewed through glasses of a somewhat darkened tint. I can only say this now – thirty years after the fact, eight years after having left the organization, and four years into having those war policies directed at me.

By way of example, until I just recently re-read the following Hubbard Guardian's Office Order, I would have vehemently argued that Scientology and L. Ron Hubbard never countenanced blackmail. Sure, they promote aggression, intimidation and fighting fire with fire, but just as surely not the commission of felonies as serious as blackmail. L. Ron Hubbard uttered the following on July 1, 1968, in a briefing to Mary Sue Hubbard about how her Guardian's Office ought to be conducting itself:

> *We try to isolate who is creating the unrest and giving the orders. But even while we're doing that, we try to collect "protective materials." Archaeological and scientific and social studies might very well result in disclosing Mr. De Gaulle's peculiar liaison with Hitler. That's protective material.*
> *All of a sudden somebody is jumping all over us in "Wango-bingo" and all it would take would be a quiet phone call. That's one way to keep order. That is an intelligence method of handling things. It's not blackmail, because blackmail is demanding money and that has nothing to do with it. "You jump on us, you're dead"— that type of material…*
> *…So, Mr. Big decides to knock us flat in Bongville. All of a sudden it cools by the simple reason that we already know that the head of the public health service at Bongville has three wives. What you normally do is leak it to him. Somebody goes out and has dinner with his daughter as a perfect stranger and says, "You know, I would be awfully careful of jumping on those Scientologists in Bongville if I were you. You know somebody ought to tell your daddy that there's some wild rumor—of course, we don't know what the truth of it is—that actually you have three mothers. And they know that over there."*

In the context of protecting the power of Simon Bolivar (read: L. Ron Hubbard) I understood this just as Hubbard said: "It's not blackmail, because blackmail is demanding money and that has nothing to do with it."

I knew these documents were written by L. Ron Hubbard because, among other reasons, Mary Sue Hubbard told me so. When I later met with her in person, she expressed her frustration about David Miscavige's hypocrisy in proudly proclaiming how he had saved L. Ron Hubbard from his "treasonous" wife and her "rogue" GO network. Mary Sue pointed out to me that she had gladly gone to jail, despite her failing health, to protect her husband. To her, and to the GO people who went to jail with her, it was for the greater good that they would take Hubbard's secrets to jail, and ultimately to their graves beyond. But for David Miscavige to brand them for life as "traitors" and "anti-Hubbard" was too much for her to stomach. No matter how painful it was to be put out to pasture and ignominiously branded as L. Ron Hubbard's enemy, Mary Sue told me the outside world would never know of Ron's link to the

Guardian's Office's illegal activities. She was the only one who could positively, conclusively link him, and she would die before doing so.

Mary Sue did not know the half of the hypocrisy of her nemesis, but I did. Miscavige was so acutely aware of the authorship of these documents that he referred to them continually, demanding they be applied by the GO's successor, the Office of Special Affairs (OSA). This even while he was demanding it be communicated to the outside world on all fronts that all such clandestine activities had died with the GO.

I helped coordinate keeping the GO convicts faithful to Hubbard and to the church, primarily to protect Ron from two outstanding grand juries that were still attempting to link him to GO crimes. However, I would soon learn the hard way that to listen to Mary Sue or GO personnel, or to consider what they had to say – no matter how well advised – would be considered by Miscavige as the most heinous of crimes.

Overall, the GO files painted a picture of a bizarre, exciting history that would shape the development of my views and life over the next two decades. At the same time, I was hamstrung by threat of expulsion if I were to reveal the content or provenance of those files. It put me in an awkward, but not unfamiliar, position of having to create my own universe; an understanding that I could not make others understand.

The GO files – in the words and hands of government agents and their target L. Ron Hubbard – made one thing crystal clear to me. It was a modern-day miracle that L. Ron Hubbard had not only survived the onslaught, but that he had kept on researching and writing prolifically all throughout it. While Hubbard had fought fire with fire – in many ways in direct opposition to the philosophy he had made his life's work – the CIA, FBI, APA, AMA and the establishment they served had drawn first blood. L. Ron Hubbard was the underdog in this saga. He was the one who first stood alone against the status quo, and he did not deserve to be forced to die alone. In my mind, L. Ron Hubbard, despite appearances in the world of 1981, deserved as strong and as loyal a defense as humanly possible.

CHAPTER SIXTEEN

MAKING ENEMIES

If you want to make peace, you don't talk to your friends. You talk to your enemies. – Moshe Dayan

In January of 1982, the Special Project was terminated in name. Miscavige, Starkey and Gamboa packed up, gathered a few finance and book marketing people, and began a new corporation to look after L. Ron Hubbard's personal and business affairs. It was part of the corporate and finance sort out; part of the strategy to make Ron's business arm's length from the church. The new outfit was called Author Services Inc. (ASI). To the outside world it served as Hubbard's literary and personal services agency. In reality, it became the headquarters through which L. Ron Hubbard continued to run the Scientology empire.

Miscavige became Chairman of the Board. He would forever after be referred to as "COB" in Scientology circles. Starkey was posted as the Executive Director, and Gamboa became the Executive Administrative Officer. ASI had offices about two miles from the Scientology complex, down Sunset Boulevard toward the center of Hollywood. ASI concentrated on raising Hubbard's income. That income was the statistic that ASI operated on – all of its rewards and penalties depended upon whether that income rose or fell. The most important income factor was royalties from Ron's books. Miscavige saw to consistently rising royalty income statistics. That was accomplished mainly by ordering the churches to buy more of Ron's books than they could possibly sell or even store. Miscavige, by virtue of still being the only communication link to Hubbard through Broeker, began to assert increasingly tight control over church management. But still, Miscavige's number one assignment was All Clear.

A new breed of Commodore's Messenger, one who had never met or worked with Hubbard, was put in charge of our All Clear unit, which was now called Special Unit. The messenger was Steve Marlowe. I was called down to ASI a couple times a day by Starkey and Miscavige to tell what was what on the litigation scene. They outright bypassed Marlowe, who also had juniors who handled corporate affairs, investigations and public relations. Miscavige, in what I would learn was his signature micro-management style, also bypassed Marlowe to visit directly with Marlowe's juniors in those other departments.

By then I was responsible for all aspects of the litigation – forming up units to service attorneys, hiring and firing lawyers, holding coordination conferences with staff and with counsel, hiring and directing investigators to flank the litigation, you name it. I was also ultimately responsible for the budget. Between July and December 1981, when Special Project reigned directly over litigation, there was no issue of budget. Church management was ordered to pay whatever expenses the project incurred.

In order to get Special Project's January estimated budget approved by top-level church management, I had to present a review and justification of the previous six months' expenditures. When I totaled the figures, it hit me like a hurricane: The church had been spending almost two million dollars per month on litigation. The first thing I thought of when I saw the total was Mary Sue Hubbard's proposed 1.6 million dollar deal. GO lawyers had proposed that figure eight months earlier. By scuttling the deal, the Special Project had incurred nearly ten times that amount of money over the ensuing eight months. If anything, the litigation had only become more complicated, precarious, and threatening during that period.

Someone heard my musing on that comparison and mentioned it to someone else. Eventually Miscavige caught wind of my comparative and went thermo-nuclear ballistic. Miscavige stormed over to my superior Steve Marlowe's office with Terri Gamboa. I could hear the shouting from down the hall.

Marlowe and Gamboa pulled me into a small office while Miscavige watched from down the hall. The two senior messengers subjected me to a six-hour tongue lashing. Such sessions were patented by David Miscavige and even given a name: Severe Reality Adjustment (SRA, for short). In effect, it was enforced thought-stopping. I was called every foul curse word imaginable, and then some. I was called an enemy of L. Ron Hubbard, a defeatist, a saboteur, a treasonous bastard, a suppressive person, a Mary Sue dupe, a GO protector, a Department of Justice stooge, and an FBI plant.

The fact that I had ever harbored even the vaguest thought that settlement was a possibility – back in May when the GO originated the idea, in July when the proposal had been scuttled, or now – demonstrated that I had deeply concealed evil intentions, probably formed in a previous lifetime hundreds of thousands of years in the past. These destructive purposes could probably only be expunged through a complete RPF (Rehabilitation Project Force) program. But because I was such a suppressive person and enemy to Hubbard, I did not even qualify for the RPF. I would be lucky to ever see Scientology again. Instead, they might just declare me suppressive and let me dwindle into a shriveled lump of black debris, floating aimlessly in the dark cold of space forever. After a threat such as that, Marlowe and Gamboa would leave me alone to stew on it for several minutes, while they went down the hall to debrief to Miscavige about the festivities. Then back they'd come, bolting into the room to shouting some more obscenities, indictments and dire predictions of my fate.

Finally, late in the evening, Marlowe came in alone to play the good cop. I think Marlowe could perceive that I was seriously contemplating taking a long hike, never to return. He told me that the reason they came down on me so hard was that they were so offended by my betrayal of L. Ron Hubbard. Ron had made it clear to Miscavige that there would be no settling with the enemy. That to settle would be tantamount to surrender and would play right into the hands of the powers that be, in their desire to keep L. Ron Hubbard away from the church, and ultimately destroy it. Marlowe then used another patented Miscavige technique. He told me that "Dave" thought I was a good guy at heart, and that he wanted to see me "trim my sails" and fly right; all presented as if Miscavige hadn't been orchestrating the entire confrontation. Marlowe said that if I showed sufficient remorse by working after hours to make amends, and by stomping out similar "defeatism" amongst those in the GO, Dave might relent and allow me to stay in Special Unit.

I was in a state of shock about the entire bizarre affair. To buy time, I told Marlowe I would do my best to warrant trust once again. I was told that first I would have to work up through what were called the lower ethics conditions. This bears some explanation. The "ethics conditions" are an application of Hubbard's philosophical work on the subject of ethics. He developed a system of ethics, which is practiced (or is supposed to be) by the church and by Scientologists. Part of this technology is a series of conditions – states of existence or functioning, ranging from low to high.

For example, when just starting a new job, one would be in a condition of "non-existence" – as far as his co-workers are concerned, he doesn't really exist yet. Not as part of the functioning organization, at least. The newbie is expected to apply the formula for the condition he is in, non-existence. A formula is a series of steps that if followed should take a person up to the next higher operating condition. The non-existence formula has the person make himself be known to others in the group, to find out from the others what was needed and wanted from him, and then doing those actions that the group members desire. If he botched an important task, or caused his co-workers and superiors inconvenience or worse, his condition would probably be "danger," – he's in danger of being disciplined in one way or another, possibly even demotion or dismissal. Following a formula for the condition of "danger" raises a person up to an 'emergency condition.' After the person has learned the ropes, and come up through non-existence, danger, and emergency, he might find the job rolling along smoothly – he's doing what others expect, performing reasonably well. This would be a condition of "normal." Ultimately a staff member is expected to work toward an abundance of production, called an "affluence" condition, and on up to the highest condition, called "power."

In Scientology organizations, staff members keep track of their job statistics, and use them to help determine their current ethics condition. They apply the appropriate condition formula in an effort to improve their job production and statistics, and so reach higher conditions. Where a staff member is not performing well, or causes trouble of one sort or another, either his or her superior or the organization's Ethics Officer may assign that staff member a low ethics condition, and require that its formula be applied. This is not (according to policy) meant as punishment, but rather as an effort to help the staff member get back on track as a contributing and valued member of the team. Using these conditions and their formulas is a routine and important part of many Scientologists' daily lives, and their use is integral to the functioning of Scientology organizations.

When first introduced, the conditions ranged from non-existence to power as outlined above. These were the only conditions (and formulas) for some years. Then, in the mid 1960s, coincident with the war mentality Hubbard introduced, also introduced what were termed the "lower conditions." These ranged from "confusion," up through "treason," "enemy," "doubt" and "liability." For staff members (and particularly Sea Org members) these conditions originally carried various penalties, such as temporary pay reductions, and being required to wear a colored arm band so that others wouldn't make the mistake of trusting them (at least not until they had worked their way up to higher conditions).

In my time on staff, I'd had plenty of experience with the conditions and their formulas, and had found them very workable up to this point. But now, for the first time, I was assigned one of the lower conditions – those below non-existence. Specifically, I was told I was in the condition of treason, and required to apply its formula.

The formula for the treason condition was "Find out *that* you are." Doing that was a bit of a mind trip, in that I had to assume (or accept) that I, in my treasonous state, didn't even know I existed – so that I could carry out the formula and "find out" that I did exist (that is, find out that I was). I weathered the mind trip, and managed to complete the formula to Marlowe's satisfaction.

Next came the enemy condition – the next up the scale from treason. In the Hubbard policy that describes this condition, it is noted as being applicable when a person has demonstrated that he is a "knowing and avowed enemy" of the group. The formula to be applied is "Find out who you really are." In a single, unguided soul searching, I was essentially being required to accomplish what the entire Scientology auditing Bridge was purported to deliver: knowing who I really was. In order to do that I first had to reckon how it was that I had been being a "knowing and avowed enemy" of L. Ron Hubbard and Scientology. In this case, my having entertained and communicated a thought that was contradictory to Ron's dictates and strategy of Ron was the "enemy" activity. In order to avoid such a pitfall in the future I would have to be someone who was incapable of repeating such "knowing and avowed enemy" behavior.

Delving deep into my own psyche, I attempted to divine who I really was. In my auditing up to that point, I had experienced some memories of past lives. For the most part, the past-life incidents I had contacted had involved deaths in battles. I had the impression that the one consistent thread in my long-term being was the role of a warrior. It was an honorable, disciplined role – abiding by the universal principles of warriordom, as outlined in the Bushido, the code of the Samurai. I reckoned it would take that level of serious, disciplined single-mindedness to shut out doubts and reservations concerning the defense of Ron and Scientology – the very reason I had been assigned a condition of treason in the first place. I decided right then and there on who I really had been, lifetime after lifetime, and who I would have to be, now and in the future, to make it on Ron's team. To me it was the most honorable identity a man could have: a warrior.

Each night, after working eighteen-hour days, I spent several more hours mopping and waxing thousands of square feet of floors, all to make amends for my destructive behavior. Making amends was a part of the formula for the condition I had now risen to, called "liability." One of the formula's steps is "making up the damage one has done by contributions far beyond the ordinary demands of a group member." Another step of that formula was to "deliver an effective blow to the enemies of the group one has been pretending be a part of." On that step, I reckoned I had better blow the whistle on anyone I knew to have evidenced any defensive, settlement-oriented thoughts. I dutifully wrote reports on two staff members from the GO that knew favored settling the FAMCO litigation.

Even though I had transformed myself into a somewhat unsympathetic and laser-concentrated warrior, I did a lot of thinking while mopping and waxing. I seriously considered doing what I'd done in the past when things got too thick: hit the road and start a new adventure. But I kept coming back to what I had studied in recent months, about what Ron had been through over the past thirty years. How he'd been condemned for advising his people, twenty-five years before, that the defense of anything is untenable and that the only way to defend anything is to ATTACK. I thought about how that passage initially offended me, and about how I was being dealt with now offended me, too. But, in the bigger scheme of things, wasn't Hubbard right? Nobody could have overcome what I saw he had overcome. Nobody. Was I simply being self-centered and weak? I knew for a fact I would never confront any challenge of the magnitude that Hubbard had. I knew I could never find another adventure with such stacked odds – one that would challenge me as much as the one confronting Hubbard and the church, right then and there.

In the end, I decided to change my mind. To recognize that I had been wrong, to believe what I was told about Hubbard's intentions regarding settlement (regardless of how irrational it seemed to me at the moment), and become what I was told Hubbard wanted on his side – a warrior. I became a warrior. I demanded that others under my command also become warriors. I demanded our lawyers become warriors, and if they faltered along that line I had them replaced with ones who were or who could become warriors.

Hubbard had sent a memo to our unit, advising that we develop what he called a "punitive defense." Hubbard reasoned that if Flynn and company could take a bunch of false plaintiffs and use the litigation process to inflict vast expense and chaos within the church, well, we could just as easily use the process more effectively in the same wise against Flynn. The end product of the punitive defense was to make the process too painful for any plaintiff to carry on.

We hired a coordinating attorney in Los Angeles named John Peterson. John had an amiable personality which helped get more recalcitrant attorneys to cooperate with our plans. John and I played an effective good guy/bad guy routine. I would rough up our attorneys with over-the-top demands for aggressive action, then John would follow up by hearing their objections, expressing his understanding of their concerns and then more gently obtaining their agreement to compromise and do something far more aggressive than they normally would do.

We had an office built for John within the complex. He worked for us full time, until his untimely death in 1987. John was in constant communication with our lawyers across the country. John and I worked out several tactical plans to inconvenience Flynn and his co-counsel. We forced him into a series of errors over the next several months. We overloaded him with paper, hearings and depositions. The FAMCO boys started missing filing deadlines, and not properly preparing witnesses we were deposing daily. Within months we had reversed the tide of the litigation; FAMCO finding itself in the state of disarray as we had been when we entered the war. By the end of summer we had chipped away at a number of cases, with portions being dismissed. More importantly, we had Flynn's back against the wall, defending two contempt proceedings for misrepresentations to courts, which we had flustered him into. Finally, in August, Flynn was held in contempt by a judge in a remote jurisdiction.

Shortly after that I was called to come over to ASI. Norman Starkey, Terri Gamboa and several of Ron's other personal staff gathered around. Starkey announced that L. Ron Hubbard had heard what I had accomplished in the litigation over the past several months, and ordered that I be promoted. I was handed my first Sea Org officer's epaulets, signifying I was now a Warrant Officer. It was nice to be acknowledged. But again I got the distinct impression Hubbard was only getting half the story. I did not see what Starkey and Miscavige were reporting to him from ASI, but I did see Hubbard's dispatches in response. It appeared he had been told that Flynn would soon be in jail, discrediting all of his litigation, essentially the beginning of the end for FAMCO. That was simply an unrealistic view of how matters worked in the courts. There was no time for rest or celebration. During the several-month blitz leading up to the promotion, I had probably read more material than I had in my entire life before that. I was sleeping about four hours a night, month after month. My eyesight was shot, to the point that I'd need glasses the rest of my life. I had also become addicted to cigarettes and coffee. On the verge of physical collapse, I knew the current offensive state of affairs was unsustainable.

I knew how tenuous our "win" over Flynn was, too; it had been a series of tactical maneuvers that had advanced the litigation. But after another year of experience I recognized that in American litigation it is a point like this at which one parleys for a settlement, with a foe one has brought into a more amenable frame of mind. It was Hubbard policy to do so, too. But what I had learned in the policy books did not seem to apply to All Clear, Special Project, or Author Services Inc. (ASI). I knew that if I raised the idea of settlement, I'd have my head handed to me, just as it had been several months earlier.

Sure enough, right in alignment with Sun Tzu's *Art of War* – which was a Hubbard-recommended read, Flynn became very resourceful once we had his back against the river. Just as it appeared he could not keep up with the mountain of paper under which our now-coordinated team was burying him, he was saved by an angel of sorts. Wayne B. Hollingsworth, recently-resigned Assistant U.S. Attorney in Boston, came on board. Hollingsworth, though not well-heeled after years of government work, outfitted Flynn's offices with the latest in computer equipment. He brought on more attorneys and support staff. And all of these new troops apparently were not asking for a dime to devote their next several years to the FAMCO plan (or, as we suspected, they were being paid by some vested interest that was inimical to Scientology).

Flynn also received a windfall, care of the fruits of Miscavige's enemy-making proclivities. Gerry Armstrong, the archivist whom Miscavige and Starkey nearly hung for trying to protect Hubbard and the church against the very claims Flynn had been making, had made contact with Flynn. We knew this because for several months Miscavige had been directly supervising surveillance of Armstrong, through a former GO intel staff member named Geoff Shervell. Shervell utilized teams of private eyes to shadow Armstrong everywhere. Shervell reported directly to Miscavige through all those months, just as I had on litigation matters from our Special Unit. On more than one occasion, Shervell groused to me about the incessant, obsessive pressure Miscavige put on him, demanding to know Armstrong's every move. He said, "Marty, he knows we're on him, which kind of defeats the purpose of the surveillance." Thinking for a moment, Geoff added, "Unless the purpose is to drive him crazy."

Armstrong became increasingly paranoid under pressure and finally got spooked enough to go to Flynn for help. Armstrong also brought with him several boxes of biography archives he had lifted from the church; documents that demonstrated to him that Hubbard's personal biography, promoted by the church, was full of holes.

I did not connect the dots until years later, but Miscavige had essentially chased Armstrong right into the enemy camp. In September, 1982, all I knew was that Shervell had evidence of Armstrong lifting the documents, and I had direct, urgent orders from Miscavige to sue Armstrong back to the stone ages. We sued, and obtained an injunction which impounded the files with the Los Angeles Superior Court pending trial (which would occur years later). But that did not stop Armstrong from – in fact it drove him to – writing long, detailed declarations claiming L. Ron Hubbard was a fraud and that the church would stop at nothing to prevent him from proving so. Flynn now had a fresh, inside witness who knew Hubbard's personal archives better than anybody on Ron's side. Miscavige's treatment of Armstrong also sent Hubbard's former Personal Public Relations Officer, Laurel Sullivan, to jump on board with Flynn.

Further, Miscavige's treatment of Bill Franks, the erstwhile Executive Director International, had prompted Franks to join Flynn and to provide even more new high-level witness declarations. With Armstrong, Sullivan and Franks aboard, suddenly Flynn could paint a credible picture, through sworn declarations, that L. Ron Hubbard was actively engaged in tight control of the church of Scientology – something we had gone to great lengths to disprove over the past year and a half. All three of the powerful new guns in Flynn's arsenal were people that David Miscavige had personally treated with aggression and vengeance.

Granted, Hubbard had directed or authorized their falls from grace, but Miscavige had an inimitable, aggressive style that produced only two possible results: a) compliance with Ron's intentions, or b) an avowed enemy of Miscavige, and usually, by association, of Hubbard and Scientology. Objectively speaking, even though I did not fully appreciate it then, in a little more than a year from the time the quest for All Clear had begun, the enemy's hand had been strengthened beyond its wildest dreams. All compliments of the man L. Ron Hubbard had charged with ultimate responsibility for All Clear: David Miscavige.

To make matters worse, Miscavige had only a month earlier supplied yet another stable of high-level, former-insider witnesses for Flynn's arsenal, and new lawsuits against Hubbard for the future. Following the Mission Holder's Conference of late 1981, disaffection toward Miscavige's heavy-handed tactics was spreading among those veteran Scientologists who owned missions. In order to stem the rebellion, Miscavige planned to intimidate the remaining mission holders into line. In response to whatever Miscavige had reported to him about the matter, Hubbard wrote back that the mission holders were historically a bunch of criminal thieves, and that they needed to be spanked back into line, hard.

Miscavige and several other Sea Org executives, including Starkey and Marlowe, ambushed the next Mission Holder Conference in August of 1982, in San Francisco. There Miscavige announced the formation of a new corporate structure. Gone was the old "mother church," Church of Scientology of California. It had been replaced by the new "mother church," Church of Scientology International. It would house all of international management, with the CMO International and its Watch Dog Committee at the top. He also announced the formation of the Religious Technology Center (RTC), a corporation to which L. Ron Hubbard gifted all the trademarks of Dianetics and Scientology. Miscavige explained that this signified Hubbard's ultimate trust, and his blessing to RTC to carry on Hubbard's role beyond the eventual end of his life.

Hubbard had legally enforced quality control and corporate compliance over churches of Scientology during his lifetime, through the ownership of the trademarks he had now gifted to RTC. From this point on, missions would be at the mercy of Miscavige and RTC, who now had the power to cancel their charters and sue them for trademark infringement if they continued to promote their activities as "Scientology." Miscavige let the mission holders know that gone were the days of peace, love and support from management. For now on, management would run a taut ship and the mission holders would toe the line, or else. Miscavige created a Finance Police unit to "audit" the missions' books and levy huge fines for supposed transgressions found.

To terrorize the majority into line, Miscavige excommunicated a number of veteran mission holders attending the conference, verbally and right on the spot. It scared people all right. Virtually every major productive mission holder left the church over the next year or two, with the most prominent of them winding up in FAMCO's camp. The Mission network would dissolve over the next decade, and this vital introduction line to Scientology, which Hubbard had painstakingly built up over decades, would never recover.

Many former member of the church have constructed a denialist story, to justify their having been on the short end of the 1982 Mission Holders Conference. These people have created and lived with the idea that L. Ron Hubbard knew nothing of the behavior and conduct of Miscavige and his management crew at the '82 conference. Their idea and story had ample credibility. After all, much of what Miscavige and his cadre lectured about at the conference, about how the church would henceforth be run, was diametrically opposed to long-standing, oft-repeating senior policy, set down by Hubbard over decades. The conference began with "church attorney" Lawrence Heller, introducing the idea of corporate Scientology. Heller likened Scientology services to Coca Cola products, promising that from then on Scientology Inc. would deal with mission holders with the same cold, business-like attitude the Coca Cola bottling company would, in dealing with its distributors and vendors and particularly trademark infringers. Corporate Scientology was born. Steve Marlowe, speaking as the first Inspector General – head of the newly formed Religious Technology Center – boasted to the mission holders that Hubbard had appointed a "new breed of management," marked by its toughness and ruthless approach; all quite at odds with tomes of Hubbard policy calling for understanding, compassionate, effective managers.

Miscavige told the mission holders that church justice procedures would no longer be followed in cases of perceived offense; instead, the church would have mission holders prosecuted under criminal law; quite contrary to sheaves of policy Hubbard had issued over the years, criticizing society's lack of swift, effective justice procedures and creating superior justice mechanisms to replace them within the church.

Guillaume Lesevre, newly-appointed Executive Director of the church of Scientology International, informed the mission holders that they were to stop running "social club" missions. They were there, he said, for one reason alone: to serve as automaton feeder outlets, introducing people to Scientology and sending ever-increasing streams of them to larger organizations. International Finance Director Wendell Reynolds told the mission holders they would be audited and assessed crippling fines for every infraction imaginable, and that they would have no recourse to church justice – those in non-compliance would be "put in the slammer."

To add insult to injury, the management team flat-out lied to the mission holders, both about corporate secular affairs and ecclesiastical technical matters of vast import to every Scientologist. Norman Starkey announced that the barrage of lawsuits against the church "is pretty much over, and the tide has definitely turned in our favor. We are winning and this is the winning side."

Ray Mithoff, holder of the highest technical post in Scientology, Senior Case Supervisor International, told of new, higher levels of spiritual attainment (the OT or Operating Thetan Levels) that L. Ron Hubbard had allegedly developed and written up: "The upper OT levels, new OT 7, new OT 8, New OT 9, 10, 11 – these levels are amazing. They are amazing beyond your belief. These things are all there and it's a very bright future." As we shall see, not only were new OT 9, 10 and 11 neither researched nor written up by late summer 1982 – they never would be, ever, to the day L. Ron Hubbard died. And the religion permitted no one but Hubbard to write up any level.

Near the end of the conference, all mission holders present were treated to forced confessions, while on an e-meter and before a group of Sea Org officers. So anathema were these actions to the basic principles of Scientology that for many, the 1982 Mission Holders Conference served as proof that David Miscavige had hijacked Scientology from under L. Ron Hubbard.

In fact, L. Ron Hubbard had advised or approved of virtually everything that was uttered by Miscavige and his management boys at that conference. And when they returned, Miscavige sent a recording of the entire conference to Hubbard. Hubbard listened to the whole proceeding. He was so thrilled with their performance that he highly commended Miscavige and his managers and ordered that a transcript of the entire event be prepared and distributed widely amongst Scientologists. His wishes were complied with, with the publication of Sea Organization Executive Directive 2104, THE US MISSION HOLDERS CONFERENCE, San Francisco, 1982.

A clue as to Hubbard's approval of the new corporate Scientology was evidenced by the identity of the first speaker at the conference. Larry Heller was not in fact a "church attorney." He was L. Ron Hubbard's personal attorney – the Heller in Lenske, Lenske, and Heller, the X attorneys retained and paid by Hubbard to attain an All Clear.

Miscavige exacerbated the gloom of the future by personally removing from post the highest authority on Scientology orthodoxy, David Mayo – the Senior Case Supervisor International prior to Ray Mithoff's appointment. Mayo had been L. Ron Hubbard's personal auditor, and was the one person with enough technical expertise and experience in Scientology to discuss the compilation and development of technology directly with Hubbard. Miscavige ordered that Mayo be put through months of grueling manual labor in the hot California sun, at Int base in Riverside County. Miscavige personally subjected Mayo to denigrating hazing, aimed at ruining his dignity and willingness to fight back. In order to "take out his connections," as Hubbard earlier advised one should do when taking out a suppressive person, Miscavige had John Nelson, the then-Commanding Officer of CMO International, sentenced to Mayo's hard labor detail. Both Mayo and Nelson would escape sometime in early 1983, and ultimately gravitate toward Flynn and his Department of Justice connections for protection.

I did not witness the Mission Holder's conference first-hand, nor the Mayo-Nelson takedown. It would be years later before I heard and read all versions of the events, from the viewpoints of everyone involved in the tiffs. I did not question any of it at the time – I was too busy in the trenches, fighting the war, and only saw memos from Hubbard directing these actions and commending Miscavige for pulling them off.

I did doubt the wisdom of the internal purges, recognizing that the Flynn suits were not all that unconfrontable as long as there were no fresh high-level witnesses to implicate Hubbard. And I did harbor well-hidden hopes that one of Hubbard's more trusted friends and associates would eventually get word to him that the baby might be being thrown out with the bath water. As of late 1982, Ron's old guard such as Mary Sue, Mayo, Nelson, Dede Voegeding, Gale Irwin, the mission holders, et al were giving Ron the benefit of the doubt. Their shared narratives targeted Miscavige and his management team for betraying Ron by false reporting to him about the alleged sabotage and treason on every hand.

But alas, Miscavige was still sole gatekeeper for communication to Hubbard, and ensured those loyalist pleas would never make it to Ron. Though not fully informed of the details of the purges while they were happening, I sensed Hubbard had sealed his own fate by his acceptance of and expansion upon a theme Miscavige presented to him. One apparent truth had gained a lot of currency within Scientologist circles by late 1982. This was that L. Ron Hubbard was being misinformed by Miscavige and his "new breed of management;" that Ron was being systematically given false reports about his closest friends and allies; that Ron only continued to back up and support Miscavige and his crew because he was operating on the lies Miscavige furnished.

As ruthless and single-minded as Miscavige could be, when it came to political power pushes he proved he could be even more diabolically clever. He began reporting to Hubbard about increasing disaffection in the Scientology field – disaffection with the new management and its actions such as hijacking the Mission Holders Conference. He interjected exaggerations about how Scientologists' objections carried an increasingly anti-Hubbard slant. Instead of accurately reporting speculations from the field that he had been lying to Hubbard, Miscavige characterized the claims as saying that Hubbard was losing his grip, and could easily be lied to. Miscavige drew connections – conjectures reported as facts – between his own internal nemeses and the very real FAMCO threat, with its roots in long-term Department of Justice, AMA, and APA hatred of Hubbard. Miscavige curried Hubbard's favor by painting a picture of being targeted himself, because of his staunch defenses of Hubbard. Miscavige artfully communicated the attacks on himself as actually being attacks on Hubbard.

Hubbard's response would guarantee his own lonely seclusion for the rest of his living days. Hubbard wrote to Miscavige and management that the whole idea that Ron could be falsely reported to was an old "enemy line" – one his institutional enemies had run in the past. Miscavige's reports reinforced Hubbard's idea that the internal enemies Miscavige was creating were in fact witting or unwitting agents of his age-old Department of Justice, AMA, and APA enemies. Hubbard mused that the idea that "Ron is being falsely reported to" was an attack on Ron himself, because it implied he was not on the ball or smart enough to distinguish fact from fiction. He concluded by stating that those who "spread the line" that Ron was being misinformed were really attacking Hubbard, and should be treated accordingly. And with that, Miscavige was effectively empowered to complete his purges, consolidate his power push and wield unquestioned authority. Per Hubbard's own decree, anyone accusing Miscavige of painting a false picture for Hubbard was by definition an enemy of Hubbard. And so he guaranteed that there would never again be even a possibility of someone providing him with any uncooked facts that might potentially clarify the macabre picture David Miscavige had painted for him.

It would take me many years to unravel the complicated web of Miscavige's Machiavellian maneuverings. Miscavige was tireless in alienating and crushing his perceived competitors for Ron's approval, and anyone opposed to his seizing control and creating his own Scientology empire. By his actions, he was in fact creating the very dangerous state of affairs he was reporting to Hubbard as already extant. Ron's erstwhile close friends and aides had not actually been in the enemy camp; but by the time Miscavige was through with them, they would all be there. And so, in his own tortured and complex way, Miscavige would eventually make true the lies that he had reported to Hubbard.

By late 1982, though, all I knew was that Hubbard was under siege, and that he was relying heavily on Miscavige – and by extension, me – to extricate him.

CHAPTER SEVENTEEN

MANUELA SAENZ REDUX

[Manuela Saenz] was utterly devoted, completely brilliant and utterly incapable of really bringing off an action of any final kind. - L. Ron Hubbard, *The Responsibilities of Leaders*

In mid-November 1982, just as Hubbard was apparently setting in stone Miscavige's position as victor of the Scientology power-vacuum contest, we were hit with a shot literally heard 'round the world. Hubbard's first son, Ronald Dewolf (once known as L. Ron Hubbard, Jr.), estranged since the late 1950s – filed a petition in the Riverside County Probate Court seeking a judicial determination that his father was either deceased or incompetent. Dewolf was represented by Michael Flynn. A great deal of the background giving credibility to the petition was provided by people Miscavige had made enemies of – Franks, Sullivan, Armstrong, et al.

The petition pled that Hubbard's alleged activities over the past year were so bizarre and uncharacteristic of the L. Ron Hubbard the world had known for decades, that the court should conclude that Miscavige and Broeker were holding Hubbard against his will in a state of incompetence, or that Hubbard was dead. It alleged that Miscavige and Broeker had effectively eliminated Hubbard's closest friends and associates, to clear the way to looting Hubbard's personal accounts and the coffers of the church while Ron was incapacitated. It was Flynn capitalizing on the "reality" – exaggerated thought it may have been – of those who knew Hubbard best, but had been alienated by him. The petition was a media sensation. Virtually every print or electronic media outlet of any size, in America and abroad, carried variations of the lurid headline: "Hubbard dead or incompetent?"

For All Clear, 1982's hard-won couple of steps forward suddenly became ten large leaps backward. Ron Dewolf had a vivid imagination and had nothing to lose; a deadly combination. After being accurately advised by Flynn that there was no way in God's green Earth Hubbard would appear, let alone sue for libel, over the next several months Dewolf's fertile imagination provided the media with the most shocking tales of his alleged madman father. The media ran with such sordid tales as "Hubbard performed coat-hanger abortions on Dewolf's mother in his presence," "Hubbard was a drug addict who wrote Dianetics and other books on amphetamine benders," and "Hubbard ordered assassinations against critics." Think of the worst possible things a jilted, drug-addled mind could dream up about a person, and Dewolf would say them about his father. All the church could say was that Dewolf had many years earlier made similar allegations, and then later swore they were lies after reaching a settlement with the church. But, as we learned the hard way, when the entire world is watching there is no putting the toothpaste back into the tube.

Miscavige and his Hubbard attorneys had no idea what to do. The church could not enter the fray. It was a family affair and the church had no legal standing. Besides, Miscavige and Broeker would be questioned under oath about where Hubbard was. The stakes were as high as they could be. The petition asked that Dewolf be appointed executor of Hubbard's estate. Since the church's wealth and power stemmed from Hubbard's ownership of the trademarks, and since the marks were part of Hubbard's estate, Flynn's (FAMCO – Department of Justice, AMA, APA) client would essentially own Scientology. Since Dewolf himself was more than a couple bottles short of a six-pack, FAMCO itself would own Scientology.

Enter once again Mary Sue Hubbard. I was on continually improving terms with Mary Sue personally, since I had helped her in preparation for the sentencing phase of her criminal case that year. I had assisted her in finding and hiring big-shot lawyer Michael "Mad Dog" Madigan of Dallas' storied Akin/Gump law firm to represent her. I served as a liaison between Mary Sue and Madigan, and prepared and delivered his briefings. I also stayed in close touch with her Los Angeles civil counsel, Barry Litt. I was his liaison point for coordinating on outstanding church and Hubbard litigation as it related to his client.

Litt recognized that nobody could challenge Hubbard's own wife's standing when it came to a probate petition. Barry was a very intelligent, thoughtful and soft-spoken man. The antithesis to what Miscavige and Starkey considered an effective advocate. Miscavige and Starkey spent many an hour – on L. Ron Hubbard's dollar – joking about and criticizing Litt with Hubbard's lawyers, Lenske and Heller. Now, all of the sudden, Miscavige and Starkey demanded I get Litt on board, since he was their only lifeline.

Barry and I spent many hours strategizing how we could overcome Mary Sue's anticipated reluctance to doing the bidding of the man who had made it impossible ever to communicate with her husband again. As Barry predicted, when she was approached with a plea to get involved, Mary Sue first responded that she was not quite sure her interests and those of the church were the same. In retrospect, she made a hell of a point. The probate petition demanded that L. Ron Hubbard appear before the court for a determination of his competence. Mary Sue Hubbard had desperately wanted to communicate to her husband, but Miscavige had prevented her from doing so. If Dewolf were successful, it was certain Mary Sue would finally be able to meet her man. Litt and I did manage to get her to reconsider by subtly pointing out that should Ron show up to court, Flynn's secondary purpose (some thought it was his primary purpose) would be achieved. Hubbard would be personally served with a couple dozen FAMCO lawsuits and maybe presented with an indictment or two. Under those circumstances Ron might not be so pleasant to talk to.

Mary Sue Hubbard was in frail health. She was facing a high-profile sentencing hearing and a lengthy prison sentence. She felt like she was being used to mount a legal attack against a petition that made sense to her in some ways – in her view Hubbard was in fact being taken advantage of by Miscavige and Broeker. But ultimately Mary Sue took her only measure of personal comfort in reckoning that her suffering was for a good cause: her husband and the religion he had created. In her view, she was Manuela Saenz to Ron's Simon Bolivar, ever faithful, even it if meant dying in infamy in some ditch.

This is what set Mary Sue apart from all of the rest of L. Ron Hubbard's long-term close friends and allies who had been denigrated and depowered by the new regime. The rest had joined or were drifting toward joining Ron's avowed nemesis – the FAMCO group – where they would receive acknowledgment and comfort as victims.

And so Mary Sue, the alleged cause of L. Ron Hubbard's legal travails, once again stepped between Ron and his enemies. Enemies who had never been so close to dragging him into the public square for a legal and media lynching.

In the first week of January, 1983, Mary Sue was scheduled to be sentenced by federal judge Norma Holloway Johnson in the Washington, DC District Court. I met her in person for the first time at a hotel in DC. We had arranged separate rooms on the same floor, paid in cash and registered under false names. Mary Sue had not been seen in public since her indictment nearly five years earlier. Her health was failing, and she looked old and gaunt – but she had a sparkle in her eye. A proud, Texas-born-and-raised woman, Mary Sue told me that she wished for only one thing. In her dimly-lit room she asked, in her soft, gravelly Southern voice, "Marty, could you see to it that the media does not see me and photograph me?" "Don't worry, I'm on it," I replied with confidence, knowing that it was easier said than done. I went to the courthouse and made friendly with the U.S. Marshall's Service personnel. They granted me the privilege of pulling our car into the judges' parking area underneath the courthouse, and using the one elevator serving the basement, reserved for judges.

Mary Sue was accompanied by a Sea Org member named Neville Potter. He was a friendly, middle-aged Englishman and a highly trained auditor. He had been appointed by L. Ron Hubbard to live at Mary Sue's home, take care of her security and help out in whatever ways Mary Sue might see fit. Neville reported every detail of Mary Sue's life to David Miscavige – particularly every nasty thing he overheard her say about Miscavige. Miscavige would often stew over Neville's reports, snarling about what a "disaffected, evil bitch" Mary Sue was. It was an odd relationship. Mary Sue was savvy enough to understand Neville was as enemy agent in her own home. But she was also resigned to suffer her lot, and managed to remain friendly with Neville nonetheless.

Neville and I conspired to distract Mary Sue from watching television the night before the sentencing. That evening, ABC 20/20 aired a special featuring Dewolf spewing scurrilous personal attacks against L. Ron Hubbard. As Mary Sue was already under a tremendous amount of stress, we did not want Dewolf exacerbating matters.

The next morning Neville drove a rented Lincoln Town Car to the courthouse. I rode shotgun and Mary Sue sat low in the back seat, scarf over her reddish- grey hair and oversized sunglasses, despite the overcast, cold weather. We followed the pre-planned route to the basement. We traveled up through the special elevator to the second-story courtroom. No media cameras were allowed above the first floor of the courthouse. While other cases were being heard ahead of Mary Sue's, I went to check on the media turnout. When I looked out the second story lobby window I saw dozens of media covering the entire walkway leading to the courthouse entrance. There were television vans lined up along the sidewalks. I had never seen anything like this – a full-blown media spectacle. I would never see anything like it again, until the O.J. Simpson trial. The first-floor lobby was also packed with media, crowding the elevator foyer and craning their necks into every elevator car that came from the second floor, looking for Mary Sue.

I went back upstairs to witness the hearing. It was a pathetic proceeding. Mary Sue, like the other ten GO defendants who had already been sentenced to five years in federal prison, was caught in a conundrum. She had sorely wanted to try the case made against her by the government, and fully present her justification defense. It would have been a complete production of much of the saga spelled out in Chapter Fourteen of this book – the struggle of one man against a trillion-dollar vested interest that was intent on keeping the public sick and consuming lots of expensive drugs. But it was too late for that. Mary Sue had forfeited the right to such a trial when she had agreed to be tried by a judge on a stipulated record. She had considered that such a course would result in the government dragging her husband into the case and so had chosen not to present it when it would have been proper, during a jury trial. Instead, she had been convicted by a judge and here she was before another judge to receive her sentence. Madigan kept the sentencing argument solely to the issues of (a) Mary Sue's alleged arms-length stance, separate from day to day GO operations and (b) a plea of mercy for Mary Sue's ailing health.

Unfortunately, when she was afforded an opportunity to speak on her own behalf, Mary Sue set herself up for an ugly smack-down by the judge. She tried to make a cursory, sketchy and thus less-than-credible case for having acted to protect her religion, in the face of a long history of government attacks. In the context of a few-minute plea, after having specifically waived that defense at trial, Mary Sue sounded feeble and bitter. And she provided Judge Johnson with the justification needed for slapping Mary Sue with a four-year sentence, noting that Mary Sue obviously showed no remorse for her crimes.

As the hearing ended, reporters streamed out of the court room, headed for the first floor where they arrayed in wait to interview, photograph and film Mary Sue. Though we were headed for the basement, there was no way to make the elevator bypass the first floor. The reporters were continually pushing the buttons to make sure all elevator cars stopped there. Madigan and I quickly devised an escape plan. We commandeered an elevator car. Mary Sue stood in a back corner of the car. I stood in front of her facing forward, totally eclipsing her body to view from the front. Madigan positioned himself right in the center, facing the opening doors. When we hit the first floor, the second the doors opened all we could see was a mass of reporters and photographers, with several flashes firing in. Madigan immediately raised his arms, and strode out of the elevator car, hollering, "Okay, boys, it's question-and-answer time!"

All eyes went to Madigan, and because his body blocked anybody from entering the car, the doors closed behind him. Mary Sue and I went on to the basement, where Neville waited with the car. We climbed in and headed out the back side of the courthouse.

Despite having been condemned to four years in federal prison, and having been treated like trash by the judge to boot, Mary Sue was giggling in the back seat of the car. I turned to her to find out what was up.

"Well, at least you got done the one thing I asked you to," she smiled at me warmly.

"I'm sorry I couldn't do more."

"Hey, do you mind if we drive around front? I'd like to see the circus."

"No problem. Neville, make a hard right, then another hard

right."

We drove slowly by the front of the courthouse, watching the ironic scene of dozens of reporters and cameramen waiting for us to walk out its front. Mary Sue, who had just lost almost everything she had, was smiling and taking a sort of victory on the one little thing her pride required of her. I was glad to see that she was happy. I would learn to appreciate such tiny, poignant moral victories; they would become life-sustaining in the face of the kind of major shellackings one inevitably took in defending Scientology.

We had a relaxed lunch overlooking the Potomac River in Virginia, where Mary Sue waxed nostalgic about the early days of Scientology with Ron. In this very relaxed and informal setting, one thing shone through, crystal clear: Mary Sue's unqualified love and admiration for her husband.

The worldwide news of Mary Sue Hubbard's jail sentence hardly distracted the runaway train that was the continuing "is L. Ron Hubbard dead, or alive?" story. If anything, it simply pumped it up with even more energy. In January alone, *Time* magazine weighed in with "Mystery of the Vanished Ruler", *People* magazine ran a cover story, "Ministry of Fear," and the *New York Times* went with "Fight Over Funds Divides Scientology Group." These stories were notable in that they began to link the internal dissension evidenced by vocal mission holders with an instability within the church that was uncharacteristic of Hubbard's leadership. In a sort of morbid backhanded compliment, the media was reporting that Flynn's allegations of Hubbard's passing or incompetence were being supported by expelled executives and mission holders who reported that Miscavige and Broeker were running the church into the ground – something that could never happen on Hubbard's watch.

As gatekeepers, and purgers of the old guard, Miscavige and Broeker were under intense and escalating international scrutiny. The judge in the probate case denied Mary Sue's initial attempts to have the petition dismissed, indicating that given the fact that Mary Sue hadn't seen her husband since 1980, only L. Ron Hubbard's appearance would dispel all suspicion.

The solution arrived at between Miscavige, the Lenske firm and Mary Sue's lawyer Barry Litt was to obtain a signed declaration from L. Ron Hubbard to present to the court. The trick was to make it sufficiently informed to indicate Hubbard knew what was going on, but without enough detail to indicate he was in the loop enough to be managing church affairs. Too much of the latter would land Hubbard squarely into the middle of dozens of other church lawsuits which named him as a defendant.

Barry Litt, the man Miscavige despised as the loyal agent of his arch-enemy Mary Sue, had to be relied upon to wordsmith Hubbard's declaration. Ironically, some of the words composed by Litt would be used by Miscavige, on into the next millennium, to defend his claimed birthright to the throne of corporate Scientology. Because the probate petition focused on Miscavige in particular as the person allegedly looting Hubbard's estate while keeping Ron ill-informed, the declaration had to explicitly dispel those charges. And so Mary Sue's own attorney wrote – while she sat helplessly in the federal correctional facility in Lexington Kentucky – the detailed outline for L. Ron Hubbard to convert to his own words, in declaration form. It included the following ode to David Miscavige:

> *Since there apparently have been specific allegations of wrongdoing by David Miscavige,* ***I wish to take this opportunity to communicate my unequivocal confidence in David Miscavige, who is a long time devoted Scientologist, a trusted associate, and a good friend to me.*** *Any activities which he may have engaged in at any time concerning my personal or business affairs have been done with my knowledge and authorization and for my benefit. The charges that he is organizing the theft of my assets are completely false and not worthy of further comment than that.*

In the year 2012, church of Scientology webpages quoted the boldfaced text above to support the proposition that Miscavige was anointed by Hubbard as his successor, to rule the scientology corporate kingdom – even though Hubbard made no mention whatsoever of Miscavige in the parting words he wrote near the time of his January, 1986 death. Of course, the church has not published the remainder of the above paragraph, since it begs too many questions.

The final, formatted declaration was sent to Hubbard along with special, forensically dated ink provided by a NASA technician, so that the time of the declaration's signing could be accurately determined. Hubbard signed the document, and placed finger and thumb prints in the margins to prove its authenticity. Another four months of fierce litigation ensued to determine whether Hubbard's current written wishes would suffice to end the battle.

While the probate case and its unprecedented media onslaught was in progress – including plenty of rehash of the GO dirty tricks documents, the church had set into motion a concerted international effort to purge GO staff members whose past actions were a potential liability. We were forming a successor to the GO, called the Office of Special Affairs (OSA). We had to be damn sure it brought none of the GO liabilities with it. For more than a year we had been claiming in courts and to the media that the GO was gone, all criminals had been rooted out, and we were flying right by the law. In late '82 and early '83, we had missions at each GO continental office (Canada, Europe, South Africa, United Kingdom, Australia, and the U.S.) weeding out anyone with a history of participation in illegal acts, and converting the remaining few staff into OSA units.

It turned out that we were a couple months too late in Canada. In February, 1983, the mission to clean out the GO in its continental offices in Toronto made some connection between two former high-ranking GO officials and a fledgling movement of expelled Scientologists who had decided to keep on practicing Scientology outside of the church. Emile Gilbert and Brian Levman were declared to be suppressive persons – excommunicated by broad public issue – for having the temerity to traffic with disaffected ex-church members. This set into motion an attack on Scientology in Canada from which it would never recover.

On March 3, hundreds of agents of the Ontario Provincial Police conducted the largest raid in Canadian law enforcement history. The target was the church of Scientology of Toronto, which housed the Canadian GO. From Los Angeles I spent that entire day attempting to locate any staff member in Toronto who could give sensible, reliable reports as to what was occurring. The efforts were fruitless, since the GO had pretty much been decimated. That night I took a red-eye flight via Vancouver, arriving the next morning in Toronto. When I arrived at the church, the raid was still in full progress – more than twenty-eight hours after it had begun. In the end, the raid lasted nearly two full days.

I retained two of Toronto's most highly regarded and aggressive criminal civil rights lawyers, Clayton Ruby and Marlys Edwardh. They immediately began what would turn into years of litigation over the legality of the search and seizure. I formed up a team of a half dozen staff as the legal unit, to service the attorneys and work to prevent charges from being laid. Early intelligence indicated that the aim of the raid was to go after high-level GO executives as well as the top of Scientology management, including David Miscavige and L. Ron Hubbard as individual defendants. The raid had been supervised by a long-time Scientology antagonist within the OPP, Al Ciampini, and was sanctioned and directed by a Scientology hater in the Crown Law Office, Casey Hill.

We would later learn, through discovery in the litigation, that Ciampini had an informant working within the GO at the time the GO clean-up mission from the U.S. was operating in the organization. When Gilbert and Levman were excommunicated, and the OPP caught wind that the files might be "cleaned up" they swooped in with a vengeance.

The evidenced seized was as damning as that in the 1977 FBI raids on GO offices in Los Angeles and Washington, D.C. From the sworn information in support of the raid, it was evident that the Crown law office was intending to indict L. Ron Hubbard as the alleged mastermind and controller of Scientology operations in Canada.

Initially I was in Toronto for several days attempting to bring order, get the church proper back into delivery, and the legal unit organized and operating. I set up a number of phone booths throughout the city to do pre-arranged payphone-to-payphone calls so I could report daily to Miscavige, directly and securely. When I reported we had learned that the Royal Canadian Mounted Police were coordinating across Canada to do similar raids at churches in the several provinces where GO offices existed, Miscavige ordered that I drop everything and, as quietly and quickly as possible, get one step ahead of law enforcement. It was not difficult to justify at the time. The Toronto raid seemed treacherous. Here we were trying to clean up the mess ourselves, a fact the OPP was clearly aware of with an informant in the GO. And then to target the founder and Miscavige, who were demanding the entire GO mess be cleaned up, seemed inherently unjust. Of course, the fact that our plans included wiping out tomes of evidence of criminal acts as part of the "clean-up" just got conveniently edited out of my thinking process. We were in the thick of the war by then, and by the nature of it my thinking became more black-and-white.

There were a couple of missionaires still in town, left over from the Los Angeles-directed GO clean-up mission. They were the only people I could think of to trust. I had no idea whether the OPP still had informants among the remaining GO staff, or even in the Toronto church organization. Operating out of a hotel, we took a map of Canada and marked the locations of all GO offices within existing churches, from Vancouver to Quebec. There were several. We divided them up and off we went – the mission was to destroy every GO intel bureau piece of paper we could lay our hands on. I went with one of the missionaires to Quebec and got him started.

I then went off to Ottawa alone. I commandeered one GO staff member I was reasonably certain was on board. The GO guy obtained a truck. After closing time at the church, he and I loaded hundreds of pounds of GO intel files into the truck. He drove us up to a remote lake shore. We found a rock-lined fire pit. We created a giant bonfire and toasted GO files in the near-freezing weather, almost until dawn. I later supervised the other teams by payphone-to-payphone calls from Toronto. Within a few days we had wiped out every last trace of GO crimes in Canadian churches. Later, with some distance from the dirty deeds, I thought in retrospect that we hadn't really accomplished a thing – aside from potentially opening us all up to fresh obstruction of justice charges. Any GO operations of any import would be reflected in the continental office files already seized by the OPP. Nonetheless, I was commended by Miscavige for such speedy, thorough, risky work.

With new criminal charges against Hubbard on the horizon, Mary Sue became all the more important. We continued to appeal to the Manuela Saenz in her to protect Bolivar. Part of our tack was to continue making her feel guilty for having creating all these threats to begin with.

After more than six months of fierce litigation, Hubbard's declaration was accepted by the probate court judge, who proclaimed that L. Ron Hubbard was alive and competent, and on that basis dismissed the Dewolf probate petition.

Celebration time? Hell no. Before the ink was dry on the dismissal, Flynn was busy filing the judgment in every church lawsuit in which Hubbard was named as a defendant. Flanked now by declarations of Franks, Armstrong, and Sullivan, he was making a formidable case that the church, through Miscavige in particular, could not only communicate with Hubbard but was in such tight coordination that Hubbard swore he knew every aspect of what Miscavige was up to.

Even more immediately pressing was the litigation against Gerry Armstrong, attempting to have the several boxes of L. Ron Hubbard archives returned to the church. Mary Sue played a critical role since once again "standing" was an important issue. Who was more qualified and entitled to the return of such personal and private material than the wife of the man that material belonged to? And so her attorney Barry Litt was the central player in prosecuting that suit. After a year of hard-fought litigation, with the documents in question held under seal in the court pending trial, Litt filed a motion for summary judgment. A summary judgment is an extraordinary remedy at law. One must demonstrate – assuming all of the affidavits and documents submitted by the opponent are true – that one ought to win the case because there is no genuine issue of fact remaining for a jury to decide. If the summary judgment could be obtained, Armstrong would be discredited as a thief, and more importantly, the myriad thorny issues of the truth of Hubbard's published assertions about his own background would be spared a high-profile public airing.

We worked intensively for a year to obtain the deposition admissions and documents required to make a convincing case for summary judgment. Litt argued the case before a Los Angeles County Superior Court Judge for a couple of hours. At the end, the judge said that he was going to grant the summary judgment in favor of Mary Sue Hubbard. Just before the hearing adjourned, Armstrong's attorney rose and ask whether the ruling also applied to the audio tape that had been impounded along with the archives documents.

The judge looked flustered and asked, "What audio tape?" Armstrong's counsel then described an audio tape recording of a meeting of church legal staff, in which they discussed what to do about the fraudulent foreign corporation that had served as a conduit for funneling millions of church dollars to L. Ron Hubbard over the years.

The judge said he had no idea about any legal conferences on tape; he thought it was all about Hubbard historical papers. Flustered and impatient, he said summary judgment couldn't be granted where there were any outstanding issue of fact, and the fact that he knew nothing of audio tapes meant there were factual issues remaining. Motion denied. Litt tried to clarify but was gaveled down, and the judge rapidly excused himself from the bench.

This was typical of the crushing blows we were continually dealt in the early eighties. We would work around the clock for months on end to research law, gather evidence, interrogate witnesses in deposition, and brief attorneys at length to prepare them within an inch of their lives. We were fueled by little more than high hopes of a precedent that would turn the tides of war. But there were so many documented past bad acts – whether technically relevant or not – that could be used by the enemy to viscerally connect with a judge, that it felt like we were continually running the length and breadth of an enormous dike, desperately attempting to plug ever-increasing numbers of leaks. There were so many salacious things to throw against the wall, something always eventually seemed to stick.

The Armstrong case would go to trial. And Mary Sue, the plaintiff, would ultimately become the center of attack – the only one standing between the enemy and the empty courtroom chair reserved for her husband Ron.

CHAPTER EIGHTEEN

WISE GUYS

Just as every cop is a criminal
And all the sinners saints
As heads is tails
Just call me Lucifer
'Cause I'm in need of some restraint
– Jagger/Richards, *Sympathy for the Devil*

Up to this point we have been able to maintain a relatively sequential timeline of events. But, by this stage of the war, where victories turned out to be losses and seeming losses turned into long-term victories, and with bullets flying with such rapidity and randomity from so many directions as to create a three-year chaotic jumble, I have found it necessary to digress. Several stories require such detail in the telling that it is not possible to weave them into a continuous history. The next few chapters cover topics that overlapped one another in time. Each is essential to portraying the timeline of Scientology's history during the final tumultuous years of L. Ron Hubbard's life.

The first such story is a wild foray into organized crime and the U.S. Department of Justice (DOJ). This is a world where criminals become saintly, cops become criminal and vice versa. This is where the concepts of right and wrong become so confused and compromised as to suggest a world gone mad.

It began six months prior to the filing of the probate petition. In early May, 1982 I was busily mounting the offensive against Flynn and his FAMCO scheme to bankrupt and destroy Scientology. Up to that point in time, several people had served as buffers between me and David Miscavige. All that changed one morning when Miscavige called me over to his offices at Hubbard's newly-formed personal services corporation, Author Services Incorporated (ASI). Miscavige was the chairman of its board. As such he was recognized as the most senior and powerful person in the Scientology hierarchy. It was understood by then that all communication to or from L. Ron Hubbard went through Miscavige's hands.

I hopped into the small Japanese car that came with the job of Special Unit Litigation Director and sped over to see Miscavige. I brought Geoff Shervell with me. Geoff was my opposite number for the intelligence/investigation function of the church. He was a short, portly fellow from New Zealand. He was handsome and friendly in looks and manner. Geoff had worked at the Guardian's Office Worldwide in England for years. The Special Project had investigated him thoroughly and concluded that he had not engaged in any illegal acts while in the Guardian's Office. His amiable demeanor and his training and understanding of intelligence had resulted in Miscavige tapping him to run all intelligence for the church. Up to that day Shervell had been reporting directly to Miscavige.

ASI was located in an office building at 6464 Sunset Blvd, two miles west of the Scientology complex near Sunset and Vermont. When I arrived I was led to a large, windowless conference room. As was Miscavige's habit, I waited for several minutes until Miscavige suddenly burst into the room, throwing the door open to bang against the wall as he made a bee line straight to the head of the fifteen-foot conference table. Norman Starkey shut the door and sat to Miscavige's side. It may have been that Norman was chosen to shadow Miscavige because of the effect it added to his presence. He rarely contributed anything to such meetings. But his South African accent and his countenance and bearing added some air of dignity and importance to Miscavige's shtick.

Miscavige seemed somberly unnerved, an attitude he rarely showed to anyone. He wore a dirty blonde mustache and glasses then. He stood about five feet, five inches, solidly built. He looked at me with piercing, intense blue eyes.

"Marty, Geoff's a nice guy, but he doesn't have the confront for this job." With that succinct statement, Miscavige put the intelligence function, and Geoff, under my supervision.

"Does the GO have any PIs you can trust?"

"I haven't worked with any, sir."

"Well, you need to find a PI that has a pair of balls and won't be compromised."

"Ok, I'll get right on it."

"Look, somebody tried to pass a forged check on LRH's account at Bank of New England. Some Arab guy named Aquil Abdul Amiar shows up at Middle East Bank in New York City with an LRH check with a forged signature. The check is from LRH's account at BNE. BNE calls us and we tell them LRH never signed any check made out to any Arab, and no check for two million dollars to anybody. They stopped payment. We keep LRH's check registers. There are no checks missing. We write all of LRH's checks and submit them to him for signature. He signs them. We mail them and every one of them is accounted for. Norman can show you all that." I looked at Norman. Norman gave a serious nod back.

Miscavige continued, "We asked BNE for more particulars. BNE won't give any. We have Sherman Lenske (LRH's corporate and finance attorney) call MEB and BNE and nobody will cooperate with him. BNE says they want to hear from LRH directly. We have all the proper powers of attorney on his accounts, but they won't recognize them. They tell us the FBI is investigating. And the FBI won't tell Sherman anything either. This whole thing smells. These fucking bankers are supposed to be working for LRH, and it looks like they are doing the work of Flynn and the FBI. You need to get a PI onto this and get to the bottom of it."

"Yes, sir."

"Okay, Norman, show him the documents we have, like the POA (power of attorney) and all. Marty, you report direct to me on this. Tell the finance people this is top priority if they give you any flack on the PIs."

"Yes, sir."

"Nobody in the GO or Special Unit or anywhere else needs to know about this, get it?"

"Yes, sir."

Suddenly Miscavige loosened up, lit a Camel with no filter (the cigarette of choice at ASI) and offered me one. "Give him a light, Norman," Dave ordered. Norman snappily complied. You always light up when offered, because usually it means Miscavige is lightening up.

"Marty, did you ever tell Norman the story about how you fucked with the Border Patrol on the way to the Super Bowl?"

"No."

Miscavige by then was smiling, "Go ahead, tell him."

I then told Norman – with Dave interjecting details I left out – about how Miscavige, his wife Shelly, and I drove thirty-two hours straight, from the Int base near Hemet, California to Baton Rouge, Louisiana. Dave's father, Ron, had managed to get several tickets for the January, 1981 Super Bowl, the one in which the Miscavige family's beloved Philadelphia Eagles were playing. Miscavige and I had taken turns driving. One person drove for eight hours while the other caught some rest in the back of a Datsun hatchback. Miscavige's wife Shelly remained continuously in the front passenger seat, and when she was awake she would keep the driver awake with conversation. Shortly after my first eight-hour shift ended, and I was attempting to get to sleep in the back, Miscavige pulled the car up to a Border Patrol check point on Interstate 10 outside of El Paso, Texas.

The green-uniformed agent asked, "Are you all United States citizens?" Shelly and Dave answered yes. Then the agent pointed his flashlight at the blanket I was lying under, and I spoke up, "Si!" Dave and Shelly froze, and when I pulled the blanket aside and showed the agent my mop-headed Anglo grin, he began laughing. Miscavige loved the story because in the split second between my answer and my cracking up the border agent, he was convinced we might be arrested and would not make the Super Bowl – and Miscavige for that split second was contemplating murdering me.

Miscavige, as was his habit, then picked up his coffee and abruptly exited the room. This vignette is classic Miscavige, circa early eighties. He is laser-precise and as serious as a heart attack when concentrating on something of importance. When business is done, his eyes turn from a grey-steel blue to a sky blue, and he is instantaneously relaxed and friendly, often playful.

That is one thing a lot of folks don't get about Miscavige. They remember him only as coming down like thunder, as he often does. They seldom see the charm, which can be engaging. I saw a lot of both. I believe one reason Miscavige kept me as a close aide for twenty-two years was the quality of my communication training routines. Unlike most people who came and went his way, I could hold my position in space, unflustered when Miscavige regularly lit up like the Fourth of July. He could vent on at me in rather dramatic and overwhelming fashion, and I would not be affected or distracted. I would hear what he had to say and acknowledge him comfortably. And that would generally calm him down and make him far more pleasant. I saw a lot of folks over the years who never made it past the venting stage. They would get nervous – which would set him off even more – or get overwhelmed and get blown away. So they never saw that at bottom he had a likable human being aspect. Maybe it was the communication training routines, or maybe it was the training I received from my dogs in childhood. In either event, I think that same ability to not get flustered was my greatest asset for my entire church career. We experienced a lot of shocking threats and losses. Generally, I was able to keep my head when others tended to flail. Having experienced Miscavige's human side I was also sympathetic to the cross he had to bear, being the only man between L. Ron Hubbard and enough seasoned enemies to easily defeat any lesser man.

The only church attorney who had previously worked with investigators was Bob Harris. Harris had worked with the GO for years on the colossal tax trial over the mother church's (Church of Scientology of California) tax years 1970 through 1972. It was the huge, pending test case that all concerned figured would determine whether the church of Scientology would ever attain tax exemption. Bob was once a fairly prominent and successful criminal defense attorney in Los Angeles. For the past few years he had pretty much moved in to church premises, working full time on the all-consuming '70-'72 case. That trial went on for several few-weeks stints over two years. Bob told me of the best private investigator, pound for pound, he had ever worked with.

According to Harris, Eugene "Gene" Ingram was a former Los Angeles Police Department street cop. Using his street smarts, better-than-average intelligence, and brash, aggressive style, he had worked overtime as an officer defense representative before the LAPD Board of Rights – where internal affairs charges would be aired out in mini trials. Ingram was so effective in securing acquittals of charged officers that he became not only a thorn in the side of the notoriously corrupt LAPD Internal Affairs Division, but also of the to-become-infamous Chief of Police, Daryl Gates. Harris told me that if we were going up against the FBI and US Department of Justice, we would be hard pressed to find anyone as qualified or as trustworthy for the job as Gene.

I met with Gene. I was immediately struck by his intelligence, healthy suspicion of bureaucratic authority, and engaging personality. Gene was in his late thirties, wore a neatly-coifed pompadour, and had tanned skin and large, brown, alert eyes. He spoke with police-business-like precision. He almost always wore neat, stylish suits and ties. I questioned Gene about his dismissal from the LAPD. Gene said that after he produced a string of acquittals of cops that Gates had sorely wanted dismissed, he began receiving anonymous death threats. In the middle of one of the biggest, most hotly-contest internal Board of Rights cases he had ever defended, personal disaster struck. While alone on a late-night call to a remote section of LA, he was shot in the back of the neck with a sniper's bullet. He showed me a huge round entry scar on the back of his neck, millimeters from his spine. While he was recovering, Gene was indicted by a Los Angeles County Grand Jury on ten counts of trumped up pimping and pandering charges. Working with Harris and another criminal defense lawyer who often worked with Gene on Board of Rights cases, they attained an acquittal by a jury on all charges. He handed me a series of articles in the *Los Angeles Times* that chronicled and corroborated much of his story.

Gene was a breath of fresh air, in that he could think with conspiracy theories. After all, he had lived conspiracies and almost died because of conspiracies. I did not have to convince him that there could be corruption within such august institutions as the U.S. Department of Justice (DOJ) and the FBI – he was already convinced there was.

After extensive briefing on all details of the case, Gene flew to Boston. He reported in that he had ingratiated himself with the secretary of the president of the Bank of New England. He sweet talked his way in to see the president by giving the impression that he might be working for interests inimical to Hubbard's and ASI's. Once in the office, Gene asked some hard questions about the bank's violations of its own policies as to customer loyalty and security with respect to Hubbard. He was rapidly shown the door. We learned from Ingram's first Boston trip that in fact Hubbard's bank was playing ball with Flynn and the DOJ – while treating Hubbard and ASI with suspicion. Miscavige was pleased with the result and entertained by the details of Gene's tactics. From then on I would be required to come give Miscavige daily, face-to-face briefings on the progress of the investigation. That led to also debriefing on other legal and public relations matters. From May 1982 forward, Miscavige bypassed my nominal superiors altogether, and I became his primary source of information for matters external to the church, and for relay and execution of his orders into the church relating to such matters.

Miscavige had an obsession with what we came to term "the check case." It had served as the anchor for the probate petition by Dewolf and Flynn. It was the one current, hard allegation that may have influenced the judge not to simply dismiss out of hand the otherwise stale, sordid allegations. In late 1983, after Flynn began using his defeat as a victory, claiming that it proved Hubbard's intimate involvement with church management – and thus his availability for service of process and relevance for depositions – Miscavige became all the more obsessed with proving that it was Flynn and the DOJ that set up the check case themselves, for purposes of dragging Hubbard out into public.

The investigation scoured every connection Flynn had ever made – most notably certain organized crime figures his legal practice had once brushed with, and most particularly those connected to his new legal partner, former DOJ attorney Wayne Hollingsworth. Ingram and I travelled regularly to Boston to pursue the investigation. Gene was putting together a somewhat tenuous conspiracy theory that Flynn had made connections through previous organized crime contacts, in order to have a Hubbard cancelled check stolen, used as a model for forgery and then passed at the Middle East Bank in New York – all under the safety of a cooperative DOJ.

The DOJ was facing monumental litigation by the church, seeking to obtain legally that which the GO had previously lifted illegally – the non-FOIA documents in the possession of the DOJ, IRS and several other agencies. By mid 1993 we were making strides in that litigation, obtaining court orders for ever-increasing disclosures. The flagship case sought millions of dollars in damages against the DOJ for a decades-long conspiracy to destroy Hubbard and Scientology, which we contended the DOJ files – if honestly shared – would demonstrate. The DOJ employed several full-time lawyers to fight against our litigation.

When the DOJ utilized the Flynn tactic of seeking L. Ron Hubbard's deposition and then asking to win by default when the church failed to produce him, it only reinforced our view that Flynn and the DOJ were in league. When I met with the Boston DOJ office attorney responsible for the check investigation, our suspicions of a grand conspiracy became virtually irrefutable fact, in our minds.

Bracket Badger Denniston III was the Assistant US Attorney in the fraud division who was assigned the case. Denniston was a snooty, thirty-something, conservative blue-blood. He treated me with cool disdain. Denniston never shared a single detail of his own alleged investigation. He listened to the results of our investigation with disinterest, and when I detailed Flynn or DOJ connections with the Bank of New England he merely smirked condescendingly.

When we had exhausted all leads and run into a stone wall with the DOJ, mild-mannered Geoff Shervell came up with an audacious idea. We would place a full page ad in the *New York Times*, offering a ten-thousand-dollar reward for information leading to the conviction of the masterminds behind the attempted passing of the forged $2 million L. Ron Hubbard check. Miscavige loved the idea and green-lighted the project.

Within days of the ad's publication, Ingram, the contact point named in the ad, received a call from a woman in Boston. She said that the brief description of the forged check passing we described in the ad sounded like something right out of her former husband's playbook. Her ex-husband was an infamous Boston con man Ala Tamimi Al Fadili. She noted that the ad said an "Aquil Abdul Amiar" had attempted to deposit the check in New York, and told us that Tamimi's brother, and sometime partner in crime, was named Aquil. The woman said her former husband was last known to be in Europe, and was reportedly in trouble with the law there.

Ingram tracked down Aquil Tamimi in the United Arab Emirates. He was able to exact a vague written confession that Ala Tamimi and

Aquil had in fact attempted to pass the forged check. Aquil was not in on the check theft/forgery end of things, but had been told by Ala that Wayne Hollingsworth (Flynn's new partner from the DOJ) had put him up to the job. Ala was in prison in Naples, Italy. When we confirmed by public records that Hollingsworth had in fact represented Tamimi in the past, Ingram flew straight to Italy see him.

Because of Italy's Napoleonic legal system, it took several months of legal wrangling to obtain a visit with Ala. When Ingram finally met Ala, the latter plied his con man negotiating skills. He demanded ten times the advertised reward for swearing to the details of the plot. Ultimately, Tamimi and Ingram settled at twenty-five thousand dollars. The Tamimi statement was of novelette length, describing the plot in detail – from being recruited by Hollingsworth, to being briefed by Flynn, to collecting a team of criminals to pull off the theft of the original check, the forging of a passable new one, to forging of the signature, to executing the plan of depositing it at the Middle East Bank. About a dozen conspirators' names were included.

Bracket Denniston III was thoroughly unimpressed with the new evidence. He said that the fact it was paid for tainted it and made Tamimi useless as a witness. I told him that surely the DOJ could use the tools it had available to corroborate the story. Why not pull some of the named conspirators in for interrogation? How about subpoenaing them to a grand jury? Denniston just looked at me like a sphinx and when I was done pleading he reiterated that we should not have paid Tamimi, and he could not tell me what they would or would not do.

I attempted to see Denniston's superior, the head of the Boston U.S. Attorney's Office Fraud Division, Robert Mueller, but was rebuffed. After several weeks it was quite apparent that the DOJ was going to do absolutely nothing with the evidence. Denniston would later become general counsel to one of America's most powerful corporations, General Electric. Mueller, of course, went on to become the head of America's most powerful law enforcement agency, the FBI.

Ingram then set about attempting to interview the players named in the Tamimi affidavit. It was not easy going. The folks named did exist. And they were clearly of criminal ilk. Ingram received death threats for even inquiring about certain names. He insisted on bringing a body guard as a second investigator for all subsequent trips to Boston. Increasingly Ingram required my presence in Boston to muster the nerve to press the investigation forward. I attended some of the interviews with some of the organized crime folks.

One of the most memorable encounters occurred after one of Ingram's associates located a New York mafioso named Joey Deciccio, who claimed to have the information and power to bring Flynn's FAMCO scheme to a halt in an instant. Geoff Shervell went to Atlantic City, New Jersey to meet Deciccio, to determine whether he was for real. He called in to ASI to debrief so that Miscavige could be in on it. Shervell said that Deciccio claimed to know the holder of enormous, accumulated gambling debts of Flynn. Deciccio was in a position to buy the debt, at which point he would effectively own Flynn. Miscavige was under so much pressure to produce an "all clear" for Hubbard that he had me booked on the next available flight to Philadelphia, to meet with Deciccio myself.

I took the redeye and was sleepless and wired on coffee when my flight arrived at 6:00 the next morning. I was picked up by a long, stretch red Lincoln limo, courtesy of Deciccio. I was barely able to stay awake during the long drive to Atlantic City. I met Shervell in a casino. He was electrified with excitement at the prospect of the danger of the folks we were dealing with, along with the hope we might be able to attain instant All Clear.

Deciccio and an associate greeted us. Both were archetypical Hollywood mobsters. Deciccio was middle-aged, with a grey pompadour, an open gaudy shirt and even gaudier gold pendant and chain across his white-haired, tanned chest. He wore a polyester suit, gold sunglasses, and talked like a seasoned wise guy. He was charming and friendly, but rough cut. His sidekick was a six-foot-four, three-hundred-pound refrigerator with no neck, introduced as Hank Lamotta. Joey said we needed to go up to their hotel room to discuss the business at hand. We took the elevator far up the hotel tower. We were led into a room and sat around a small round table overlooking the Atlantic City boardwalk. Hank immediately closed the drapes.

"Look, this Flynn bastard is in some bad kind of trouble. Seems he's addicted to playing the numbers and ponies," Deciccio started in.

"I can get his debt transferred to me for a discount. Then Flynn has to play by Brooklyn rules." Deciccio paused for effect.

"What are the Brooklyn rules?" I asked.

Deciccio traded grins and chuckles with Hank. Hank never sat down. Aside from the grin on cue, he just stood behind my chair with a menacing look on his face and his arms crossed – apparently to add some fear to the mix.

"Well, the first level is when a guy don't pay his debt, he gets a visit from some of our boys. They hold him by his feet and dangle his head in the sewer till the rats start gnawing on his face. Usually that brings out the entrepreneur in him and he finds a way to start paying down."

"What if that doesn't work?"

"Well, then we up the ante. We start by taking a finger, starting with the finger that has a rock on it."

"What's next if that doesn't work?"

"We take the rest of his fucking fingers," Deciccio boomed, as if frustrated that my questioning was ruining the effect of his rehearsed intimidation play.

"Well, I don't see how that makes the Flynn problem go away."

"That's easy. Rather than exercise the Brooklyn rules for the collection of the debt, we do them to make the litigation go away."

"There is a problem with all this. We will not engage in or condone any illegal acts."

"Well, too late for that, pal. We had a deal."

"You can't have a deal, because I am the only one who is authorized to make any deals."

Suddenly, from behind me Hank's ham of a hand slammed the small table, *THWAPP!*

"This is bullshit!" yelled Hank.

"Oh, no, now you've done it," Deciccio said, as Hank stormed out of the room, slamming the door behind him.

"You really screwed the pooch, pal," Deciccio said to me with a great deal of concern.

"What are you talking about?" I asked.

"He's gone to get his gun."

Deciccio and I looked one another in the eye for thirty seconds. Then we heard a key in the door and Hank lumbered back in. I turned and looked Hank in the eye as he stormed toward me. I reckoned if I made a move to resist him, the laws of physics would not be in my favor. So I decided to simply confront the situation I was in – do nothing else but face it as comfortably as I could.

Hank stopped in front of me and looked down while biting his lower lip, as if restraining himself from beating me to a pulp. Once it was clear that I was not retreating and they were not killing, the discussion resumed between Deciccio and me. Now it was more civil, and Deciccio retreated by appealing to my sense of fairness. After a while it became evident to Deciccio that they misestimated their encounter and played the wrong hand. He started making a pitch for the future. "Listen, stay in touch, maybe we can come up with some more legally acceptable ways of doing business."

Hank was assigned to drive Geoff and I back to New York La Guardia airport. Now that the intimidation game was over, Hank was a big old pussycat. We talked sports and politics all the way back and punctuated our trip with a pleasant lunch stop.

Miscavige was none too pleased to hear we hadn't worked out the end of FAMCO. But the story of what happened was a great consolation to the kid from near Philly who prided himself on being raised by the "city with no pity."

After a year of constant rebuffs from Mueller, Denniston and the DOJ, we finally got their attention as a result of some rather peculiar events. We began investigating a key player in the Tamimi story, the man once dubbed the financial wizard of organized crime in New England, George Kattar. Kattar was in his sixties and most considered him retired. He owned a golf club in Andover, Massachusetts and spent most of his time golfing and telling war stories in its diner. But Kattar had heard of our investigators' interest in him and put the word out he'd be willing to talk. The problem was that no one in our growing ranks of private investigators was brave enough to meet him face to face. So I arranged to have the meeting myself, accompanied by Shervell.

We pulled up to the Andover golf club in a rental. It was a crisp but sunny morning. When we walked into the diner it looked like a scene from a rat pack movie. Twenty booths lined the walls, each filled with two to four middle-aged men with Brylcreemed, combed-back hair and attired in natty, colorful golf outfits circa 1962. We were seated in the booth farthest from the entry. After we had sipped a couple cups of coffee and I had quietly calmed Shervell's nerves, the entire place suddenly went silent. George Kattar, whiting hair combed back, impeccably dressed in a model golf outfit, strode easily through the entry. He briefly stopped at each table as the grown men said to him, "Good morning, Mr. Kattar." Kattar finally made his way to our booth, graciously introduced himself in his gravelly Boston accent, and sat down across from me. Kattar said that he knew exactly what we were looking for. And he was right.

Kattar tested me out by asking what it was I thought I was doing, looking into a man of his stature. He gave a brief bio of how he was a self-made man, the son of immigrants from Lebanon. The gist of it was, "treat me with respect, or lose your own." After I passed his decorum test without toadying in propitiation to him, Kattar got down to business.

"The fuckin' feds won't do anything unless you force them to. And without the inside man at the bank you can't prove the chain of custody on the check – and you don't have a credible witness to finger Flynn. You, Mawty (Kattar's pronunciation), need the inside man."

"Well, you've proven your great wisdom – you know the score exactly."

"What maybe you are getting around to finally figuring out is that I am the *only* one in a position to give you the inside man."

"That pretty well sums it up, Mr. Kattar."

"No, no – it's 'George' to you, Mawty."

"What will it take?"

"It'll cost you one hundred large."

"A hundred grand? No can do, George. The DOJ won't accept evidence we got for one quarter that amount. Paying anything at this stage is an impossibility."

"Listen, fuck the DOJ. Once you get it out, the public at large, the media, Flynn will be ruined. He'll be ruined in the courts."

"George, can't do it. Can't be accused of buying evidence after what we've been through."

Kattar tried to bargain. He brought the price down to twenty-five thousand. However, I remained firm. Kattar attempted to maintain his friendly demeanor and tact. But his disappointment was not well veiled. Finally, he ended the meeting with a threat, "I tried to help. If I find you stabbing me in the back by continuing to poke around my affairs, it won't be pretty for you."

I briefed Bracket Denniston on the encounter. Rather than commend us for our persistence in the face of danger, he too threatened me. "If you continue with this investigation, you may well be indicted for obstruction of justice."

Having been banned from Boston by both sides of the law, we carried on. Soon the local Boston church of Scientology was receiving calls from Kattar, "Tell Mawty I'm gonna send him home in a garbage bag." The death threats were too much for Ingram. He flew home to LA and refused to return to Boston. Still Shervell and I pressed on. After several weeks, I was called back to LA on urgent business.

One night Shervell called from Boston. "I've got good news. I made the deal with Kattar without church money. Harvey Brower negotiated the whole thing."

Harvey Brower was a disbarred attorney and ex-convict who had apparently cooperated with Geoff in the past, showing him the ropes in the Boston organized crime community.

I responded, "Geoff, tell me you are lying."

"No, I borrowed the money from Larry Byrnes." Byrnes was a Scientologist with a lucrative computer company in New Hampshire, and a former GO associate of Shervell's.

"Geoff, hold on to it. Kattar is a snake and so is Brower."

"It's ok. The money is safe."

"Where is it?"

"It is totally secured. It's in a safety deposit box. Harvey and I rented one jointly. I have a key."

"Does Harvey also have a key?"

"Yes."

"Well, say sayonara to the twenty-five k."

"No, it's there. Harvey wouldn't screw me."

"Harvey is a convicted felon and disbarred attorney. You've been had, brother."

Sure enough, when Geoff checked the next day, the twenty-five thousand was gone. Harvey explained that he made the deal with Kattar and Kattar wanted to meet with Geoff to deliver the goods.

When Geoff met with Harvey and Kattar, the only goods that were delivered were more threats from Kattar. "The deal was 100 large, see? Now I want the rest of it," Kattar demanded. He threatened to kill Geoff and Mawty if the other 75 wasn't delivered by the end of the week.

I took the redeye to Boston. I marched Geoff down to see

Bracket Denniston. Finally, we had his attention. "George Kattar? You've got George Kattar extorting you for a hundred grand?"

"Yes."

"The department has been after Kattar for thirty years, with nothing to show for the effort. Excuse me," he said, reaching for the phone. Denniston barked out orders for several assistants and FBI agents to be assembled.

Geoff met at least a dozen FBI agents and DOJ attorneys in a conference room. All listened attentively to the details as Geoff recounted them. To our surprise, they literally worked out a sting operation plan, not only in front of us, but with us. Geoff would arrange a meeting with Kattar. An FBI agent would pose as Larry Byrnes, ostensibly there to deliver the rest of the seventy-five thousand, but in fact to tell Kattar he wanted the twenty-five thousand back. An elaborate, commando-like operation was devised and carried out. FBI agents manned outposts surrounding the hotel pool where the Shervell-Kattar meeting was supposed to occur. Shervell and the agent posing as Byrnes were wired for sound.

When the meeting took place and Shervell demanded the twenty-five thousand back, Kattar – as predicted – came unglued. He let out a three-minute tirade, leveling death threats if seventy five thousand dollars wasn't delivered right then and there. He told Shervell that the bodyguard who accompanied him, the three-hundred-pound fellow he affectionately referred to as "Tiny" would sit on and kill Geoff's mother.

Kattar was indicted for violation of the federal extortion statute and for fraud. Notwithstanding our great, albeit accidental, favor to the DOJ in delivering up Kattar, we still received no cooperation in resolving the original crime. In fact, the DOJ gratuitously set up the Kattar case to serve as the ultimate discrediting of the notion that Flynn was involved in the original two million dollar check conspiracy. They had Kattar dead to rights on extortion, in living color and captured on tape. The additional fraud count alleged, however, that Kattar had committed fraud by attempting to sell what he knew to be false information, to wit that Flynn had any involvement in the original L. Ron Hubbard forged-check case.

While Miscavige's best resource, me, was being sent around the country on what seemed to be turning into a quixotic quest, any hope of an "all clear" was being blown out of the water in Los Angeles. I was urgently summoned back to the West Coast.

CHAPTER NINETEEN

COGNITIVE DISSONANCE

In modern psychology, ***cognitive dissonance*** *is the feeling of discomfort when simultaneously holding two or more conflicting cognitions: ideas, beliefs, values or emotional reactions. In a state of dissonance, people may sometimes feel "disequilibrium": frustration, hunger, dread, guilt, anger, embarrassment, anxiety, etc. The phrase was coined by Leon Festinger in his 1956 book* ***When Prophecy Fails****, which chronicled the followers of a UFO cult as reality clashed with their fervent belief in an impending apocalypse.* – Wikipedia

I would discover over decades of practice that the heart and soul principles that make Scientology effective, when it is effective, were summed up in a few short paragraphs in a 1954 L. Ron Hubbard writing, aptly titled *A Summary of Scientology.* Hubbard wrote then:

> *CONSIDERATIONS TAKE RANK OVER THE MECHANICS OF SPACE, ENERGY AND TIME.*
>
> *By this it is meant that an idea or opinion is, fundamentally, superior to space, energy and time or organizations of form, since it is conceived that space, energy and time are themselves broadly agreed-upon considerations. That so many minds agree brings about reality in the form of space, energy and time. These mechanics, then, of space, energy and time, are the product of agreed-upon considerations mutually held by life.*
>
> *The aspect of existence when viewed from the level of Man, however, is a*

> *reverse of the greater truth above. For man works on the secondary opinion that the mechanics are real and that his own personal considerations are less important than space, energy and time. This is an inversion. These mechanics of space, energy and time, the forms, objects and combinations thereof, have taken such precedence in Man that they have become more important than considerations, as such, and so his ability is overpowered and he is unable to act freely in the framework of mechanics. Man, therefore, has an inverted view. Whereas considerations, such as those he daily makes, are the actual source of space, energy, time and forms, Man is operating so as not to alter his basic considerations. He, therefore, invalidates himself by supposing an Other-determinism of space, energy, time and form. Although he is part of that which created these, he gives them such strength and validity that his own considerations thereafter must fall subordinate to space, energy, time and form, and so he cannot alter the universe in which he dwells.*
>
> *The freedom of an individual depends upon that individual's freedom to alter his considerations of space, energy, time and forms of life, and his roles in it. If he cannot change his mind about these, he is then fixed and enslaved by barriers of his own creation. Man thus is seen to be enslaved by barriers of his own creation. He creates these barriers himself or by agreeing with things which hold these barriers to be factual.*

My experience with Scientology proved to me that when processes were applied and learning was imparted consistent with this foundation, people got better. However, when this foundation was departed from – whether by misapplication or by compliance with Hubbard's later words to the contrary – people got worse. In the middle of defending this foundation with my life, Hubbard published a number of words that seemed diametrically opposed to this philosophy. In the early eighties, as Hubbard's situation *vis a vis* the outside world became increasingly desperate, so too did the writings he issued to the church.

As more long-time Scientologists left the church during and in the wake of Miscavige's power plays, Hubbard had occasion to review matters of policy that hampered keeping folks on the reservation. First, Hubbard detected that excommunication orders issued against veteran Scientologists who were resigning from the church lacked punch. Specifically, they did not detail the crimes of the individuals targeted, and so did not effectively discredit them. Miscavige reported that he was hamstrung by Hubbard policy prohibiting the publication of crimes learned about through the confessional auditing process. Hubbard wrote back that this was a misinterpretation of his technical and policy writings. He wrote and issued a new policy describing how to write ethics and declare orders. Such orders were to include details of specific crimes the subject of the order committed. He also removed any ambiguity on where that information might be derived by issuance of a technical bulletin/policy letter on March 10, 1982. It was entitled CONFESSIONALS – ETHICS REPORTS REQUIRED.

The bulletin made it firm policy that any sins confessed in the auditing process that could be construed to be a violation of the vast, ambiguous "codes of the church" must be reported to church officials called ethics officers. By other long-standing policy ethics officers were expected to act on such reports, and punish the offender where called for. This could include publication of the person's "crimes" if doing so was deemed necessary to protect the group.

By mid 1983, many veteran Scientologists had been expelled in the Miscavige purges. Hundreds of them formed up a splinter movement, setting up Scientology centers not connected with the church of Scientology. Such acts had historically constituted High Crimes or Suppressive Acts in the church's ethics codes, leading to excommunication and fair game status for the offender. Scientologists were directed that such people could be lied to, cheated, or destroyed with impunity. The heretic movement had become so prevalent that its influence reached into church of Scientology organizations by way of long-term friendship and family connections. The organizations were shrinking, with staff and public (non-staff Scientologists) jumping ship in increasing numbers. Noticing a pattern amongst the numerous reports coming his way, Hubbard queried Miscavige as to why it was that church staff and management were allowing staff and public in good standing to remain in communication with excommunicated heretics. Miscavige replied that church policy had been modified over the years so as to effectively cancel the policy that Scientologists were required to disconnect (cut all ties and all communication) with those who had been declared SP (Suppressive Person), a status that comes automatically with excommunication. Hubbard wrote back that the cancellation of "disconnection" as a policy was another of the growing list of discovered crimes of Mary Sue Hubbard. He reminisced a bit about the government inquiries of the sixties, and how Mary Sue's GO was so ineffective in handling them that he had to relent, temporarily allowing cancellation of "disconnect" in order to survive the inquiries (several of them had focused on the practice of disconnection causing the systematic break-up of families). He expressed dismay to be learning only now that the policy had remained effectively cancelled.

To terminatedly remedy the situation, Hubbard wrote a policy titled *PTSness AND DISCONNECTION*. PTS stands for Potential Trouble Source, someone susceptible to disaffection with Scientology by virtue of being connected to a suppressive person. It begins as a well-reasoned essay on the fundamental societal rights of an individual to communicate or not, with whomever he or she wishes. By the end of the policy letter, "disconnection" is fully reinstated. It was even taken a step further with this injunction:

To fail or refuse to disconnect from a suppressive person not only denies the PTS (person connected to a Suppressive Person) *case gain, it is also* ***supportive*** *of the suppressive – in itself a Suppressive Act. And it must be so labeled.*

So, as of August 1983, any Scientologist who refused to comply with orders to disconnect from a person previously labeled a Suppressive Person would, by continued non-compliance, be labeled a Suppressive Person himself.

While these policies laid the foundation for Scientology's subsequent degeneration into an insular cult, several other writings issued between 1981 and 1984 implanted beliefs that would raise the ante on its "ends justify the means" approach to the outside world. These writings were very likely a response to learning, through Special Project reports, that the dozens of lawsuits confronting Hubbard included a stable of FAMCO expert witness psychiatrists and psychologists, readying to testify to Scientology's alleged deleterious mental effects upon the plaintiffs. Hubbard was likely also influenced by reports of the tight lines of coordination that were discovered between FAMCO and the U.S. Department of Justice (including the FBI).

On September 15, 1981 – one month prior to the original All Clear target date – Hubbard issued a technical bulletin titled THE CRIMINAL MIND, which laid down the law: "THE CRIMINAL ACCUSES OTHERS OF THINGS WHICH HE HIMSELF IS DOING." I found this datum, on its own, to have a high degree of truth, and so very useful in analyzing and combatting attacks against Scientology. However, in the same bulletin Hubbard also proclaimed the following "facts:"

> *As an example, the psychiatrist accuses others engaged in mental practice of harming others or worsening their condition, yet the majority of psychiatrists maim and kill their patients and, by record, in all history have only worsened mental conditions. After all, that's what they seem to be paid to do by the government.*
>
> *The psychologist accuses others of misrepresenting what they do and lobbies in legislature continually to outlaw others on the accusation of misrepresenting but there is no psychologist who doesn't know that he himself is a fake, can accomplish nothing of value and that his certificates aren't even worth the printing ink. The psychologist goes further: He educates little children in all the schools to believe all men are soulless animals and criminals so that when the possible day of reckoning comes and the psychologist is exposed for what he is, the population will not be the least bit surprised and will consider the psychologist is "normal." The psychologist accuses others of sexual irregularities when this is, actually his entire profession.*
>
> *The FBI agent is terrified of being infiltrated and accuses others of it when, as standard practice, he infiltrates groups, manufactures evidence and then gets others charged for crimes his own plants have committed. The FBI acts like a terrorist group posing as law enforcement officers…*
>
> *..Doctors, psychologists, psychiatrists and the government form a tight clique. Only the government would support such people as the public hates them…*

On May 6, 1982, Ron went further, with the issuance of a technical bulletin to all staff and public Scientologists, entitled THE CAUSE OF CRIME. He wrote,

> *They say poverty makes crime. They say if one improved education there would be less crime. They say if one cured the lot of the underprivileged one would have solved crime. All these "remedies" have proven blatantly*

> *false…*
> *…So what IS the cause of crime? The treatment, of course! Electric shocks, behavior modification, abuse of the soul.* ***These*** *are the causes of crime. There would be no criminals at all if the psychs had not begun to oppress beings into vengeance against society.*
> *There's only one remedy for crime – get rid of the psychs! They are causing it!*

When combined with a technical bulletin issued a couple of years earlier, *CRIMINALS AND PSYCHIATRY*, Hubbard had set the stage for a culture bent not only on the destruction of mental health professionals of any stripe, but also the mistrust of virtually all government, educational and public betterment institutions. He pronounced:

> *The instigators, patrons and supporters of these two subjects (psychiatry and psychology) classify fully and demonstrably as criminals.*

On August 26, 1982 Ron issued yet another bulletin, this one entitled *PAIN AND SEX*, that probably caused more cognitive dissonance with true-believer Scientologists than anything else he had written to date. He wrote:

> *There are two items in this universe that cause more trouble than many others combined. One is PAIN. The other is SEX…*
> *…Despite the false data of Freud, psychologists, psychiatrists and other criminals, they are not native to a being. They are only artificial wavelengths. They have exact frequencies that can be manufactured. A being or a machine can synthesize either one…*
> *…Destructive creatures who do not want people big or reaching – since they are terrified of punishment due to their crimes – invented pain and sex to shrink people and cut their alertness, knowingness, power and reach…*
> *…Pain and sex were the INVENTED tools of degradation. Believe it or not, a being can be so overwhelmed by either that he or she becomes an addict of it. Priests become flagellants and cut themselves to pieces with self-whipping. Torturers drool over pain. Lovers are seldom happy…*

He went on to identify the creatures that created pain and sex:

> *...Under the false data of the psychs (who have been on the track a* ***long*** *time and are the sole cause of decline in this universe) both pain and sex have been gaining ground in this society and, coupled with robbery which is a hooded companion of both, may very soon make the land a true jungle of crime...*

And in case any Scientologist questioned the truth of this pronouncement, Ron wrote:

> *...These are data which emerged from recent thorough research of the whole track [*the entire span of time from the beginning of time to the present]. *This is not theory or some strange opinion. It is provable electronic fact. The waves are just synthesized...*

Upon reading these writings, my own cognitive dissonance was palpable. There was likely no one in Scientology who had as much experiential reason to believe that the psychs (as psychiatrists, psychologists, and psycho-therapists were collectively referred to in Scientology) were the cause of crime and chaos in society. The same could be said for Hubbard's more extreme statements about the FBI, given my experience in Boston. But the Hubbard pronunciamentos were so absolute and they were so strongly conflicted with understandings I had derived from Scientology itself, that they prompted a lot of logical questions. If psychs were a special breed of thetan, how did they keep the continuity of suppression alive through billions of years? Where were they before the late nineteenth century, the period which Hubbard himself had pegged as the birth of psychology and psychiatry? How did they know to continue running their control operations from one lifetime to the next?

Hubbard answered these questions in a dispatch he sent to Miscavige concerning the need to abolish psychiatry and psychology altogether. It was marked "Secret." In it, Hubbard said that Miscavige ought to share this dispatch only with those whose cases could handle it. That is, those who were sufficiently high on the Scientology grade chart to receive this type of shocking truth without becoming de-stabilized and overwhelmed spiritually and mentally. Even though I had only received the most rudimentary, introductory levels of Scientology auditing, Miscavige deemed it necessary for me to see this information, since Hubbard's directive would be executed through me. I was now in charge of all aspects of the Guardian's Office's successor organization, the Office of Special Affairs (OSA), and it was OSA's duty to carry through on the abolish-the-psychs project.

In the dispatch, Hubbard matter-of-factly detailed how psychs are a special breed of being. He said they were raised and trained on a planet called Farsec. They were sent to Earth in order to keep its population under control, ignorant, obedient and slave-like. Earth is a prison planet, he said, and most of its inhabitants were pirates, rebels or artists, millions of years before being deposited here by a repressive inter-galactic government. The psychs were also assigned to see that no mental or spiritual technology arose that might expose the nefarious plot. They had always been with us on Earth. Before the advent of psychiatry, they had been priests and shamans. The long and short of it was that this brand of being was programmed to carry out the above mission, was incapable of understanding anything to the contrary, and would act on an automatic, stimulus-response basis – no matter how strenuously they might try to rationalize their activities as well-meant and beneficial.

My mental dissonance was heightened by the fact that during the few years in which Hubbard issued these bulletins, he also issued hundreds of others that were lucid, rational, even brilliant, on the technology of Scientology auditing. He also wrote inspiring and useful advice on such far-flung subjects as art, morals, diet, drugs, administrative technique and logic itself. The bulk of these other writings were consistent with the axioms and logics upon which Scientology is predicated. And those fundamental laws reinforced the idea that every individual is ultimately responsible for his own condition, that his mental and spiritual health is directly proportional to the degree to which he recognizes that fact.

In contrast, the psych writings increasingly laid the travails of humankind at the doorstep of an invisible inter-galactic (and thus overwhelming) exterior source. In his secret Farsec dispatch, Hubbard noted – and Miscavige emphasized – that if what he was saying did not make sense to someone, it would all become clear to them further on up the Scientology bridge. And so, as the cognitive dissonance intensified, I took refuge in the *belief* that it would all make sense further on up the road. I became a true believer, a religious crusader.

That warrior, crusader mindset was necessary to survive and perform in the All Clear war environment. That idea too came from Ron. While Hubbard distanced himself from Mary Sue and GO criminality in his written dispatches, in some of those same dispatches he also began to betray his own role in the GO criminality. He did this specifically in some, and by omission in all of them: Not a single mention was ever made of repairing or making good on any damage done to even one of the hundreds of people whose lives had been destroyed by GO operations. In fact, his prohibition of even considering settlement of any such cases could be interpreted as condoning those acts.

We were to treat the litigants as enemy combatants. We were instructed specifically on the "fact" that every person who had ever criticized Scientology was a criminal, guilty of crimes for which they could be punished. Hubbard wrote a lengthy dispatch directing that we "set the PIs (private investigators) loose" on Flynn and his litigants to prove as much. We were to study and apply his policy and instructions to the GO, since the reason for the GO's failure, according to Hubbard, was Mary Sue's and the GO's refusal to follow his directions. I learned to walk a difficult line. On the one hand, I had to direct a very aggressive, offensive defense, while at the same time avoiding any action that would establish evidence that might contradict the assertion that L. Ron Hubbard and the church were aghast at GO atrocities, and that any violation of the law whatsoever, under whatever circumstances was prohibited by church policy.

On several occasions we engaged in acts which, if not criminally prosecutable, certainly would subject us to civil liability if discovered. For one, Miscavige instructed me to never allow damning evidence to be produced in civil litigation discovery. On several occasions during the early eighties, we conducted massive shredding parties after catching wind that there might be a DOJ or IRS raid (much like the Canadian mop-up described in the previous chapter). When I balked at the idea of destroying evidence, Miscavige accused me of being a GO-influenced idiot. "Don't you get it that LRH was pissed that the GO got caught?" he asked impatiently. "I was there when the raid went down and he was first informed." He described the scene in some detail – Ron in his bathrobe at the Rifle house in La Quinta, being told of the simultaneous raids on church premises in Los

Angeles and Washington, D.C. in July, 1977. "He was in shock – shock that they were so stupid as to get caught. Read his dispatches, damn it. It is clear."

Reading the entire body of Hubbard's writings about Mary Sue, the GO and the criminal case, it *was* rather clear. Whether Miscavige made up the story about Ron's first reaction was sort of irrelevant, in light of the tone and emphasis of the written directions we had received on the subject of Mary Sue, the GO, and their criminal case. Miscavige's refrain which went like this, "Mary Sue and the GO stabbed LRH in the back by getting so cocky they got caught. They didn't follow policy. It's right in *The Responsibilities of Leaders* [the "Simon Bolivar" policy]. Now it's *our* responsibility! But we have our hands tied because we have to keep it legal. All because they got caught."

After that I never thought twice about destroying evidence. I had no problem with running intelligence agents in on enemies, provided they did nothing that could get us into trouble. L. Ron Hubbard was the source of any power we might have. He was the only power worthy of defense, since his power was exclusively directed at clearing the planet of war, insanity and criminality. Therefore, all future warlike, insane and criminal behavior on our part was justified, in that it was the only way to end warlike, insane and criminal behavior on planet Earth. It was cognitive dissonance supreme.

CHAPTER TWENTY

THE TIPPING POINT

If you tell the truth, it becomes part of your past. If you tell a lie, it becomes part of your future.
– Origin uncertain

Up until the spring of 1984, we still held out hopes for some game-changing victory that would turn the tide toward a rapid All Clear for L. Ron Hubbard. After a respite during much of the course of the probate case where Ron laid low for a while, he was back on the lines during the latter part of 1983 and early 1984. He was reviewing international Scientology statistics and sending detailed analyses and responses to managers of the church about them on a weekly basis. He was sending dozens of memos to ASI about his books and investments, and more broad-overview type advices about the church to David Miscavige, ASI's chairman.

In May of 1984 I was promoted to the post of Legal Executive ASI. As such I was working directly for and being paid by L. Ron Hubbard. I sent a dispatch to Ron informing him that I was on post and asking what he needed and wanted from me personally. I never received an answer, for in 1984, Ron went under the radar for several months when he again became the focus of a battle royal.

I had been summonsed back from Boston urgently because of that conflict. It was the Armstrong trial, our lawsuit against Gerry

Armstrong seeking the return of the L. Ron Hubbard personal archives. At the time I had left Boston earlier in the year, the case had, in our estimation, been set up for a win. To assuage Miscavige's fears that Mary Sue's attorney, Barry Litt, was "too defensive" to handle the rough and tumble of a trial, we had brought litigation gunslinger Bob Harris on board to represent the other plaintiff, the church of Scientology of California. On the advice of counsel, we had opted for a bench trial, obviating the chance of an easily prejudiced jury. A judge, serving as trier of law and fact, would be a lot less susceptible to extraneous appeals to prejudice than a jury would be. It seemed like an open-and-shut case of conversion (civil theft) and invasion of privacy.

The early going in the trial was rough. As much as we denigrated Michael Flynn as a patsy with the DOJ and media on his side, we underestimated his ability as an advocate and propagandist. Probably never in the history of Scientology battles had an adversary been so well prepared and so well equipped to change minds about Scientology for the worse. Ultimately, in twenty-two years of battles, I would never see another as competent and effective as Flynn. In addition to a smooth style, a commanding – if irritating – voice, and a sharp ability to string established and embellished facts into a compelling story, he also had no compunction about inventing facts to fill any gaps. He had an innate ability to weave in irrelevant and extremely prejudicial details, bolstering a good argument into an overpowering one. For example, though he had no physical or corroborating evidence for the charge, he always seemed to get away with claiming in court – with a strong prejudicial effect created – that the church had attempted to assassinate him. Flynn blew away every one of our most-expensive attorneys in court. Bob Harris was an accomplished and tough trial lawyer, but even he did not hold a candle to Flynn. Exacerbating matters was the fact that the judge bought into and allowed Flynn to present a "justification" defense. The theory went that Armstrong had held onto the documents for his own self protection from anticipated church harassment. When Miscavige's private investigators did in fact harass Armstrong he forwarded the documents to Flynn.

I was briefed that while we were still in the plaintiff's case in chief portion of the trial, Flynn had already apparently visibly soured the judge on Scientology and our case. It was due in part to Flynn's masterful opening arguments, painting this trial as the one chance to expose to the world an elaborate fraud that had escaped all previous scrutiny due to institutionalized intimidation tactics. He was able to convincingly portray himself and his client as two altruistic whistleblowers fighting a courageous fight with a foe who had slain all who had come before.

Flynn had also torn apart our witnesses so thoroughly on cross examination that our side was consumed with worry over the downsides of calling any further witnesses. Harris had warned of this possibility before trial, noting that going to trial at all in a Scientology case had two huge downsides. First there was the long history of documented bad acts the opposition could dredge up to color the proceedings. Second, as he put it, "Scientologists are too honest." He explained that virtually anyone else who testifies in court knows how to hedge and forward and protect his own position, and has no qualms about treating the opposition attorney as an enemy, showing no cooperation. But Scientologists, he maintained, are so trusting and honest that they wind up cooperating with and even assisting their cross examiners. Harris had created a "witness school" for the very purpose of coaching Scientology witnesses to handle themselves better. Apparently this had backfired under Flynn's blistering cross examinations; he made those coached look contrived, exposing them as playing games with the truth.

And so, it was reported that Judge Breckenridge of the Los Angeles County Superior Court seemed to be leaning in the defendant's favor, even during the plaintiffs' (Mary Sue and church of Scientology) case, before the defendant had even begun to present his case. Miscavige was livid, and called such reports from Litt and Harris the result of the apathetic defensiveness of a couple of losers.

I was directed to attend a couple of days of trial to supply another viewpoint. Since I was working for Ron and had daily contact with Miscavige, it was not an easy task. If I was subpoenaed, Miscavige warned, it would sabotage an All Clear since my testimony could help lead the enemy to himself and Hubbard. For two years I managed to slip into and out of courtrooms like an invisible man – drawing many glances and whisper conferences by the enemy. But I developed a knack for sliding in quietly after proceedings began and quietly stepping out before the next break. On more than one occasion I saw enemy players head for the clerk's office for a subpoena, which was my cue to make myself scarce. In this wise I managed to catch glimpses of the Armstrong trial.

I reported that Breckenridge indeed seemed disaffected with the plaintiffs, but that it may have been in part due to the defensiveness with which the lawyers were conducting themselves. It seemed that every communication interchange in the courtroom was being dictated by Michael Flynn. He would start the day with a number of "housekeeping" items. These are mundane little evidentiary and procedural affairs. But, in Flynn's inimitable style, he could turn an objection about a mis-numbered exhibit into the Nuremberg trial, part II. Before the first witness was called, he interjected unanswered suspicions that the judge's office was infiltrated by the church, that the defendant may have been the target of an assassination attempt the night before, and that the Earth was in grave danger of going off its regular orbit any second now, all because of the church of Scientology.

We, in our inexperienced youth, and in our "always attack" policy frames of mind, mistook this as a simple matter of *our* counsel's lack of aggressiveness. And so, at Miscavige's direction, I vehemently demanded Litt and Harris ratchet up the attack, crank up the righteous indignation, and beat Flynn at his own game. Being wholeheartedly in disagreement, their halting, intermittent outbursts only served to alienate Breckenridge further.

Ironically, again we were forced to bank on Mary Sue Hubbard as our last great hope. Mary Sue made a heartfelt plea from the stand for the return of her husband's papers. She characterized the theft of her husband's archives as the commission of "mental rape" against her. As compelling as she was on direct examination, she was pathetic under Flynn's cross examination. He had a field day contrasting her plea that she was being victimized with the well-documented decades of heinous crimes perpetrated by her own Guardian's Office, including thefts and invasions of privacy of the most shocking kind.

Even sadder was Flynn's peppering Mary Sue with questions about false representations Ron had ordered the publication of. Mary Sue seemed to be in the dark about the particulars, and instead of addressing them she kept expressing a blind faith in the honesty and integrity of her husband. In a perverse sort of way, Flynn was using Mary Sue to prove the effectiveness of the false representations – Ron's own wife was clearly ignorant of the facts about his background.

Litt and Harris saw the handwriting on the wall. During the mid-trial break, between presentation of the plaintiff's and defendant's cases, they demanded a meeting with whoever would have the final word on settlement. That person ostensibly was David Miscavige. An extremely tense meeting was held in the ASI conference room. Harris and Litt spelled out the disaster that was about to become part of the public record – the smearing of Hubbard's life and character – if the case was not settled at once. In his inimitable style Miscavige made it painful for either attorney to provide any particular allegation about Ron's character. "That's bullshit! You are so defensive, even you believe Flynn." Therein lies how the case could be so ill prepared. We were aware of many of the allegations Armstrong was making, but when it came to presenting Miscavige or Starkey with plans for witnesses to produce to counter them, staff and attorneys were met with being accused of being weak and defensive. That came with demands that we just needed to discredit Armstrong, "he's a lying punk!"

Finally, it seemed the attorneys might have been getting through to Miscavige. He asked what the attorneys thought the case could settle for. The attorneys estimated they could settle it by paying the defendant – who also had a counterclaim against the church that would be tried later – a couple hundred thousand dollars. Miscavige lost his composure. He tore into Harris and Litt, accusing them of being defensive losers and being walked all over by Flynn. On at least two occasions Miscavige bolted from the room, his face beet red, so as to restrain himself from some ugly outburst at the lawyers.

Norman Starkey, as was his role, supported Miscavige, calling the plaintiff's witnesses – former staff for the most part – a pack of criminals and liars. "Get in there and prove it," he demanded; "don't be pussies." Not only were Litt and Harris becoming discouraged, they were clearly becoming disaffected with Miscavige. Ultimately, I had to use my diplomatic skills to bring the lawyers somewhere closer to agreement with Miscavige, a difficult role I found myself playing for the next twenty years with professionals hired by the church.

And so the show went on. It was far worse than Litt and Harris had even projected. It wasn't that they did not fight like wounded steers; they did. It wasn't that the staff didn't do their part – dozens of us worked around the clock for weeks preparing each day's cross examinations and the plaintiffs' rebuttal case. The catastrophe was brought on by the facts. And our hands were tied by the same factors that had shackled Gerry Armstrong himself, when he was archivist a few years before. As noted in the judge's ultimate decision concerning the defendant's state of mind while in the church, "Defendant Armstrong was devoted to Hubbard and was convinced that any information which he discovered to be unflattering of Hubbard or contradictory to what Hubbard has said about himself, was a lie being spread by Hubbard's enemies. Even when Armstrong located documents in Hubbard's archives which indicated that representations made by Hubbard and the organization were untrue, Defendant Armstrong would find some means to 'explain away' the contradictory information."

And so it was with the legal staff, right up to me, Starkey and Miscavige. We were busy rationalizing and justifying how anything found in the archives that seemed unbecoming was simply so because of the "twist" being put on it by Flynn, Armstrong, and their several witnesses. Nobody, from me on down, dared imply that even one of the allegations or characterizations had any merit.

Starkey's treatment of Armstrong (at Miscavige's direction) while Armstrong was working as an archivist and raising such concerns, was echoed in the loud-and-clear message to our present legal team: If you even *think* there is anything slightly "off" about Ron's representations about himself, you are by definition disaffected – and if you persist with such thoughts you are an enemy.

So, the following short list of disproved representations and unbecoming historical facts about Ron came into the public record, with only a sort of knee-jerk, hysterical response on our parts:

"LRH was never married to Sarah Northrup, his second wife" – in fact he was, bigamously.

"LRH was a war hero" – in fact he was not.

"LRH was 'wounded, blind and crippled' during World War II" – in fact he was not.

"LRH was a nuclear physicist and a civil engineer" – in fact he never was.

"LRH never engaged in black magic rituals" – in fact he did, at a branch of Aleister Crowley's Ordo Templi Orientis (O.T.O.) in Pasadena.

While none of these things meant much to me personally, given my lack of reverence for stamps of approval from officialdom, something that occurred during the course of the trial hit me in the gut, hard.

In the mid seventies, the daughter Ron had sired with Sarah Northrup, Alexis Valerie Hubbard – then a college student on the East Coast – reached out to her estranged father to reconcile. Hubbard prepared a letter to her, to be read to her by an agent of the Guardian's Office. The letter informed Alexis that her mother was a hallucinatory tramp, and had been sleeping around quite a bit at about the time of her conception; that her mother only dreamed up the idea that Ron was her father in an unethical attempt to profit from his fame and fortune and thus Alexis was not his daughter.

Sure, we fought the good fight in attempting to discredit the notion LRH had fathered a child with Northrup, and during that fight I was certain he had not. However, during the trial, Flynn kept alluding to the idea that he might produce Alexis to testify before the court. Then one day Alexis showed up to court. As she entered the courtroom, I turned to look her in the face. My jaw dropped. It was as if L. Ron Hubbard himself had walked in, in drag. She was the spitting image of LRH. Right down to the unmistakable, large Roman nose and almost caricature-like oversized mouth and lips (neither of which I had ever seen the like of, except in portraits of L. Ron Hubbard). Worse still, Alexis did not look spiteful. She did not joke around with members of the Flynn camp. She looked contrite, polite, courteous and curious.

Alexis never did take the witness stand. She did not need to. Instead, Flynn entered into evidence the dedication page of the original 1951 first edition of Hubbard's book, *Science of Survival* – a dedication which was removed from subsequent editions. It read:

> *To ALEXIS VALERIE HUBBARD, For Whose Tomorrow May Be Hoped a World That Is Fit To Be Free.*

More damning, Flynn entered into evidence what were called "the affirmations." These were dozens of handwritten pages from the Hubbard archives. They contained some sort of self-processing Ron had been engaged in, in the late forties. They were called the affirmations because for the most part they seemed to be a sort of positive thinking Ron was writing down, to boost his own self-confidence. They began with this statement of purpose, '*The purpose of this experiment is to re-establish the ambition, willpower, desire to survive, the talent and confidence of myself.*'

There were a number of entries acknowledging Ron's sexual and living relationship with Sarah Northrup, and his close personal friendship with Jack Parsons, the rocket scientist who had headed the Ordo Templi Orientis black magic group Ron had participated in.

Flynn harped on the following passage to give credence to his former-staff witnesses, who had testified about slave-like conditions in the Sea Org:

> *Material things are yours for the asking. Men are your slaves. Elemental spirits are your slaves. You are power among powers, light in the darkness, beauty in all.*

The passage that perhaps had the greatest overall effect, in a trial about whether L. Ron Hubbard's archives proved him to be a self-promoting liar, read:

> *You can tell all the romantic tales you wish. You will remember them, you do remember them. But you know which ones were lies. You are so logical you will tell nothing which cannot be believed. But you are gallant and dashing and need tell no lies at all. You have enough real experience to make anecdotes forever.*

The affirmations were highly personal, detailing Ron's sexual problems, physical deficiencies, fears and phobias. I felt like they were a precursor to some Scientology confessional processes, and felt sorry for LRH that they were being bandied about in open court. However, one of the first exhibits Flynn entered into evidence was a Guardian's Office order authored by Mary Sue herself, which directed that preclear folders (supposedly confidential notes from auditing sessions) of Scientologists deemed "security risks" be routinely culled for information, for use against them should they become a problem for the organization. We would be receiving no sympathy from the court over the airing of Ron's secrets.

Despite having become rather accomplished in the technique of thought-stopping, I couldn't get the image of Alexis out of my head. I would do something that became a regular practice, throughout my involvement in the church. I would evaluate my own personal gains and the gains I had seen others obtain through Scientology against such seemingly incongruous acts of cruelty as Hubbard had carried out against his own daughter. For better or for worse, though not totally incognizant of the bad, I would remain loyal to the man for what he had done for me and for others I knew.

In the middle of the trial I received a phone call from Pat Broeker; it was the only time we would speak before Hubbard's death. It was extraordinary that someone physically present with L. Ron Hubbard would find the case of such import that he found it appropriate to talk to the man on the ground about it. Pat gave me a rallying pep talk right out of the Knute Rockne story. I don't know exactly what Pat had been briefed on, but it was clear that the view from the top was that it was all a matter of mustering greater intention than the enemy. "Come on, get those attorneys in their pitching for LRH! It is not a matter of they can't do it. They just *think* they can't do it. Your job is to get them to realize that they can."

The talk went on for several minutes, with no interest whatsoever expressed for my view of the affair, or the facts of the matter. I only had time to acknowledge now and then, when Pat would pause momentarily with a "You know what I mean?" Though Pat was inspiring, I was scarcely in need of any inspiration on the subject of coaching and inspiring attorneys.

After weeks of Flynn's attacks on the credibility of witnesses, unrelenting blows to the character of L. Ron Hubbard and decrying of Mary Sue and the Guardian's Office's crimes, we were prepared to deliver our own counter-blow. It was something that I, Miscavige, Starkey, and the rest of the legal team were convinced would throw question on the entire Flynn-Armstrong presentation. The star witness we had waiting in the wings would blow Armstrong's and Flynn's credibility out the water. He would just prove that L. Ron Hubbard had seen combat in World War II; he would also attest that Ron was a war hero.

Thomas Moulten had served on a naval vessel captained by Ron, which Ron had claimed had sunk two Japanese subs off the coast of Oregon during World War II, after two days of pitched, fevered battle. Moulten testified that regardless of official naval records determining that there were no subs and that Hubbard had led a wild goose chase, lobbing depth charges into empty water for two days, he had in fact seen oil bubbles rise to the surface – indicating subs had been struck.

There is no question Moulten was a decent man. And there is no doubt he thought very highly of Hubbard, even though he had neither seen nor heard from him since the war. However, much like Mary Sue before him, he was hoisted by his own petard as far as credibility was concerned. First, he sounded somewhat eccentric telling a story utterly contradicted by all available documentary evidence. And, like Mary Sue, he did not leave well enough alone. He testified that Ron had seen a lot of action previous to the alleged Oregon battle. He described how Ron had sustained torso bullet wounds by Japanese machine gun fire; even though there was no record anywhere of Ron ever having been fired upon. On cross examination, Flynn had a field day with the fact that Moulten's only source of knowledge about Ron's alleged stellar combat record was Ron himself. Flynn was able to paint a convincing picture of Moulten as just another person misled by Ron's great story-telling skills.

The decision to waive a jury trial came back to haunt us. Judge Breckenridge was able to do something no jury had the power to. That was to issue a written decision. Breckenridge decided that while the plaintiffs had made out *prima facie* cases for conversion and invasion of privacy against the defendant, Armstrong was exonerated because the plaintiffs came to court with unclean hands, and Armstrong was privileged to violate their rights because of his need to defend himself against Scientology threats, and because his actions served the public interest at large. The written decision was the worst indictment of L. Ron Hubbard and Scientology ever published. Breckenridge issued judicial findings that included the following:

> *In addition to violating and abusing its own members' civil rights, the organization over the years with its "fair game" doctrine has harassed and abused those persons not in the church whom it perceives as enemies. The organization is clearly schizophrenic and paranoid, and this bizarre combination seems to be a reflection of its founder* LRH. *The evidence portrays a man who has been virtually a pathological liar when it comes to*

> *his history, background and achievements. The writings and documents in evidence additionally reflect his egoism, greed, avarice, lust for power, and vindictiveness and aggressiveness against persons perceived by him to be disloyal or hostile.*

Far more significant legally, and deadly to the prospects of an All Clear, were these findings:

> *Notwithstanding protestations to the contrary, this court is satisfied that LRH runs the church in all ways through the Sea Organization, his role of Commodore, and the Commodore's Messengers. He has, of course, chosen to go into "seclusion," but he maintains contact and control through the top messengers. Seclusion has its light and dark side too. It adds to his mystique, and yet shields him from accountability and subpoena or service of summons.*

The decision rendered Mary Sue Hubbard next to useless for future attempts to buffer Ron from legal problems:

> *On the one hand she (Mary Sue Hubbard) certainly appeared to be a pathetic individual. She was forced from her post as Controller, convicted and imprisoned as a felon, and deserted by her husband. On the other hand her credibility leaves much to be desired.*

Just as devastating for the future prospects for All Clear were Breckenridge's credibility findings for Flynn's stable of witnesses, who would be central to all pending outstanding litigation:

> *...credible, extremely persuasive...In all critical and important matters, their testimony was precise, accurate, and rang true.*

Breckenridge's order called for the unsealing, and thus public availability, of the archives documents that had been used in trial, and served as the foundation for his findings. However, over the next two years I would personally direct forty-two separate, related and continuous extraordinary legal actions to keep the seal on the documents. Those actions were lodged in the Los Angeles Superior Court, the California Court of Appeals, the California Supreme Court, the U.S. District Court, the US Court of Appeals, and the

United States Supreme Court (several of those courts were appealed to multiple times, for temporary stay orders). I went through several teams of lawyers keeping that chain of sealing unbroken. The necessary stretching of legal theories and the continuous overreaching nature of our pleas for temporary relief resulted in our lawyers eventually refusing to be associated with such actions, for fear of harming their own credibility with the courts. Nonetheless, I was somehow able to keep the documents under seal for the remainder of L. Ron Hubbard's life.

We also battled collateral attempts by other litigants to obtain access to the sealed material. The most notable was the U.S. DOJ's plea for access to the transcripts of the infamous conference wherein church legal representatives characterized corporations set up to mask payments to Hubbard from church funds as "a classic case fraud." We too kept that transcript under seal for the remainder of Ron's days through dozens of extraordinary legal actions.

Keeping under seal documents concerning lack of corporate and financial integrity was vital to the prevention of criminal charges being filed against Ron and his associates during the final years of his life. A large part of the All Clear strategy was restructuring the churches of Scientology into a sensible corporate structure that aligned with its ecclesiastical management. It also entailed thousands of hours of lawyer and accountant work, creating a paper trail to justify payments of millions of dollars from the churches to LRH over the years.

Just as with the GO dirty tricks history, Hubbard's dispatches about church corporate and finance matters were laden with his shock and dismay. Yet a review of church records indicated that for the most part the GO had been trying for years to stay in close compliance with Ron's wishes on those subjects. For example, Hubbard once boasted about the maze-like nature of church structure:

> *If anybody tried to attack a Scientology organization and pick it up and move it out of the perimeter or go over the hills with it today (1961) – this happened to us once – why, they would find themselves involved in the most confounded weird mass of legal – well, it's just like quicksand. Quicksand. It's an interesting trick. Every time they shoot at you on the right side of the horse, you're on the left side of the horse; and then they prove conclusively*

> *you're on the left side of the horse, you prove conclusively that you're on the right side of the horse. They go mad after a while. This is what the basic legal structure is.*

Even though our scorched-earth litigation efforts to keep damning evidence out of the hands of enemies no doubt worsened the courts' already dim view of Scientology's credibility, it might well have saved L. Ron Hubbard from spending his final days in jail, alongside his last chosen close associates, Pat Broeker and David Miscavige.

CHAPTER TWENTY-ONE

THE JUGGERNAUT

Juggernaut: in colloquial English usage is a literal or metaphorical force regarded as mercilessly destructive and unstoppable. – Wikipedia

For all of his alleged faults, L. Ron Hubbard was a keen observer and writer on the human condition. He once noted that "the bank follows the line of attack." "Bank" is Scientologese for the reactive mind, the stimulus-response portion of the mind that seeks destruction of others for survival of self. With the devastating strike upon Ron and Scientology delivered in Los Angeles, all roads to L. Ron Hubbard's bunker led through Flynn and Armstrong. It seemed that anyone with a score to settle was drawn like a magnet to the duo. Those combined forces took on the appearance of an overwhelming juggernaut.

The DOJ duplicated Flynn's latest legal tactic: ask courts in Scientology litigation to order the church to produce L. Ron Hubbard as the "managing agent" of the mother church. Flynn assisted the DOJ to procure sworn declarations from his growing stable of former high-level official witnesses in support of the move.

David Mayo, the expelled former auditor to L. Ron Hubbard and erstwhile top technical authority in Scientology, had created a thriving Scientology splinter operation in Santa Barbara, California. Former high-level messengers – including two former Commanding Officers of CMO Int (Commodore's Messenger Organization International) served as executives of his operation. Until the Armstrong affair, they had steered clear of the L. Ron Hubbard-bashing Flynn/FAMCO circles. But by 1984 they were supplying declarations to the DOJ and Flynn in support of their motions to compel Hubbard into depositions in lawsuits across the country.

Breckenridge's Armstrong case decision, bolstered by a dozen declarations by former Hubbard messengers and aides, made the allegation of Hubbard's "managing agent" status virtually uncontestable. Miscavige and Broeker were clearly established as the last links to Hubbard, but they could not provide countering declarations because it would subject them to depositions – which would lead Hubbard's enemies directly to him.

Worse, the Breckenridge decision destroyed any chance of winning, in courts across the U.S., our vast array of pending motions to dismiss Flynn's lawsuits on the basis of First Amendment rights to freedom of religion. The twenty-one-page Breckenridge indictment was devastating to our three years of expensive efforts at positioning much of the Flynn litigation for pre-trial dismissal.

Worse still, the decision pumped new life into what we thought by then to be criminal investigations losing steam. The Internal Revenue Service's Criminal Investigation Division (CID) had been actively investigating the church, as well as LRH, Pat and Ann Broeker, David Miscavige and other church officials as named targets for criminal charges. Until the Breckenridge decision we had kept the CID somewhat at bay through litigation combatting their summons power, and a team of lawyers attempting to negotiate with IRS counsel and DOJ officials. But our intelligence lines were reporting that the LA-based CID group was once again gearing up to indict Hubbard and his aides.

The Ontario Provincial Police had, after their March, 1983 raid, steered clear of targeting Hubbard. Now they were reconsidering, in light of the outcome of the Armstrong case.

Our intelligence network reported that Gerry Armstrong was feeling drunk with power, given the sudden attention he'd received and his new importance in the anti-Scientology community. It seemed Armstrong and Flynn had worked their way up to being the axle to which all anti-Scientology spokes were linked. Per reports, Armstrong was talking of bringing all Scientology's enemies together in a concerted effort to take over the church. The man who had prevailed in his case because of his alleged "fear for his life" was beating his chest and promising to take the very life of our church, and convert all its assets to outside control.

Our only shot at staving off indictments against LRH across North America, and of keeping him out of the couple of dozen pending lawsuits was to take out the axle and so depower its spokes. It was this desperate state of affairs that drew me directly into the shadowy world of intelligence. Throughout his litigation Armstrong had remained in periodic communication with a Scientologist who knew a thing or two about intelligence. Dan Sherman had published a number of spy novels, and had struck up an acquaintance with Armstrong. Armstrong looked up to Sherman and envied his literary success and intelligence acumen. Armstrong believed that Sherman – like so many other Scientologists during the tumultuous early eighties – was disaffected with the church and no longer considered himself a member. In fact, Sherman was cultivating a friendship with Armstrong in order to glean intelligence from him about the enemy camp. Up through the trial their communications were infrequent and mundane. All that changed when Armstrong became an overnight anti-Scientology sensation. Because of Armstrong's newly won stardom, Sherman began giving him more face time. Armstrong began sharing some of the details of his activities as a coordination point for all camps inimical to the church, from the Ontario Provincial Police, to the IRS CID, to the DOJ, to the Mayo splinter movement. Armstrong asked Sherman to see whether he could locate some church insiders who might aid in a take-over coup inside the church.

Gene Ingram and I concocted a rather elaborate game plan. Gene would tap one of his old LAPD comrades to obtain written permission to covertly video record conversations with Gerry Armstrong. Technically, it was a lawfully given permission since we had a witness attesting that Armstrong was suggesting taking over and destroying the church by questionable means.

Gene obtained a recreational vehicle which had a wide rear window with reflective coating, making it one-way vision. A high-powered camera could record what was going on outside without being seen. We planned to record meetings with Armstrong to obtain evidence showing that not only was he not afraid for his life, he in fact was a well-backed aggressor and an operative of government agencies out to get Scientology. After taking circuitous routes to lose any possible tails, Sherman and I met Ingram in the RV in Long Beach. We worked out every detail of Sherman's cover. We would bring in a former GO operative and have Sherman introduce him to Armstrong as a church insider, plotting the overthrow of the Miscavige regime and willing to play ball with Armstrong, Flynn and their government allies. That would hopefully prompt Armstrong to repeat and elaborate on some of the provocative takeover and take-down ideas he had alluded to in earlier conversations.

The chosen venue for the meetings was Griffith Park, inside LAPD jurisdiction and with plenty of opportunities for positioning the RV to capture the action. Sherman met with Armstrong and whetted his appetite. He told him he had made contact with an ally who had a number of well-placed contacts, currently on staff in the church. He told Armstrong he could only be identified by his first name, Joey, for security purposes. Joey was formerly of the Guardian's Office and was connected to a number of former GO people who were bitter about being ousted by Miscavige, and sympathetic to Armstrong and the Mayo splinter movement. Armstrong was visibly overjoyed at this opportunity gratuitously falling into his lap.

Sherman arranged a meeting between Armstrong and Joey to take place on a park bench in Griffith Park. Joey wore an audio wire which transmitted the conversation back to the RV, parked a hundred yards away and video recording the event. Armstrong and Joey both wore sunglasses; both attempted to look as nonchalant as could be, as they introduced themselves.

Joey explained that there was serious disaffection within the church, and a forming cabal of veteran staff ready to take out Miscavige and the current management. He called this cell the Loyalists. Armstrong was clearly excited, and believed Joey's cover – no doubt because of Sherman's story-telling skills and credibility with Armstrong.

Armstrong shared with Joey the master plan, which he represented as his brainchild, along with Michael Flynn. He explained that the plan was backed by the Ontario Provincial Police, the DOJ and the IRS. Flynn would prepare a lawsuit on behalf of the Loyalists, asking the Attorney General of California to take the church into receivership on their behalf. The DOJ, FBI, and IRS would conduct a raid on church premises to get fresh evidence of illegalities, in support of the Loyalist action. The raid would be coordinated to coincide with the filing of the receivership action. The public relations fallout and the possible arrests of leaders would all but cripple the church.

Joey played his role well, feigning fear and nervousness that Armstrong could make good on the government back-up. In order to prove his representations, Armstrong opened a notebook and started naming his government contacts, representing that each was briefed, coordinated and ready to roll with the plan. He cited the following agents as close personal friends and in constant contact and coordination with him and with Flynn:

Al Ristuccia – Los Angeles office of the IRS Criminal Investigation Division

Al Lipkin – Los Angeles office of the IRS Criminal Investigation Division

Richard Greenberg – U.S. Department of Justice, lead counsel in defending civil litigation brought by the church against DOJ, FBI and IRS

Tom Doughty – DOJ associate of Greenberg

Al Ciampini – Ontario Provincial Police

Armstrong provided Joey with phone numbers for each, including home numbers for some – and urged Joey to get in touch with his team members from these agencies.

Over time, Armstrong told Joey that the IRS CID was the most active government participant, and served as the main coordination point between agencies. He told Joey the CID agents had been briefed about Joey and the Loyalists, and were excited and supportive. The CID would grant them informant status, offer immunity for any crimes they might commit in assisting the government, and had even talked of providing safe houses for insiders. Armstrong then asked Joey to get his contacts to go into church files and find evidence of illegalities, so that the IRS and DOJ would know where to search. Joey then brought into the mix someone whom Gerry had known from his Sea Org days. Mike Rinder was a Commodore's Messenger who had once worked directly with Ron. He was then heading up the U.S. branch of the Office of Special Affairs. Joey introduced Mike to Gerry. Mike reported to Gerry that the files were relatively clean – there were no big smoking-gun documents being created after the 1977 FBI raids. At this point Armstrong's macho bravado provided what would be our greatest defense against the indictments being issued against Hubbard, Miscavige, et al. Armstrong suggested that the Loyalists *create* evidence of illegalities and plant them in church files for the IRS and DOJ to find in a raid, and use against church officials.

All of Armstrong's representations about government conspiracies to take down church leadership and close down the operation were duly recorded.

David Miscavige was ecstatic with the results. He had me make a presentation of the evidence to a team of criminal lawyers, assembled to represent L. Ron Hubbard, Miscavige, Pat Broker and Lyman Spurlock (Hubbard's accountant at ASI) to prevent IRS CID indictments and convictions – the potential charges we took most seriously. These attorneys – most from white-shoe Washington, D.C. law firms – were scaring the hell out of Miscavige. They were suggesting the IRS CID case was so serious that they recommended working a deal with the IRS for Miscavige and Spurlock to do time in halfway houses, so as to prevent indictment of Hubbard. At the root of the IRS CID case was the evidence of millions of dollars of church monies being funneled to Hubbard through fraudulent means. And at the heart of the case would be the infamous MCCS taped conference in which church attorneys and staff acknowledged the fraudulent nature of the transfers.

My presentation horrified the team of criminal attorneys. They were hired because of their conservative, Reagan administration contacts. They did not want anything to do with such an aggressive investigative move. They were concerned about the propriety of the means Ingram and I had utilized to obtain the evidence, and thought it would reflect badly on their own reputations. One attorney who represented Miscavige personally took me aside, though. He said he did not know how to use it at the moment, but that the evidence I had obtained would ultimately save the day for Hubbard, Miscavige and the church. Gerald Feffer was the former Assistant Deputy Attorney General for taxation during the Carter administration. He was becoming a dean of white-collar criminal case dismissal prior to indictment. He would become a senior partner in the venerable D.C. law firm Williams & Connally. Gerry told me to work with some of our more aggressive civil counsel to figure out a way to make the information public, and he would use it to make the IRS criminal case go away.

Another disclosure from the Griffith Park meetings cut to the quick with both Miscavige and me. Armstrong had told Joey that another Department of Justice player was in on the grand plan to close down Scientology: Bracket Deniston III. Armstrong said that Deniston was not investigating to find out who attempted to pass Hubbard's check, and he was not investigating the evidence we had provided to him. Instead Deniston was out to nail our investigator, Gene Ingram. Deniston had represented to Armstrong that he was setting traps to nail Ingram and the church for attempting to frame Flynn with purchased evidence.

This was particularly disconcerting, given events in the check investigation while all this Armstrong business was going down. After I had been ordered out of Boston by Deniston, I had been lured back in by a man being prosecuted by his office. Larry Reservitz had been charged in a case very similar to the one involving LRH's check. One of Reservitz's connections who had access to Bank of New England records had used his access to fraudulently transfer money from random accounts to Reservitz. While under indictment, Reservitz reached out to me for the $10,000 reward we had previously advertised in the *New York Times*, claiming he had inside information on the Hubbard case and could identify the inside man at BNE. We had a number of phone calls and several meetings attempting to negotiate the deal. The jockeying was due to my suspicion that Reservitz was shaking us down, and I was searching for facts that would indicate he knew what he was talking about. Reservitz was continually attempting to characterize my questioning as an attempt to make the deal an exchange of cash for handing us Flynn.

In the meantime, Robert Mueller, Denniston's superior and head of the Boston U.S. DOJ office fraud division, had flown to Italy to visit Ala Tamimi. He bought Tamimi's retraction of his original statement in exchange for dropping a number of outstanding indictments the DOJ had pending against Tamimi for a variety of fraudulent schemes he had previously executed. I attempted to confront Mueller with what we had learned, but he refused to meet with me. Deniston outright denied that any visit or deal had been carried out by Mueller. In either event, Tamimi's retraction caused Miscavige to turn up the heat to get me to turn up fresh evidence of Flynn's involvement in the crime.

I was caught between a rock and a hard spot. Miscavige wanted Flynn at any cost. Yet I felt that Reservitz might be attempting to frame me for attempting to frame Flynn. I walked a tight rope between pursuing the investigation to Miscavige's required degree of aggressiveness, and not stepping over the line with Reservitz. I even visited the Boston FBI agent in charge of the Hubbard check investigation, Jim Burleigh. I pointedly accused Burleigh of having covertly made a deal with Reservitz to attempt to sting me. Burleigh brought in another FBI agent to witness his categorical denial that the FBI or DOJ had made a deal with Reservitz: "We would never cooperate with the likes of Larry Reservitz." Deniston likewise denied that Reservitz was working for the DOJ. Still, I had my suspicions, particularly when we learned Deniston had become pals with Armstrong and Flynn.

With the sharks circling in and our waning confidence in our civil lawyers (having their heads handed to them in the Armstrong case) and criminal lawyers (advising Miscavige that he resign himself to doing time, at least in a halfway house), Miscavige ordered I find a new breed of lawyer. He wanted someone tough as nails, not some nervous Nellie. He wanted someone who could figuratively kick Flynn's butt in court, and scare the hell out of his DOJ and IRS backers. After an exhaustive nationwide search and many candidates eliminated, I thought we had finally found our man – in, of all places, Boston.

Earle Cooley was bigger than life. He was a big, red-haired knock-off of L. Ron Hubbard himself. His gravelly voice was commanding. His wit was sharp. He was perennially listed in *The Best Trial Lawyers in America.* He could spin a yarn that charmed judges and juries and took easy, great pleasure in viciously destroying witnesses on cross examination. After I had interviewed Earle and reported to Miscavige, I arranged for us to watch Earle in action. Miscavige and I flew out to Boston to see Earle perform in a high-profile art theft trial. We saw him decimate a seasoned criminal government informant so thoroughly on cross examination that the fellow, in a trademark Cooley expression, "didn't know whether to shit or wind his watch." Earle's client – whom the government had dead to rights, and who was as unsympathetic a defendant as could be – was acquitted by the jury. We had found the horse for the course.

Earle was like a breath of fresh air to Miscavige. He took a similar black-and-white view of matters – we are right and good, the enemy is wrong and bad. Miscavige had long since lost his patience and his tolerance for our teams of civil lawyers and the civil-rights-experienced opinion leaders among them. He referred to them as the "pointy heads," short for "pointy-headed intellectuals." To him, our only problem was our counsels' timid, second-guessing, defensive frames of mind. And Earle reinforced that view. Cooley attended a few civil litigation conferences with our other counsel. He ruffled their feathers by readily agreeing with Miscavige's simplistic sum-up of what was wrong and the solution to it, aggression. The existing lawyers' nervous objections and eye-rolling reactions to Earle's sermons only reinforced Miscavige's view. "They are nothing but a pack of pussies," he regularly groused to me; "what we need is for Earle to sink his teeth into those Flynn witnesses and that'll be the end of this nonsense."

Miscavige was nothing if not resilient. While never giving a hint that the overridingly important goal was the attainment of All Clear, by late 1984 it was quite evident to all involved that we were fighting an entirely different battle now. It was a fight for survival. We were desperately staving off the barbarians storming the walls of whatever compound L. Ron Hubbard might reside behind. It was evident too that Hubbard himself might have quit fighting – we no longer received any dispatches from him about the legal front. He was only sporadically sending ASI advices concerning his personal business, and to the church about Scientology matters. Miscavige had a team feverishly marketing Hubbard's new science fiction books, the *Mission Earth* series. He was putting just as much pressure on church marketing folks to market *Dianetics: The Modern Science of Mental Health*, the broad public re-release of the 1950 book that had launched the entire movement. All titles were making it back onto the *New York Times* bestseller lists. So the incongruity created another level of cognitive dissonance. How could government officials across the continent be so feverishly pursuing a man who was so wildly popular with the public at large? It would be years before I would find out that the sales were given a mighty boost by teams of Scientologists sent out to bookstores to buy them in bulk. In the meantime, Miscavige was adept at keeping me and the troops motivated, inferring that we were buying Ron time to bail out the church's disastrous public image and to complete his final researches at the highest levels of Scientology.

With Miscavige's solving of the "why" behind our failures to attain an All Clear – i.e., the outside lawyers' blatant counter-intention to Hubbard's advices on using the enemies' tactics against them, only more cleverly and more aggressively – our defeat-battered hopes were rehabilitated. Earle Cooley, the great Scientology hope, would soon be unleashed.

CHAPTER TWENTY-TWO

THE BATTLE OF PORTLAND

Men in general judge more from appearances than from reality. All men have eyes, but few have the gift of penetration. – Niccolo Machiavelli

Everything hung in the balance at the spring, 1985 trial of Julie Christofferson-Titchbourne vs Church of Scientology. This was the very case that my brother's friend had tried to tell me about in 1977 in Portland, when he was making an effort to get me out of Scientology. Christofferson was a young woman who had taken a simple Communication Course. It was the very Communication Course that I had taken, at the same Portland mission I'd attended. Christofferson had, however – according to her – an experience completely opposite to my own in taking the course. She and her Flynn-allied attorney Garry McMurry claimed that she was defrauded into taking the course in the first place, by false representations about L. Ron Hubbard's credentials and Scientology's scientific guarantees to bring her health, joy and happiness. According to the lawsuit, the course hypnotized Christofferson and the mission subsequently used that hypnotic state to turn her against her family. The case had originally gone to trial in 1977, and a Multnomah County jury had returned a verdict in her favor for more than two million dollars.

In 1982, the Oregon Court of Appeals reversed and remanded the case for new trial. The appeals court decision was one of our first major religious recognitions. While Miscavige took full credit for the victory with L. Ron Hubbard, in fact he had served as little more than a nuisance to its accomplishment. The case had already been argued and was pending decision when Miscavige's Special Project came on the All Clear scene in 1981. His then-deputy Starkey had attempted to intervene in the matter, and wound up blowing off the attorney who would ultimately win the great precedent, Charles Merten.

Merten refused to re-try the case because of his disgust with the church's new order. But he had already briefed and argued the appeal of the 1979 verdict, so there was no way for the Special Project to mess that up. Had it not been for the original Christofferson case appeals court decision, we likely would not have attained several of the more minor – but useful in their cumulative effect – religious recognition precedents we did wind up achieving through the perilous fight for an All Clear.

A new trial lawyer had been retained in Portland to try the case. Ted Runstein was a personable, seasoned and successful trial attorney. He was, however, demoted to ride shotgun to Earle Cooley and keep his mouth shut as local counsel after saying something for which Miscavige never forgave him. Runstein had suggested that "the jury needs to hear from some real Scientologists from the witness stand." Miscavige replied that we have plenty of Scientologists on our witness list. Runstein countered, "Those are all Sea Org staff; I am talking about having them hear from Scientologist parishioners who live and work in the same community as the jurors – *real* Scientologists." Miscavige snapped, "Sea Org members are *real* Scientologists, public Scientologists are dilettantes." Miscavige ruminated on this affront by Runstein throughout the trial, calling him a "theetie-weetie, airy-fairy idiot" behind his back.

So when Earle Cooley rolled into town he had free rein.

David Miscavige, as the chairman of the board of Author Services, would spend the next several weeks in Portland supervising and dictating every last detail of the trial. He was going to show me, the dozens of other attorneys he categorized as "defensive losers," and the entire OSA network how a trial was conducted, Scientology style. No more counter-intention from lawyers who knew best. He had a soul mate in Earle, so that in his view L. Ron Hubbard's slash-and-burn policies with respect to detractors and attackers would run into no internal interference. David Miscavige would prove to Ron once again why he needed him to ramrod his intentions through. Hubbard himself was apparently incommunicado, as evidenced by little to no dispatch traffic arriving – which made Miscavige's two-month, full-time battle of Portland stint possible.

We rented a number of units at a downtown condominium, walking distance from the courthouse. One unit was inhabited by Earle, his long-time mistress Jeannie and their fourteen-year-old son. Another one-bedroom unit was occupied by Miscavige and me. Another was reserved for a couple of Office of Special Affairs staff, and served as a document preparation area and repository. We had a dozen more staff working out of the offices of the mission, which were only a few blocks away. One more condo unit was occupied by Earle's partner and protégé, Harry Manion.

Harry would prove pivotal to the case, though he did very little speaking in court. Harry was in his early thirties. A big, strapping man – if overweight, like Earle – with a boyish face and an infectious smile and personality. Harry was the archetypal hale fellow well met. He had a glib, friendly word for everyone he encountered, and a natural ability to make people feel comfortable and light. Harry had something else going for him. He was a former college and minor-league professional baseball player, and that really meant something to the judge.

Judge Don Londer was respected by many locally. But because he was Jewish, he was not really accepted into Portland's traditionally WASP judicial circles. Londer consider himself an old jock, often reminiscing about his boxing career during his younger days in the Navy. He was also a decent, considerate man. However, he was not very bright. In the condo we used to joke that maybe he had his lights knocked out one too many times during his boxing career. But because Harry was a real professional athlete, in Londer's eyes Harry could do no wrong. Harry struck up a relationship gradually by arriving a little early to court, and thus "bumping into" the judge regularly. The latter always wanted to hear jock war stories from Harry. Harry was the son Don Londer wished he had fathered.

In Miscavige's view, the Christofferson case was the perfect test case. Christofferson had only ever had a few months engagement with Scientology. She had spent a total of $3,000 on auditing and courses. She had not been harassed by the Guardian's Office. The court of appeals had already ruled that she could make no case for infliction of emotional distress/outrageous conduct. Her only remaining cause of action was for fraud. The court of appeal had even narrowed the issue to whether the representations made to her were motivated by sincerely-held religious belief.

In retrospect, it was probably the stupidest move imaginable to not settle the case before trial, for those very reasons. Christofferson claimed fraud primarily based on alleged false representations about L. Ron Hubbard's pre-Scientology credentials. These were the very issues aired in the Armstrong case, which had made an All Clear all but unattainable. By going to trial, we were affording a woman – who effectively had no damages to claim – a worldwide platform to replay the Armstrong inquisition all over again. Except this time Flynn's stable of witnesses was bolstered by the former Executive Director of International Scientology, Bill Franks, and the former head of the organization Christofferson had interacted with – the Scientology Mission of Portland, Martin Samuels.

Samuels had been the owner of the Portland mission when both Christofferson and I were parishioners there. He was the owner of the Portland mission when the first Chistofferson trial played out. Samuels had joined the Flynn camp shortly after being expelled, during Miscavige's mission holder purges of 1982. Samuels testified in the first Christofferson trial on behalf of the church. In the second trial we knew that he would testify that the mother church had not only run every single detail of the trial, but even forced Samuels to lie on the witness stand. And thus Christofferson II was rather a cinch for the Flynn camp to hit the mother church with a sizable judgment (something that had not occurred in the first trial).

But Miscavige – and thus we – looked at it in the simplistic, black-and-white, good-vs.-evil worldview of L. Ron Hubbard. This was our big opportunity to play it all over again. In our view, the 1979 Chistofferson verdict had been what motivated Flynn and FAMCO in the first place.

All of the testimony in the Armstrong trial (including that of Armstrong and Laurel Sullivan) came pouring into the record. More horror stories were added by Samuels and Franks, and by a host of other witnesses. Miscavige and I directed a couple dozen staff, frenetically working through each and every night to provide Earle with material to discredit each witness on cross examination. While direct examination was still in progress, I, Miscavige and several other staff would pore over the real-time transcripts being relayed from court, marking them up for every bit of discrediting documentation we had available in a massive file room at the mission. When the court day ended, we would huddle with Cooley and outline the preps required for the cross exam the next morning. The crews stayed up until 1 or 2 every night, putting the material together and getting final ok from me and Miscavige. Then we would sleep for two to three hours, wake up at 4 a.m. and prepare to meet Earle in his condo at 5 a.m. We would spend the next three hours briefing him on details about how each witness had lied, exaggerated, and twisted the truth or was somehow morally reprehensible. We liberally used material from the ethics records from their days in the church, even copying internal reports to use on cross. This went on for weeks. We continually engaged in echo-chamber, confidence-reinforcing sessions, reviewing how Earle had so thoroughly destroyed each witness' credibility.

There were external indicia to support our overconfidence. Earle Cooley brutalized the plaintiff's witnesses on cross examination. So dramatic were his cross exams, that each day Earle was up, the courtroom was packed with local lawyers. They had no interest in the case itself, but Earle's cross examinations were so dramatic that word had spread through the legal community that Cooley was the best show in town. They were there only to watch a master of their own trade at work. What we were blind to was the cumulative impression that so much manhandling conveyed.

We received a wake-up call of sorts in the middle of the plaintiff's case, but collectively chose not to heed it. We had planned to enter the covert Armstrong-Griffith-Park surveillance tapes into evidence during the cross examination of Armstrong. Earle set up Armstrong masterfully, leading him to deny that he had ever talked to anyone about taking over the church, orchestrating federal raids, and least of all manufacturing and planting documents in church files. Then Earle started quoting Armstrong from transcripts of the surveillance tapes, clearly demonstrating he was lying from the witness stand. The warning we did not heed came in the form of Judge Londer's reaction to the courtroom spectacle. In chambers he loudly chastised the church's behavior in being involved in such cloak-and-dagger activity to begin with. Londer, who clearly did not think much of

Chistofferson's case based on comments he had made up to that point in the trial, was more disgusted with the secret video-taping than the lies they revealed. Had we not been so thoroughly in the throes of a thought-stopping, alternate-reality creation, we might have given thought to how the jury felt about the aggressive, "gotcha" manner we were using with all the plaintiff's witnesses.

Even though it backfired in the case at hand, getting the Armstrong surveillance videos on the public record would serve as a major step in dealing with the more serious government threats of criminal indictments then still extant. The stakes were far higher than merely the Chistofferson case, and there was a great deal of tension in getting the tapes put on the record. We did not want to submit the producer, private eye Gene Ingram, to cross-examination, for fear that he would be forced to disclose anything about the increasing number of operations he was privy to. In the course of coordinating the transportation of the tapes to Portland and into the hands of church coordination attorney John Peterson, Miscavige insisted upon bypassing me and speaking directly to Ingram – something he had not done up to that point in time. I advised him that was a bad idea, should Ingram or he ever be subject to deposition.

I picked up the phone to make the call to Ingram, and Miscavige came flying at me – tackling me into a sofa and attempting to wrestle the phone from my hand. I would not relinquish my grip even though he was strangling me. I threw my chest out to buck Miscavige from me. He violently stabbed his fist into my chest and said menacingly, "Don't you ever cross me, motherfucker! I'll have you declared [excommunicated] in a heartbeat if you ever fuck with me again." I looked Miscavige in the eye for a moment and considered the weight of that statement. For four years no one on planet earth could communicate to L. Ron Hubbard but through Miscavige – not even his wife. Miscavige was the recipient of personal communications on a weekly basis from Hubbard – but for the extended periods the latter went incommunicado entirely. He was right, he could have me declared in a heartbeat, and all I'd fought for to date would have been for naught. I handed him the phone. He had established himself – much as he had done with Mary Sue Hubbard – as boss buffalo.

So dramatic were Earle Cooley's cross examinations that we were all swept into the sweet oblivion of the drama of it all. We heard from Judge Londer, through Harry, and we heard from dozens of lawyers who attended as spectators and students: Earle Cooley was magnificent. Earle huddled us up in the condo one evening over beers.

"Have you guys ever heard of Percy Foreman?" Earle asked us.

We all replied that we had not.

"Foreman was one of the premier trial lawyers in American history. He once defended a woman who was up for a murder rap in Miami. The government brought a bunch of scumbag convicts in to bolster their case against her. Foreman demonstrated on cross examination that the testimony was obviously paid for. When he saw the jury understood that, he surprised everyone. After the case in chief, he rested the defense without calling a single witness. He wanted those cross examinations fresh on their minds when they went to deliberate."

"Brilliant!" exclaimed Miscavige. "We don't want to serve up our people to McMurry anyway."

"Exactly," Earle replied, "sending in Runstein and his 'real Scientologists' would be like sending sheep to slaughter."

"You're fucking-A right, Earle!" Miscavige proclaimed, as final authorization of the strategy.

And so Earle Cooley shocked the judge, the plaintiff's team, and all who were watching when he announced the next morning in open court that the defense would call no witnesses, and rested. Judge Londer thought it was a great idea. He didn't want to sit for another several weeks on this case. And he agreed with Earle that the plaintiff had never made a case worth a hill of beans. It was judge Londer's nonchalant manner of dealing with jury instructions that helped set us up for the shock of our lives. Londer told Earle and Harry to relax on their stressed arguments to attempt strict control of the jury before their deliberations began. He said, "Hey, what has she got, three grand in damages? The jury isn't stupid." And so, with the judge's assessment of the merits, we were optimistic – albeit nervous – as we awaited the verdict.

Nobody was prepared for the result. On a Friday afternoon the jury awarded Christofferson $39 million. That not only buried any idea of an All Clear, it put the church's very future at risk. Earle Cooley wasn't sure why he did it, but he asked the judge to hold off on recording the verdict for a few days. The judge wasn't sure why either, but he granted Earle's request.

Miscavige had flown back to Los Angeles after closing arguments. Cooley left that night for Las Vegas to blow off steam and to try to deaden the devastating loss with a weekend of amnesia-inducing recreation. In a way, I was left alone holding the bag at the scene of the crime. Early Saturday morning I met with two associates of our local counsel in their Portland office. We frantically traded ideas for challenging the verdict before the case went up to the court of appeals for the two-to-three-year appellate process. One of the associates was a cheery, bright British woman. She came up with a wild idea. Since the verdict had not yet been recorded, we could still make a motion concerning the case before the lower court. That court retained jurisdiction until such time as the verdict was recorded.

We reckoned that since there were motions brought by our side continuously, against prejudicial matter being entered into evidence throughout the trial, and since those motions had been consistently denied, there was no way to challenge rulings already made along the way. However, what if we brought a motion for mistrial based on what was put before the jury during closing arguments? That was the one small window of trial history we had not already brought legal challenges to. With Cooley incommunicado, we got busy dissecting the transcript of the closing arguments to find something, anything we could hang our mistrial motion on. We noted some particularly prejudicial statements that plaintiff's counsel had made, and drafted a motion for mistrial on the basis that the statements were so outrageous and prejudicial as to have potentially caused the jury to act on passion and prejudice, rather than on the evidence presented over several weeks of trial.

When Cooley returned at the end of the weekend, he thought the motion was brilliant. We filed it early the following week. Harry Manion artfully used his weeks of informal credibility-and-sympathy-building with judge Londer to obtain his agreement to set a hearing for a few weeks down the road, to consider the motion. Londer would not and did not ever record the jury's verdict.

Miscavige returned to Portland and we had a conference in Cooley's condo with a couple of legal staff. Miscavige was distraught and desperate. He talked of moving L. Ron Hubbard and Scientology management to a South American country in order to assure the church's future survival. We discussed how with a 39-

million-dollar judgment being publicized internationally, the three dozen similar FAMCO suits heading toward trial, and the DOJ and IRS champing at the bit to clean up anything remaining after the damage was done, the United States was about the least safe territory in the world for Scientology.

Miscavige railed about the stupidity of Judge Londer, how he continued to allow the trial to go out of control while reassuring us that the worst-case scenario was a few thousand dollars in damages. He ruminated how a mighty institution like Scientology could be brought to its knees by a group of degraded "wogs" (non-Scientologists) from a cow town. His own characterization prompted a lightning bolt from the blue.

"I got it!" he exclaimed. "We'll take over this shit-hole town. I'll bring in one hundred thousand Scientologists from around the world and we'll surround that courthouse and *make* this town comply. We'll overwhelm them. We'll overwhelm not only the judge but every other criminal judge he talks to in his town. "

The battle of Portland had only just begun. We called in every Public Relations officer assigned to every church of Scientology in the world (several dozen) and gave them orders to call every person who had ever taken a service at each local church and order them to get to Portland for the biggest, most important event and contribution they would ever make to Scientology. Ken Hoden was pulled out of mothballs and put in charge of the "religious freedom crusade." Hoden had been the Guardian's Office person in charge of external affairs in Portland during the original Christofferson case appeal. Miscavige and Starkey had busted him and relegated him to backlines PR work in Los Angeles back in 1981, when they decided he had screwed up the appeal of the original case (the result of which was ultimately the vacating of the original two-million-dollar judgment, and Scientology's strongest religious recognition to date). But now Hoden was integral – he was the only one who knew the ropes in Portland, as well as all allies of the church and public officials in the Portland area. Hoden was instructed to wear a religious "dog collar" shirt and coat at all times in public. He would be the spokesman and he would position all utterances along the line that the Christofferson judgment was the worst assault on religious freedom in the United States in modern times.

Within days, several hundred Scientologists had shown up in

Portland. Hoden organized them up, made signs and began regular marches around the courthouse. The trademark chant of the crusade echoed down the streets of Portland:

Hoden: "What do we want?"

The crowd: "Religious freedom!"

Hoden: "When do we want it?"

The crowd: "Now!"

Initially, the protesters came across as angry, in compliance with Miscavige's orders to intimidate the city into compliance. As Miscavige was back in LA, and there was no allowance for discussion of mitigation of his ideas, instead Hoden discussed with me the need to tone it down and create a far less threatening and far more dignified presentation. I told Ken he was right, and told him follow his instincts, just learn to report to Starkey and Miscavige in the language they liked to hear. That was to emphasize, in briefing them, how loud you were, how numerous you were, and how shocked and awed the public watching was – while taking a slightly different approach in conducting affairs on the ground. It was an art I had come to learn out of necessity, to avert many church catastrophes over the years.

Ken got the knack of how to play shock absorber to the brass – and did a masterful job in controlling the masses in a fashion that had maximum impact. Over the next week, thousands of Scientologists showed up and the regular protest marches easily surrounded the entire block the courthouse occupied, with parishioners marching in ranks of several abreast. Hoden took care to brief each arriving Scientologist on the importance of being polite and friendly, cleaning up after themselves and generally creating a good impression of "regular Scientologists."

We wound up having two hearings before judge Londer, separated by several weeks. As much as the crusaders were creating the impression we wished they would, Londer could not wrap his wits around the constitutional arguments we were making. In one chambers meeting with counsel, he uttered something which, despite the public relations gains we were making with the "religious freedom campaign," flagged our hopes of success. Earle Cooley had made a lengthy presentation, backed by citations to court case precedents. Londer had seized on one particular case that Cooley cited, buoying our attorneys' hopes that he might understand and adopt our position. After a back-and-forth conversation about its parallels to the case at hand, Londer shocked them all by saying, "Wait a second. That was a court of appeals decision; this isn't a court of appeals." Of course, all legal precedent is created by opinions rendered by courts of appeal, and these are binding law for the lower courts to apply and follow. Londer's statement belied a challenged cognitive capacity. As Earle Cooley put it, "Oh my God, we're in the hands of the Philistines!"

We kept orchestrating Harry's having "chance" encounters with Judge Londer, hoping to divine where he stood and hoping that he might begin to understand this case was not only important to the church and Earle, but to Harry's future. Try as he might, Harry would come back from his meetings befuddled. His refrain was that Londer was as dumb as a sack of rocks, and he couldn't tell whether anything we were presenting was getting through.

On the afternoon prior to the final hearing and the announcement of decision on the mistrial motion, Earle, Harry and I sat in Earle's hotel room in Portland preparing our arguments. We had a last-minute brief to file, and had purposely waited until mid afternoon, when we knew Londer took a break. That way, when Harry was bringing the brief into the clerk, Londer might see him and invite him into his chambers for a chat. That went like clockwork. Earle and I beseeched Harry to call in any chips he might have with Londer. Earle told Harry to tell him outright that Londer needed to do this for Harry. Harry reported back that he had schmoozed with Londer, but that it wasn't appropriate under the circumstances – open chambers doors – to make his ultimate personal pitch. However, Londer had invited Harry to come to his home that evening to meet his wife, since it might be the last time they would see one another. Harry had not committed, out of concern for doing something that would smell of impropriety and could come back to haunt us.

Earle and I discussed the matter in some detail. He explained the downsides of a visit – if it were ever found out it could raise the ugly specter of the decades of GO improprieties we were attempting to live down. "On balance," Earle said, "this is up to the client. You need to brief the boss [Miscavige] and I'll trust his instincts." I called Miscavige and briefed him on all that had transpired. He said, "What is your hesitance? It's a no brainer. Of course he sees Londer, and he does whatever he has to do to get the product." I told Earle the verdict. Earle told me, "Okay, now it's between me and Harry. I'm going to protect you and Dave. Leave it to me."

Earle did report that Harry had gone to Londer's home. He did not give particulars beyond saying that Londer was thrilled with the visit. He gave no guarantee of any particular outcome, "But," Earle added, "tell Dave to relax." And then Earle told me an anecdotal aphorism he would repeat several times to Dave and me over the next couple of years. He said, "Here is my only test of friendship. I know you are going to testify tomorrow in front a grand jury investigating me. Do I sleep tonight…or don't I?"

Even though Earle said he would sleep well that night, I did not. Of secondary importance was my own life. I was so thoroughly invested in the crusade to protect LRH and Scientology that the possible impact on them loomed larger than my own spiritual death – which would be a virtual certainty if we did not win. As I had learned by then on Hubbard's lines of operation, there had to be a head on a pike after a catastrophe of this magnitude. And I had been around Miscavige long enough to know that regardless of his having micro-managed every move in the trial, down to strangling me the first time I attempted to counter him, it would not be Miscavige's head on this particular pike.

The next morning, the Multnomah County Courthouse was surrounded by Scientologists. The hallways and wide stairways inside were packed with Scientologists, from the front door, through the lobby, up to the third-floor courtroom of Judge Londer. Londer gave a touching soliloquy about how well the "real Scientologists" who had descended upon Portland had conducted themselves. He said he might not have been so gracious and polite had his own religion been compared to botulism soup, as plaintiff's counsel had done to the jury. He found such conduct to be extremely prejudicial, and in violation of his own orders – having already determined that Scientology was a religion. The judge granted the mistrial motion, wiping out in one breath the $39,000,000 judgment.

After having survived a nuclear explosion by, among other things, successfully defrauding the court as to L. Ron Hubbard's inaccessibility (Ron had been a named defendant, but we managed to get through the entire trial without the issue of his personal liability ever being adjudicated), Ron had two handwritten messages relayed to Miscavige. The first was a short note to the "real Scientologists," the crusaders, commending them for having pulled off a feat of historical proportions by influencing the winning of the mistrial motion. The second consisted of two words and a single letter, sprawled across a full page in Ron's signature style. It read, "Earle, congratulations! – R." The "R" stood for Ron, a signatory he had used for years on internal church dispatches.

Two months later, at our annual Sea Org Day celebration, Miscavige and I would be awarded special medals of honor, of a type never before issued by Ron. We had slipped on a banana peel and somehow managed to fall on a fur rug.

CHAPTER TWENTY-THREE

THE END TIMES

The mark of your ignorance is the depth of your belief in injustice and tragedy. What the caterpillar calls the end of the world, the Master calls the butterfly. – Richard Bach

There were two critical All Clear litigation issues with which we sought to establish precedents for the future protection of Scientology. These were: a. Scientology is a religion, and b. Scientology is not a fraud. As the litigation evolved, and as we became more familiar with constitutional law, issue "a" became more important than issue "b" for two reasons.

First, if Scientology were established as a religion, then it was in large part protected from issue "b." That is, if Scientology is a religion and is presented as such, there is very little leeway to judicially question whether representations about its efficacy are in fact misrepresentations. Under First Amendment precedents, the government, including civil courts, may not make determinations about the truth or falsity of religious beliefs. If an inquiry about a representation made about the efficacy of Scientology would entail a determination of the validity of Scientology religious practices, that inquiry would constitute excessive entanglement by the government in religious affairs.

The second reason that firmly establishing Scientology as a

religion became the most important goal was that when we had been forced to defend the truth of representations made about Scientology, it had resulted in catastrophe. Witness the Christofferson case. Witness the Armstrong case. And witness as we would, the Wollersheim case.

The Lawrence Wollersheim vs. Church of Scientology case would result in one of the largest disasters in Scientology history. What few people know is that in 1982, L. Ron Hubbard's All Clear team brought the matter upon themselves by zealously executing L. Ron Hubbard's philosophy that the right thing to do is never nothing.

By February 1982, the All Clear team, headed by David Miscavige, was frantic. Two previous All Clear dates had been promised to L. Ron Hubbard, meaning that there would be no outstanding criminal or civil litigation which could hinder his open participation in activities at the church of Scientology's headquarters. Hubbard was growing impatient, and the tone of his dispatches concerning legal matters was becoming more sour. Norman Starkey was the Special Project's Legal Director at the time. He came barreling into my office one morning, after having his head chewed off by Miscavige for lack of an All Clear. Starkey demanded a rundown on the status of every outstanding case naming LRH as a defendant. I systematically went down the list, reporting on where each case stood.

When I was done, Starkey snapped, "What about the Wollersheim case?"

"It has not been served on any defendant. Our intelligence sources tell us Wollersheim is off on his latest con-man deal, and quite probably lost track of it. It has been a year and a half since it was filed. Counsel advises that if we wait a few more months, we can move to have it permanently dismissed for lack of prosecution."

Starkey frantically took notes during my explanation. He turned on his heel and went back to report to Miscavige. An hour later Starkey returned and tore into me, "Get rid of that CI [counter-intentioned], loser attorney on the Wollersheim case, boy! Get a real attorney on it and file a motion to dismiss it on First Amendment grounds, like all the other cases."

"But sir…"

"Knock off your backflash, boy! You are lucky you are still in the Sea Org after that defeatist settlement shit of yours a month ago. Dave wants to know from me whether we ought to kick your ass out right now. How do you want to settle it now?"

"I'll get an attorney on it and get the motion filed."

"You're goddamned right, sonny! Now, move!"

And so, the "offensive" mantra took a case which, with a little patience, might never have been, and turned it into a devastating defensive. Three years later, after the predictable defeat of our ever-flowing stream of legal motions, the Wollersheim case was poised to go to trial. And David Miscavige was poised to take advantage of that fact to vindicate all the previous losses.

His reasoning went along this line. "Wollersheim is no sympathetic plaintiff like Christofferson. He was and is and always will be a con man. LA Superior Court is no Multnomah County, Oregon court. No bumpkins in LA, only street-smart jurors who will have no use for a con man. We now have an attorney who thinks just like me, and who has a written commendation from L. Ron Hubbard himself. Now, after the Portland religious freedom crusade, we know how judges, and presumably jurors, respond to "real Scientologists." So with Earle ripping Wollersheim and his witnesses to shreds, plus a phalanx of real Scientologists surrounding the courthouse (just like Portland) and on the witness stand, this is a sure victory."

For several months the "Religious Freedom Crusade" staged marches, concerts and protests in front of the LA County Courthouse. Several hundred people attended. But a few hundred people gathering in downtown Los Angeles is less noteworthy than the crime blotter for any given single night there. Miscavige's demands that the crusade make a greater impact escalated. Since the crusade's leader, Ken Hoden, was no longer 1,500 miles away in Portland, he found it more difficult to manage things quite the way he would have liked to. At Miscavige's prompting, Hoden stood in the courtroom to defy one of the several judges who sat on the case during pre-trial and trial. When that had no impingement, Miscavige insisted that I bypass the attorneys and argue directly to the court. Twice I was dragged out of courtrooms by four LA County Sheriff's Office deputies. The second time, the judge was so impressed that I continued my argument while clutching onto the doorway, preventing the four deputies from dragging me out of the building, that he ordered them to unhand me. He then afforded me another couple of minutes to complete my argument. That might possibly have had some influence on the judge, as he later dismissed the fraud counts from the case that I had argued. The dismissal of these fraud counts marked the end of "fraud" as a threat in Scientology litigation.

But the two counts remaining, intentional infliction of emotional distress and negligent infliction of emotional distress, were enough to prompt the judge to hear the defendant's case. That would mean we would put on a two-month parade of "real Scientologists" describing the benefits of Scientology and the horrors of Larry Wollersheim's character. But first, Wollersheim's attorney, Charles O'Reilly, indicated the plaintiff might be interested in settling after having presented his side of the evidence.

It was the perfect time for us to settle. The warhorse Earle Cooley had done his usual yeoman's job of attacking the credibility of Wollersheim and his witnesses. However, he was literally worn out. He had been diagnosed with blockage of a coronary artery and was scheduled to receive an angioplasty treatment that could not be delayed. Earle met with me alone one night, in the condo we had rented for him by the courthouse. Earle had driven a hard bargain with O'Reilly and obtained his agreement to settle the case for $500,000.

The facts of the matter were these: We were hit with a $39,000,000 judgment in the last trial. Essentially the same Flynn dog-and-pony show as we had seen in Portland was now on display in the Wollersheim case. We would spend probably three times that much just in attorney's fees to complete the trial (let alone future appeals). And finally, Earle would be out of action for the defense case. In light of these factors, Earle reasoned that it was the deal of the century.

Earle had been unsuccessful with those arguments in attempting to garner Miscavige's authorization to settle the case. Earle pled with me, "Marty, please, you have got to exert whatever influence you can on the boss to get this thing settled. It is insanity to continue on with this. The jury is poisoned. The judge has let it get completely out of control." I replied, "Earle, you are preaching to the choir. I was asked for my vote, and I voted with you. And the response I got was that I was a pussy." Earle sighed, "Jesus."

And so that battle raged on, from late 1985 until the summer of 1986. Ultimately, the jury awarded Wollersheim thirty million dollars. For the next fourteen years we litigated appeals, at a cost of several million dollars, and wound up paying Wollersheim eight million dollars to go away.

As 1985 came to a close, I began to sense that L. Ron Hubbard was not long for the world. There had been no written traffic from Ron for months. Miscavige was having an increasing number of meetings in the office next to mine, with Lyman Spurlock – ASI's corporate director and Ron's accountant. I overheard a lot serious talk about modifications in Ron's last will and testament. Miscavige took on a haunted, deeply contemplative mien. Ray Mithoff, the Senior Case Supervisor International and highest technical expert in Scientology, was spending most of his time at ASI. He was also having subdued, confidential meetings with Miscavige.

L. Ron Hubbard's attorney and I had earlier traveled to Toronto to meet with the Crown Law Office and made an impassioned and documented plea against the wisdom of indicting LRH. Around Thanksgiving the Office announced its indictments. To our great relief, the indictment was limited to GO staff who had participated directly in the crimes in question and the local Toronto church. Ron was spared. Oddly, though Miscavige seemed relieved (he too was a potential defendant who had been spared indictment), his usual enthusiasm at scoring a huge victory was absent. It seemed as if this good news had come too late.

We had fought vigorously, in cases across the country, against motions to force LRH into depositions. It was part of Flynn's ploy to set the cases up for default judgments, for failure to produce Hubbard once he was ordered into deposition. Two federal judges had ordered the church to produce Ron for deposition as its managing agent. We delayed the ultimate loss in both cases through tying them up on appeal, while we sought favorable rulings in other cases on the same issue.

In November, I was called upon by Miscavige to obtain compliance with L. Ron Hubbard's three-year-old order to terminatedly take out his erstwhile auditor and senior technical wizard, David Mayo. When Mayo set up a splinter group, Hubbard had ordered that the church "squash him like a bug." In 1982 a group called Religious Technology Center (RTC) had been formed under Miscavige. Hubbard had gifted the trademarks of Dianetics and Scientology to RTC, along with instructions to utilize them in perfecting the monopoly on the subjects. Until late '85, the small team at RTC had answered directly to Miscavige.

But now two events brought me into the mix. First, a private investigator phoned me to report that RTC executives had ordered him to plant drugs on a Mayo associate travelling in Thailand. The investigator had done church work before, and though he was now working for RTC, he had heeded my emphatic earlier instructions to engage in "nothing illegal." The second event was a series of RTC harassment operations against Mayo getting out of control. Miscavige and RTC had Scientologist spies placed in Mayo's group, acting as *agents provocateurs*. Though these people had created a great deal of disruption and internal turbulence, Mayo's group kept growing. Miscavige and RTC then formed a network of Scientologists calling themselves the "Minute Men." The Minute Men overtly harassed Mayo's group by protesting in front of its premises and following and aggressively confronting Mayo and his associates wherever they went. The harassment got so overt and continuous that Mayo was able to obtain a temporary restraining order against the church, prohibiting continued harassment. When he learned of the two incidents – the proposed drug planting and the temporary restraining order – Miscavige hit the roof. He acted surprised and dismayed that RTC would be so "criminal" and "rogue," allegedly unbeknownst to him. He did his best impression of Captain Louis Renault from the movie *Casablanca*: "I am shocked – *shocked* – to find that gambling is going on in here!" He issued a blanket order that RTC was not to breathe without clearing their actions with me. And so, I was now straddled with the additional problem of closing down the splinter movement.

I worked with RTC attorneys and with Earle Cooley to come up with a lawful means of executing Hubbard's intention to squash Mayo. We had RTC file suit in federal court and sought a temporary restraining order and permanent injunction against David Mayo and his Scientology delivery group, the Advanced Ability Center. We sought to enjoin them from using upper-level, confidential Scientology materials, under the theory that he was in receipt of stolen copies of those materials. After a full day's evidentiary hearing, Federal Court Judge Marianna Pfaelzer in Los Angeles entered the injunction, finding that Mayo had lied about how he had come into possession of the material.

Mayo, his back against the wall, then joined ranks with FAMCO and the DOJ, and moved the court to order the church to produce Hubbard for deposition. We prepared for and defended against the motion. We held high hopes that the judge's ruling would counter the ones by other judges that went against us.

A number of lawsuits were filed by the church, attempting to keep the upper-level Scientology material out of the public record. While I had received no formal auditing on such levels, I was suddenly exposed to their most guarded, arcane secrets, out of the necessity of defending their secrecy. It was church doctrine that if anyone who had not achieved the lofty level of Clear were to be exposed to these secrets, he ran the risk of becoming ill or even dying.

At the time of my first exposure – while litigating the right to maintain the material's secrecy – I did not become ill or die. The exposure was, however, a bit of a shock. At the time, I thought the material had nothing to do with Scientology. Even years later, after attaining the highest spiritual states and levels of training in Scientology, I would finally conclude the secrets were in conflict, in fundamental ways, with the very axioms that form the philosophy's foundation.

However conflicting the materials seemed to me, the first judge to study them in detail was singularly effected by that study. Ironically, her interpretation perhaps best explained why I felt the material conflicted with the rational, even scientific, grounding of the Scientology I was familiar with. Judge Pfaelzer said that there was no denying that this was religious scripture; it could not be characterized in any other wise. She would not even entertain arguments seeking to prove anything to the contrary. Her view apparently was that credulity had to be suspended in order to take this dogma seriously; in other words, religious belief was required. Ultimately, even though it was an unintended consequence of bringing the Mayo litigation in the first place, it was Pfaelzer's determination that would turn the tide toward universal acceptance of Scientology as a religion. Even when we lost an appeal of the original inunction in the Federal Appeals Court, the basis for the ruling was that the upper level material, being indisputably religious, could not be protected from unauthorized use by way of commercial law.

Had it not been for that tide shift, the church of Scientology would not exist today. It would have been liquidated by waves of damages claims by former members and by the Internal Revenue Service. The subject would likely be little more than an historical footnote by now. Given the fact that Scientology owes its virtual legal immunity today to these materials, and given the fact that ultimately L. Ron Hubbard's demonstrated belief in what those material state (which speaks to the issue of his ultimate sincerity), a short synopsis of that secret scripture is important to this narrative. It demonstrates that Scientology *is* a religion and that L. Ron Hubbard sincerely believed in it. Thus, in whole it could not possibly constitute fraud.

The materials state as fact that what is wrong with humanity stems from events that occurred seventy-five million years ago. At that time, we were transported (as spirits) to earth from a far-off, ancient, yet technologically sophisticated civilization. Here we were put through a process of having thousands of other live, unconscious beings grafted to us. Those beings, designated "body thetans" or "bts," have been connected to us ever since. At the upper levels of Scientology, one audits these engrafted bts to a state of alertness and Clear, at which point they drift off as free spiritual beings. The Earth holocaust was orchestrated by an evil inter-galactic villain called Xenu. The story goes that ultimately Xenu was captured and imprisoned by military officers who had remained loyal to the citizenry. While Hubbard never connects the dots, it could be presumed that the Sea Org might represent the modern-day meeting ground of those loyal officers. After all, Hubbard had given the Sea Org the motto "*Revenimus,*" Latin for "we come back."

When stripped of its space-opera story line, Hubbard's account of the origin of electronic disturbances connected to a being, as located and identified with the electrical resistance detecting e-meter, parallels a number of ancient, traditionally accepted philosophies. These would include the Gnostic movement that followed Jesus Christ immediately after his death and before the advent of "Christianity," with their established belief in and practice of exorcising demons. It would also be in agreement with the story of the Buddha's ultimate enlightenment by facing down "Mara and her armies" (described as hundreds of disembodied beings, influencing an individual but unbeknownst to him) under the Bodhi tree.

That Scientologists swore to take Hubbard's sci-fi context backstory literally led judge Pfaelzer, and a federal appellate court which reviewed her ruling, to conclude that Scientology was not science. It could be characterized as nothing other than religion; clearly, the matter it treated required a significant measure of faith or belief to embrace.

I was not sure what to make of this secret doctrine at the time. But two things were absolutely clear to me. First, the intensity with which I was being directed from the top communicated that the potential exposure of this material was a life-and-death issue – not just my life, but the life of Scientology and Man's only hope for salvation. Thus it was a matter of the future life of every person on the planet. Second, I believed that should the material be made publicly available, Scientology might be ridiculed out of existence.

We fought for the next fifteen years – spending millions of dollars – to keep the material sealed, through a number of court actions. The materials did remain sealed during L. Ron Hubbard's lifetime and for many years beyond, until the new millennium. With the advent of the Internet, the toothpaste was forever out of the tube, never to be held secret again.

In late December 1985, I was instructed by Miscavige to perform a rather tricky task. I was to have Earle Cooley, LRH's estate attorney Sherman Lenske, private eye Gene Ingram and another armed investigator placed on 24/7 call, indefinitely. That team had to be prepared and willing to drop whatever they were doing on a moment's notice, to leave Los Angeles for at least twenty-four hours on a secret mission. I obtained everyone's agreement, and kept them on call for nearly a month.

On Friday, January 24, 1986, we received the best news and the ultimate worst news of the whole four-and-one-half year All Clear campaign.

First, Federal Judge Pfaelzer issued her ruling on the motion to compel L. Ron Hubbard's deposition in the Mayo lawsuit. Pfaelzer ruled that Hubbard would not be compelled to attend. In keeping with her unalterable view that Scientology was a religion, she wrote that while Hubbard clearly was revered by members of Scientology management as the founder and spiritual leader of the religion, that did not equate to being a "managing agent" of a commercial corporation. Judge Pfaelzer had articulated our argument as a federal court written precedent. David Miscavige and I felt this vindication of our position with respect to LRH could be the turning point toward All Clear. As fate would have it, our optimism lasted for only a few short hours.

That evening Miscavige came to see me in my office. He said to me somberly, "LRH dropped his body." Before the tears made it half way down my cheeks he added, "Get the attorneys and PIs over here, now." And just like that, we were back into action. We mustered the professionals in the conference room. Miscavige told them that Pat Broeker had called and informed him that Ron had died peacefully that evening, in his Bluebird motor coach home at his ranch in Creston, in central California. Hubbard's personal doctor, Scientologist Eugene Denk, was attending and said that Ron had died of a brain aneurism. We had to get there to view the body and determine what to do in terms of reporting the event. Obviously, the media would be all over this, and there would be accusations of foul play from the Flynn camp, *a la* the Dewolf probate case. Security was of the utmost importance, as we would want no leaks before we could learn the full circumstances and be the ones to announce it to Scientologists and the world at large.

We arrived at Creston before dawn. The ranch was 160 acres of rolling hill country, located thirty minutes north of San Luis Obispo. A house under renovation sat on top of a prominent hill. Below it was a pond. At the pond's edge were stables with a tack room and adjoining apartment. And next to this modest structure sat L. Ron Hubbard's custom Bluebird mobile home bus, and a trailer occupied by Dr. Denk.

Denk entered the bus with Pat Broeker, Miscavige, Cooley and Lenske. I went to the apartment and met Annie Broeker and my old friend and former mentor, Steve "Sarge" Pfauth. Annie was LRH's constant companion in his last years, taking care of all of his domestic and professional needs. Pat was the liaison to Miscavige and the church, and was absent from Creston much of the time, arranging communication drops with Miscavige. Sarge was the handyman. He was in charge of upgrades to the ranch and to the home on the hill. Sarge and Annie were pretty much consumed with grieving.

Miscavige, Cooley and Lenske met with me after viewing the body and questioning Pat, Annie, Dr. Denk and Sarge about the circumstances leading to Ron's death. It seemed there was no evidence of anything suspicious. Ron was seventy-four years old, and his health had been deteriorating over the past year. Sherman and Dr. Denk determined that a local funeral home should be phoned to arrange pick-up of the body for cremation, in accordance with Ron's written wishes.

The local sheriff (who doubled as coroner) arrived with the funeral home folks to view the body. He was briefed on the international media firestorm that announcement of the death would ignite. Miscavige told him that there would likely be allegations of foul play, consistent with the Dewolf-Flynn probate petition controversy of a couple of years before. The sheriff commented that he had never felt a body still as supple as Hubbard's was, after having expired ten or more hours earlier. The sheriff suggested that a blood sample be drawn so that a toxicological study could be done, to eliminate any suspicion of foul play. Miscavige and Cooley discussed it with Dr. Denk, who agreed. Denk let it be known that traces of Vistaril would be present, since he had prescribed the drug for acute pancreatic pain Ron had been suffering over the past year. Fingerprints were taken, blood was drawn and the sheriff then authorized cremation of L. Ron Hubbard's body.

Pat Broeker and David Miscavige would spend the next two days joined at the hip, planning the funeral event where Scientologists would be the first to learn of Ron's passing. The event was held at the Hollywood Palladium, and was video-taped for re-play at events for Scientologists across the world. Miscavige, Broeker and Cooley would speak, and Norman Starkey (who had been named executor of Ron's estate) would perform the Scientology funeral rites. Scientologists would be presented with the impression that Ron had rationally determined to leave his body, because he had discovered it was a hindrance to further researches above and beyond what he had so far accomplished with Scientology. He had left the church of Scientology to the Broekers and Miscavige, to continue to manage with his full blessing.

Broeker announced to Scientologists that Ron had been fully in control of his mental and physical faculties when he had decided to leave his body for the final time. He had fully written up the next higher OT levels. OT VIII was in the hands of international management. They were preparing a ship and training staff so that this new level could be delivered at sea, away from the distractions of the world. Beyond that he said, "OT IX and OT X are also written up, finished. There are several other OT levels it is my job to compile. The task consists of taking what he has written and putting it essentially in paragraph form, and then adding the appropriate technical bulletin references that go along with the auditing necessary to the levels. Once complete, they'll be released in due course. We have materials that are in this form, in his, in his…in a thick sheaf of notes, per folder, for OT XI, OT XII, OT XIII, and so forth. And then about…oh, a stack about this high [indicates five feet high], to be sorted out for subsequent OT levels. We also have, by the way, the OT level that is going to be done immediately after every thetan discards his or her body. He wrote that up before he went."

Broeker told the Scientologists that "There's not much else to say. What he came (to Earth) to do, he did. Now, now that he's out there, he embarks upon his further OT research at a completely new level."

And so the church of Scientology's resurrection myth was firmly implanted into the minds of Scientologists. Ron had painstakingly spent the final years of his life exploring the farthest reaches of spiritual attainment – and had written it all up for their benefit. And then, after the minor hiccup of discarding the body, he was back at it strong as ever – in parts, apparently, unknown. Miscavige even commended me for having fought the good fight successfully over the past four years; after all, we had afforded Ron the protection and seclusion he required to complete his OT research.

Shortly after the funeral event and Broeker's verbal rundown about stacks of purported L. Ron Hubbard writings on states of awareness far beyond anyone's imagination, the one, single scrap of paper Ron had left behind for issuance was broadly published:

SEA ORGANIZATION
FLAG ORDER 3879
19 January 1986

THE SEA ORG & THE FUTURE

I, LRH, Commodore, am hereby assuming the rank of ADMIRAL.
The rank of COMMODORE IS RETIRED FROM ACTIVE SERVICE in the Sea Organization at this time. As we move on up the track the Commodore rank will be reinstated as will be needed.
A new rank of LOYAL OFFICER is created directly above the rank of Captain.
Pat Broeker is hereby promoted to the first LOYAL OFFICER rank.
Annie Broeker is hereby promoted as the second LOYAL OFFICER.

There are several Sea Org Officers they will want to promote.
The SEA ORGANIZATION will always be the Sea Organization, no matter that we may leave the surface of this planet when we're finished and operate on others (hopefully not too many devoid of seas — joke) and no matter what, we will operate, in general, throughout the universe — solid, liquid, gaseous, and yes, — there are other states of matter, which are ours for the taking because nobody else seems to know about them.
I'll be scouting the way and doing the first port survey missions. I expect your continuing backup. You've got a little under a billion left on your current hitch, and it is hoped you will sign up again — veterans are valuable!
So, there it is. You know what to do. You know how to do it. Hold the form of the S.O.! You've got the watch!!
I will be in comm.
We will meet again later.
L. RON HUBBARD
ADMIRAL

As predicted, Flynn and company alleged variously that L. Ron Hubbard had been murdered, and that he never died and was being held captive somewhere. Challenges to Ron's estate were litigated into the late nineties. But his written wishes, to take care of his family while bequeathing to the church the bulk of his estate, including his intellectual property rights in Scientology, were complied with.

CHAPTER TWENTY-FOUR

MEANWHILE, BACK AT THE RANCH

It is better to conquer yourself than to win a thousand battles. Then the victory is yours. It cannot be taken from you, not by angels or by demons, heaven or hell. – Buddha

Pulitzer prize winning author Lawrence Wright's book, *Going Clear: Hollywood and the Prison of Belief,* is essentially a biography of L. Ron Hubbard from an outside researcher's perspective. One of the book's central themes is Hubbard's propensity for depowering and alienating those who were once close friends and aides. From his second wife Sarah Northrup to his son L. Ron Hubbard, Jr. in the fifties, to high-level Sea Org officers in the sixties and seventies, Ron demonstrated an intolerance for anyone potentially competing with or overshadowing his genius and absolute authority and control. It seems that my narrative here has brought that theme forward through Ron's final years – from the Hubbard-ordered demise of his own auditor and top technical man David Mayo, to his most trusted messengers Dede and Gale, to his wife and church Controller Mary Sue Hubbard.

David Miscavige and Pat Broeker, the last of L. Ron Hubbard's closest confidantes, apparently were no exceptions. Upon Broeker's announcement that he was holding all the control cards for the foreseeable future – the OT levels he purported to possess – David Miscavige immediately began a quest to obtain them.

Broeker and his wife Annie, the alleged First and Second Loyal Officers, at first kept Miscavige at bay by playing the "Ron said" card. Ron, they alleged, was mightily disappointed with Miscavige for never attaining the All Clear. At first Miscavige demonstrated appropriate contriteness and respect to the only Loyal Officers. However, before long it became apparent that Pat was not so much interested in compiling and issuing OT levels as he was in trading in expensive quarter horses and playing lord of the L. Ron Hubbard ranch. At Creston, Pat literally created a cult within the cult. He kept ordering new personnel be put at his disposal for his important work in forwarding Ron's legacy. After several months he had been sent nearly two dozen church staff. However, virtually no Scientology work was done at Creston. Instead, the staff became ranch hands, cooks and domestic servants, to wait hand and foot on the First and Second Loyal Officer.

Broeker's overreaching ostentation would ultimately spell his demise, and would seal Miscavige's fate at attempting to play Scientology's Brigham Young to LRH's Joseph Smith. After LRH's death, the IRS criminal investigation refocused on Broeker and Miscavige. Because Broeker could not account for $1.8 million he had been handed in cash by Miscavige over the years, meant for the running of the Creston operation during Ron's final years, and because of his continuing to spend cash like an irresponsible Saudi prince, Miscavige was the only one with the power to prevent the IRS from putting Broeker in jail and taking over all church assets through jeopardy assessments. Since Miscavige had learned the ways of the external world so well during the All Clear war, and had managed to earn the loyalty of all church lawyers (by, among other means, controlling their paychecks), Broeker ultimately became beholden to Miscavige for his continued freedom.

While I was busy creating a war machine that would sock the IRS with more than two thousand lawsuits, waves of investigations, series of exposés and Congressional oversight hearings, Miscavige was busy frightening Broeker into submission with threats of letting the IRS at him.

I led two raids on the Creston ranch and on the L. Ron Hubbard back-up hideaway at Newberry Springs, California, to recoup the alleged OT materials that Broeker had promised all Scientologists would soon be available. When we had confiscated all of L. Ron

Hubbard's remaining papers, including his own personal counseling folders, and they had been gone through with a fine-toothed comb, there was no sign of any OT levels above OT VIII.

Finally, during our second raid – backed by a team of armed private investigators – Annie Broeker broke under Miscavige's pressure. She turned on her husband and sided with Miscavige in their epic power struggle. We finally squeezed the last of Hubbard's remaining random notes out of Pat. Still no sign of any OT levels. At that time Annie confessed that The Sea Org and the Future bulletin, purported to be L. Ron Hubbard's final published words (the one-page farewell included earlier in this book, appointing Annie and Pat as Loyal Officers) was a fabrication of Pat's. According to Annie, Hubbard had not at first authorized its issuance. But he had finally given his okay, simply to rid himself of Pat's death-bed pestering, after Ron was no longer competent physically and mentally. Annie confessed that Pat was seldom even in Hubbard's presence during the last year of his life. Ron had ordered Pat to leave the ranch, and Pat had willingly obliged – spending months in parts unknown to Annie or to Miscavige and the church.

Once Annie turned on him, Pat Broeker fled Miscavige's rule. Miscavige had Pat covertly surveilled (an operation I set up and ran for five years) for the next twenty years, worried he might resurface to challenge Miscavige's unquestioned rule of Hubbard's Scientology empire. Annie voluntarily served in minor positions under Miscavige, until her death from cancer in 2011.

Because of the cosmic politics of paranoia that reigned within Scientology's Sea Org, and because all those who worked directly for Hubbard in the line of command did in fact wind up as Ron's enemies – at least as far as he was concerned, it has been hard to come by relatively neutral, unbiased accounts about the man. In 2009, four and a half years after I left the Sea Org, I finally ran across someone in the unique position of having been L. Ron Hubbard's friend during his final years, without ever having run afoul of Ron by being part of the chain of command – and so in Ron's line of fire. That person was my old pal and mentor, Steve "Sarge" Pfauth. The same Sarge who had taken me over the rainbow in 1978, and taught me the ropes of securely handling communications to and from Ron's secret locations. During the last ten years of Hubbard's life, Sarge was continuously stationed wherever Hubbard was staying, or was responsible for securely relaying his communications. Sarge served Ron as a ranch hand, handyman, cook, and friend during his final two years in Creston.

When I met up with Sarge again, he had been away from the Scientology organization for almost twenty years. He lived a quiet life, taking care of his mother and working as a handyman at a Christian church, in a small town on Lake Michigan's eastern shore. Sarge had kept his inside knowledge of Ron's final years to himself through all that time. However, he felt a need to speak up when he learned that many of his old friends and comrades were being manipulated and even imprisoned by Miscavige, through perpetuation of the myth that Ron intended to come back in a new body to resume control of the Sea Org.

Sarge is particularly credible in that he holds no grudges against L. Ron Hubbard, the church of Scientology, or any other players in the drama. He was never a participant in the perpetual power pushes that are part and parcel of the Scientology organization. In the following passages from our discussions, "S" stands for Sarge and "M" stands for Marty.

S: I was in Creston from '83 till '88.

M: I didn't know you were there that early, '83.

S: Oh, yeah. Right after Pat bought it. It was him and me. We did a lot of work there. We had contractors come in and we did a lot of work ourselves. But he'd leave and come back, leave and come back.

M: So you guys were there before LRH and Annie were there, then?

S: Oh, yeah. We had to set it up for the RVs. There was no RV set-up. We had to put water lines in. I dug the water lines. We bought a tractor.

M: How may acres was that place?

S: A hundred and sixty…Pat threatened me just before LRH came; he told me, "Sarge, if you ever blow from this place, I'll hunt you down and I'll kill you. And I'm not joking. I'll kill you."

M: Are you serious?

S: No, he told me that. Because Pat and I were so close, it shocked me. Why does he think I would blow to begin with? Do you know what I mean?

M: Right, right.

S: It just totally shocked me. And so I said, "Okay. Fair enough."

He said, "Now, you understand me?" And I said, "Yep." And I just wanted to drop the subject. I didn't want to get into a row with him. Because he had guns, ok?
M: Yeah, I know. So did Dave.
S: Sometimes you kind of wonder. You know?
...Through those years he [Ron] liked me. It was obvious. When he first came to Creston he came bounding off the Bluebird, and he said "Saaaarrge!" You know, real loud. And I'm looking around because there are wogs [non-Scientologists] around, because we were all using phony names and all. He was like a little kid, he was so excited.
M: Tell me what he said.
S: Well, he said, "Who do I look like?" And I didn't want to say anything. I stammered and stuttered a little bit. He said, "Come on, who do I look like?" And I said, "Well…" And he says, "Colonel Sanders! Don't I look like Colonel Sanders?" He had long white hair. He had a beard. And of course he was dressed up. He had his hat on and stuff. He used to dress up a lot. He was almost giggling because he was so happy to see me and he said, "What's your handle?" And I said, "Joe Carpenter." And he *laughed*, he thought that was so funny. Joe Carpenter, what a classic name for a ranch hand. So he says, "Guess what my name is." And I said, "I don't know." And he said, "Jack Farnsworth." And he got a kick out of that. He was into that intrigue. He loved security. The phony names and all that. I think that's why he got such a kick out of me, because I did that so much.
M: I know, you were the guy. I learned all that stuff from you, Sarge.
S: I know. See, I was trained. You gotta understand, I didn't come up with all this stuff. I just used what I learned from him because he used to send me dispatches about security, and he wanted to make sure I was trained in security…I think that's why the old man liked me so much. But I screwed up, just like everybody screws up. The point I'm making is, he never came down hard on me. He gets a reputation of being a real hard-nosed asshole and all that. And I am sure that some people may have taken it that way. But like I said, he had a temper. But he didn't hold onto that.
M: Right. No grudges.
S: No grudges…Maybe it's because I had a different relationship with him, because I was security. I was usually the security guy. You

know, I did comm runs, I did security watches, I did capers with phony names…I was the PR guy that knew all the neighbors and stuff. I did all the stuff downtown, did all the shopping…

…LRH wrote the tech, he lived the tech. To my knowledge he audited every day. He wrote. He did drums. He was into music. He lived what he preached. From my perspective, I loved the man (tears). He was special, one of a kind. It hurt me when he died. He wanted to be on the lines so bad…

…I was on his lines but I was kept off the Sea Org lines. I was Joe Carpenter there. I carried comm, because I would go out and meet Pat a lot [to relay it]…I did know that he wanted All Clear real bad. I heard Annie say that and I heard him say it too, because he desperately wanted to go back to S [International Scientology HQ] and wanted to be on the lines… He wanted to be running the show. That was LRH.

M: I'm getting the impression that the ranch was nice, but it wasn't a big enough game for him.

S: No. Yeah. He felt like he was being deliberately kept off the lines. And I think that's probably one of the reasons Pat quit coming out so much. He would come in the middle of the night and I'd meet him at drops and stuff. I think LRH had it out with Pat a few times. I think there was a little bit of friction there. LRH could have said – now, I'm not saying he said this, but it's possible in my mind – that LRH could have said, "I don't want to see you again until you bring me an All Clear." I could have seen that happening.

M: You could have gotten that impression based on what you saw.

S: I could have got that impression – but that is just my opinion.

M: Being on the other end of it, that might make sense to me too.

S: He was frustrated that nobody could handle this. That was very upsetting to him…I have a feeling that sometime in early '85 there was something going on between LRH and Pat [Broeker] so Pat wasn't coming out to Creston as much.

M: Where was he?

S: Off handling things. There was some friction there between Pat and LRH. LRH got sick, I believe it was in early '85. He had pancreatitis, he had to go to the hospital. We had [Dr.] Gene Denk there. So, basically what happened was Pat didn't come out that often. He would come in the middle of the night, drop off comm [communications], talk to Annie for a little bit, and then split before

LRH was up. Anyway, what happened there, it was mainly Annie and I there. Gene was in a trailer, he wasn't supposed to know where he was at. He told me, though, that he knew right where he was. On Sundays we go out and shoot skeet. When all the workers were gone in the evenings when I got back from town, because I'd go out shopping and stuff, we would go out and play badmitten before dinner. I would cook all the dinners. And I got videos for him and books for Gene and the old man. Gene was cooped up in the trailer [the Country-air].

M: And where was Annie?

S: Annie took the bedroom that I used to stay in. Pat and Annie were in the Country-air, and when Gene came, Gene went into the Country-air and Pat and Annie moved into the bedroom that I used to have in the stables. So I got bumped into the living room on a little fold-out couch. LRH was living in the Bluebird [bus]. So basically what happened was, when LRH came back from the hospital…Pat wasn't there a lot. And Annie would page Pat, and a lot of times Pat wouldn't answer. Annie used to get frustrated over that. But there was, I think, a falling out between Pat and the old man. I think it had to do with All Clear. I think you know what All Clear was…

M: Right, I worked on All Clear. Was all of 1985 a downer with him? What was it like the last year?

S: No. He quit smoking and stuff and he would come out after he got back from the hospital. Of course he was recouping and he was on medication, I know that. I don't know what he was on. I wasn't privy to a lot of that stuff. That is something that Annie and Gene would know…He didn't get out quite as much, but every now and then he would come out for a walk. I remember one time he came out for a short walk. He wasn't doing that well. It was early evening. You know how the sun starts to go down and you can see a few stars?

M: Yeah, twilight.

S: Yeah, twilight. And I remember him going for a short walk and I happened to see him so I walked out there and I said, "Hello, sir." He liked to tell stories. I remember him looking up at the stars, and we saw a missile; it might have been more than one missile. The stars were starting to come out. He was looking up at the stars, and he said, "There's nothing but a bunch of cowboys out there." He said,

"Yeah, they're all cowboys, they kill each other and shoot each other, and they're just a bunch of cowboys out there." You know, just little things like that, you are out there walking around and he'd tell stories. I wish he was still around. I loved him. And it's not just respect. You know, a lot of people love him because of the tech and everything like that. But I love him more on a personal level. Because he was more like, you know, he was my boss, my father, he was like that type of thing.

M: Didn't he get you some stuff?

S: Well, he thought I dressed bad so he ordered Pat to get me some clothes. You know, I wore jeans, you know, I was a cowboy. I wore jeans, and cowboy shirts, and once in a while a cowboy hat. The thing is he was a very thoughtful man. And he was a giving man. And a lot of people can say that. Some of the people that knew him early on, maybe they just never saw the real LRH. Maybe they were just on a business level with him. That makes a big difference.

M: Yeah, you had kind of a unique thing in that your business was domestic. Maybe you had a special kind of thing over those couple of years that nobody has ever had.

S: That's what I'm thinking. You see, Annie was too close in.

M: Right, because she would have to handle all the Scientology traffic and all that.

S: Yeah. She had a lot of responsibility. That is why I love Annie so much…I wasn't an angel, and Annie would berate me a bit. But then, she was also loving. I remember she found this little bird. She was feeding it with an eye dropper. That little bird was important to her. I remember when the bird died, and I gave her a big hug. She smoked and I smoked. And I used to borrow some of her cigarettes. She used to smoke Canadian cigarettes.

M: The old man used to like to give you his cigarettes.

S: Yeah. The stale Picayunes. He was smoking Picayunes. They were very, very strong cigarettes. They were non-filters. And he would give me his old ones. If they were stale, or they had been around for a while he'd say, "Give those to Sarge." He knew I smoked Camels at that time. That was kinda nice. And we exchanged books. I gave him some Louis L'Amour books. And then I used to buy him books when I went shopping. He loved, he loved stories, you know. Good writers. He loved the Horatio Hornblower stuff, man, with the big sails and the swashbuckling stuff. He was really into that. He was one heck of a good guy. ...But, I knew there were problems [in 1985] because he would just come out like twice a day. He would go out and drive around, Annie would drive him all over the property. He had a [Subaru] Brat. Toward the end there, what happened is, Annie said to me, "LRH wants to see you." And I said, "Okay." And I used to drink beer with the contractors and stuff. That was something Pat set up. I had to set up a fridge and keep it stocked full of cold beer. And I had to go and have beer with them. Believe me, that wasn't something you had to twist my arm to do. That was kinda cool. Hot day and cold beer, there's nothing better.

M: Yeah.

S: So, I came back and I smelled like alcohol and Annie got all upset. She said "I'm going to send you in there, just like you are." And I said, "I'm not drunk, Annie." She said, "I don't care." So she got a little upset over that. And I understand it, okay? So, anyway, he wanted to see me. So I went into the Bluebird and sat down. And he sat across from me and he said, "Sarge,"...boy I wish I had written it all down because I don't want to goof it up, because this is kind of important. Basically he said, "Sarge, I need you to do something." He wanted me to build him a machine that would get rid of the bts [body thetans] and kill the body.

M: Wow.

S: Yeah. It's kind of heavy. It struck me real hard. He told me a few things. He said, "Yeah, I've done all I can do here and I'm just... I'm not coming back. I'm leaving and I am not coming back." He wanted to die, basically. You know, his body was going to hell and all that stuff. He was having trouble with bts.

M: And you say that was in late '85?

S: Yeah. Fall of '85. Yeah, it was right around October.

M: Like three months before he died.

S: Yeah, like three or four months. So, I didn't want to do it. But I didn't tell him that. And I was hoping I could talk to Pat because Annie insisted that I build the machine. And I said, "Annie, I don't know that much about building machines that fry people, you know what I mean?"

M: Well, did he describe how it should be done?

S: Basically, he wanted to hook it up to the e-meter. And he wanted enough voltage in there that it would get rid of the bts. And I asked

him about voltages and I asked him some questions…it was so long ago. And, uh, well, I gotta tell ya, it upset me a lot.
M: I bet. So, the idea was that you'd be holding the cans…
S: Turn the thing on and then, in other words, he was gonna audit the bts away and the body was gonna die.
M: Right. So there would be enough voltage to kill the body?
S: To do it all. How he figured I was going to figure that out, I have no idea. You gotta understand, he wasn't well at that time. I'm not saying he was nuts or anything at that time. I'm just saying he wasn't well and he was very, very frustrated about not being able to come back to S [International Scientology Headquarters near Hemet, California] and be on the lines. He wanted to be on the lines, very, very bad. And I know they kept telling him all kinds of crap because of all that stuff. I mentioned the argument that Pat and LRH had because he was frustrated. Well, I gotta tell you something else that happened earlier on that same year. He wanted to move to the coast. So I went down to Pismo Beach and I found this fabulous place, Marty. God, I don't know what it was, like three million dollars or something. Big, huge old house, sat on a big old hill overlooking the ocean. With a small guest house and then stairs that went down to a boat landing.
M: Wow. He would have loved that, huh?
S: He would have loved this place. Pat put a big nix to it. "No, no, that's the first place they are going to look is the ocean." You know how much ocean there is in California?
M: Yeah. Like eight hundred miles of it?
S: He didn't want him to leave Creston. Oh, he put a big nix on that in a hurry. But I got all the information and I gave it to Annie and stuff and I'm sure she gave it to the old man. That may have been part of the thing with Pat. That could have been part of it. I know he got a little frustrated at the end. Anyway, after the thing with him telling me he was going to leave and he wasn't coming back and all that stuff, it hit me kind of hard. I did the dinner thing, cooking dinner for Annie and Gene and me. You know, went to town and did the dinner thing and all that stuff.
M: And Annie took care of LRH's meals?
S: Yeah. Earlier on I cooked for LRH. He thought I was a good cook. And then he got sick. Anyway, what happened was I was very upset. So I got pissy-ass drunk and Annie found me about four

o'clock in the morning with beer cans all over the green truck, out at the racetrack. I had passed out on the seat. And she was screaming at me, "Oh, you son of a bitch!" Oh man, she laid into me. And I said, "All right, Annie," and my head was hurting. But I was upset, I was very upset. I was crying and everything. That was a rough time. Very rough. Uh, so anyway, then days went by, okay? And Annie kept saying, "He wants to know about the machine, he wants to know about the machine. What are you doing on the machine?" Annie says, "If you don't do anything on this Sarge, he's going to get the local electrician to build one for him." Can you picture that?
M: Wow. That would have been a…
S: I said "No way, man." So I had to show some progress. So I went to an electronics place in San Luis Obispo and I bought some Tesla coils and some up-transformer things and I got all sorts of things. I basically built him a battery-operated automotive coil type thing. This is my reasoning now, Marty. If he gets zapped by that sucker, it's gonna shock him but it ain't gonna kill him. Okay?
M: Okay.
S: It'll shock him but it ain't gonna kill him. It'll scare him and he won't want to do it again.
M: These are like 12-volt batteries?
S: Yeah. But the voltage is going to go way up on a transformer. It's like an automotive coil sort of thing.
M: So your thought, what you understand is that he is not going to get…
S: I'm not frying him!
M: Exactly. I gotcha.
S: I didn't want anything that is going to plug into the wall. I didn't want to fry him, but I didn't want to tell him I didn't want to fry him. You know what I mean?
M: Yeah, I think about what you are saying right now, and I try to put myself into your position and I…
S: It was very difficult. I didn't want to kill the old man. So anyway, he used the thing and he fried up my Mark VI [e-meter]. I had a Mark VI that got fried.
M: He used it?
S: Yeah.
M: LRH actually used it?
S: Yeah, it was my Mark VI, yeah. And it fried the Mark VI. I knew

that was going to happen. Fried it.
M: You mean he actually tried…
S: Oh, yeah. It had burn marks on it and everything.
M: He didn't get burnt?
S: He may have. But after that there was no more mention of any machines. And that was my intention. That was my intention.
M: He probably got a good, hard jolt.
S: I think it scared him, or something.
M: And it burned the plastic?
S: It was burnt. It was fried. The insides were gone. Because, you know, those things are like a computer. You can't put that much power into them without zapping them…I do think people need to know. I just wish at the time when I first blew that I would have written it all down. But I carried it because I had no terminals [people to talk to].
M: I know the feeling. Mine was a mini thing. Mine was for four years, yours was for 18 years. So I know what you are talking about.
S: So anyway, it wasn't long after that – so when he did the machine – it must have been November, December. Early December or late November or something like that.
M: What happened to his pancreas, did he have it removed, or…?
S: No. He had some treatment for it. They put him on medication. He only spent a couple days in the hospital. Gene was with him and Annie. And then I held down the fort, and Pat was gone.
M: So, it is late '85 when this incident happens with the fry machine?
S: Yeah. And it wasn't much longer after that things got a little bit strange. LRH was in the Bluebird a lot, because he wasn't well. I would be mucking out stalls and he'd come out in his nightgown and slippers. And you know, for a disguise he grew a beard and long hair and all that for a disguise, all right? But you could tell he wasn't feeling well. He was shaking a little bit. He had lost some weight. And he was walking around in his nightgown and he would follow me around. And I would say, "Yes, sir," and "no, sir" and that sort of thing, listening to him. He was ranting and raving about psychs and rose perfume.
M: Rose perfume?
S: Rose perfume. Yeah. Rose perfume is his… the smells that they put in shampoos, and soaps, and things like that. That's all part of the psych conspiracy, is the rose perfume. And this was not LRH,

okay? He was… this was weird. And I'd say, "Yes, sir," "no, sir," and he'd say, "You have to be careful of rose perfume; those goddamn psychs," and he'd just rant and rave and walk around while I was cleaning out the stalls.

M: At night?

S: No, it was in the afternoon. And when he wasn't feeling good he wouldn't dress. See, LRH *loved* to dress. He wore capes, and the hats, and the whole bit. I mean he dressed. When he was getting sick and he wasn't right, he would wear nightgown, slippers, he didn't get dressed. You know, it was different. It was not the same LRH everybody knew. Okay? But then one day, God I am trying to remember when. He died, in the middle of January '86, I believe it was…

M: The 26th.

S: Was it the end of January? Then it was… this must have been sometime early January.

M: Or the 24th.

S: Must have been sometime early January, Annie called me. "Sarge, Sarge," she was all excited, very upset, and she says, "LRH wants you to go to the south gate of the pasture and tell me if the bt is there."

M: *The* bt?

S: Or *a* bt. "Look for the bt on the south gate" or something like that. It was something like that. It's something I don't like telling people. But I think they need to know where he was at during that period of time, because he had had a stroke and I didn't know it. I didn't know he'd had a stroke.

M: What ever happened with that thing? Did you go down and check it out, or…

S: I did it several times because I checked it, and I told Annie I didn't see any bts. So she went in the Bluebird and he said, "No, it's the wrong fence." So I went, checked another… or it was a gate, the gate, I'm trying to remember, was it the south gate? Anyway, I checked like three gates, or something. Each time I would come back and report to Annie that I didn't see any bts and she would tell him. So I don't know what that was all about. That was so weird.

M: So here is what I want to ask you. You went into the Bluebird to witness the revised will. Do you recall how close that was to death? How soon after was the death?

S: Oh, my God. It couldn't have been two days. Because Ray was there to assist in the death and Ray wasn't there that long before. And I'm sure LRH requested someone there to come and do that. I don't know whether he requested Ray or just said that he wanted somebody. I don't know.

M: Did you talk to Ray at all when he was up there?

S: No.

M: Okay.

S: You gotta understand, Marty, that I had to keep the place running. So I was in and out, you know? They were mostly right down there. I had to keep all the locals away. When the bt on the gate, that was going on with Annie, Annie was just a wreck, right, Dave Barker [non-Scientologist local contractor working on the ranch] shows up. And I go, "Oh no, man," I tried getting rid of him. I said, "Dave, this is not a good time. Can you come back another time?" First thing I did was I sent him out to refill the ground squirrel trap poison, because we had a ground squirrel problem. I sent him out to do that. And he was gone for about ten minutes, then he came back and said, "Oh, they're all full." I then asked him, "Please, can you just go and do something else?" He said, "Well, I got pretty much everything else done." I said, "Well, you can go home early if you want." And he says, "I can help. Do you want me to clean the stalls for you?" He wanted to know what was going on, basically. And I wasn't about to tell him, so I just kept shooing him away. And Annie says, "Get rid of him!" Finally, I just said "Dave, can you just leave us alone? You know, go home early or something." And he said, "Okay, but I want to do whatever I can to help."

M: So he knew that there was a problem with the old man.

S: He knew something was going on because Annie was upset. He saw me down there doing stuff.

M: This is when, just before he died?

S: Yeah, well it was before, see, Pat wasn't there or anything. Pat brought Ray there about a week before. So it had to be about a week or two weeks. Because right before that episode, Annie kept trying to page Pat. She had to go to a pay phone in Creston. He had a pager. He wouldn't respond. She waited and waited and waited there. Wouldn't respond. She had to get back. So then she'd go out later. She'd wait 'til he (LRH) was taking a nap or something and she'd go back out. Annie was very upset. She would throw things down and say, "I hate security, I hate this fucking security!" Yeah,

that was a rough time. It was a little shocking, you know?
M: When did you subsequently learn he did have a stroke?
S: I don't know. Gene would know. Gene's dead now.
M: Gene's dead?
S: Oh yeah.
M: When did he die?
S: Well, I went looking for him. There was a memorial thing by his family on a website. I did a Google search for him.
M: I'll be damned.
S: Yep. I'd say four or five years ago. Yeah, he's been dead for a little while now. Yeah, that kind of slammed me because I wanted to get a hold of him. Because he was there. He would know a lot more. I mean, he would know what medications. People think LRH was murdered. I saw that where people say "Oh, they murdered him." No, nobody murdered LRH.
M: Well, it sounds like it would be completely pointless from what you are telling me because it sounds like he was sort of wrapping up his life those last few months.
S: Oh, yeah. Absolutely. He said, "I am going to drop the bod, Sarge. I am going to drop my body, Sarge." And he said, "I'm not coming back." I think I asked him, "Uh, where you gonna go?" He told me something about what it was they used to do was go out and he'd – what is that when you run around the pole? He's gonna go out and then to a star and go around it like this [makes circular motion with finger] or something. He was trying to explain this to me, but I didn't quite understand. But that's what he planned on doing.
M: But he made it clear a couple of times that he's not coming back here.
S: Oh, no. You know what surprised me, Marty, about this whole thing? What surprised me was I assumed other people were told. Until I started talking to Sinar [former Sea Org member and Hubbard's personal chef]. Sinar was saying "Yeah, he's AWOL." And I said, "What do you mean?" It surprised me. I thought, "Pat didn't know about this, Annie didn't know about this? DM [David Miscavige] didn't know about this?"
M: About?
S: About LRH not coming back. Saying he wasn't coming back.
M: Right.

S: Maybe he didn't say that to Pat or Annie. But I can't imagine that.
M: Well, see – let me tell you two things that you may not know about. Or maybe you do. But there was one thing that was early on, it was around 1980 or something, because it was around the beginning of the All Clear time. There was a dispatch, actually it was to Mayo. I think it was to Mayo, in like '78, where he said "Look, once I move on, you are going to have about twenty years to get stuff…"
S: Oh yeah, I knew about that.
M: But then later than that, according to DM and Norman [Starkey] they had something from him [LRH] that was much more recent, much closer to the time of death, that he was talking about how he was going to come back in twenty years. He's going to be a twenty-one-year-old blonde guy who is going to show up in Las Vegas and there was some means to recognize who he was.
S: See, I never heard anything about that.
M: See, because I don't have a date on that, when that allegedly was. You know, it could have been '84, it could have been '83. I don't know when it was.
S: Well the thing is, see, I have no proof or anything like this, but I know there were some things that I think were fabricated by others. You know what I mean? Like, I wouldn't put it past DM to lie about anything, really, to be able to control people. You know, so I want you to take that with a grain of salt.
M: Oh, I agree. Let me tell you. Dave used to do things like go down to Int [International Management] and say things like, "The old man said when this planet is going to end. And believe me, it is a lot sooner than you guys think." Now think about that. That's cult stuff. He doesn't show you anything, he just says it. He could just make that stuff up.
S: Exactly.
M: But you are right. You said he could do it for control. Clearly, that was totally for control. He was freaking everybody out.
S: And so I was really surprised when I started talking to Sinar. Because I wasn't going to tell anybody about the machine or our talk in the Bluebird. I mean, you know, why bring it up? I'll tell you one thing, I didn't want anyone thinking that I built a machine that caused his death. It was close to that time, see what I mean?
M: Right.
S: And not only that, it's a little bit embarrassing because it seems

strange. Right?

M: Right. I can have it either way. I mean, to me, I mean, it's like here's a guy who is seventy-four years old. He has done what he has done. I mean a person is entitled to go out the way they want to go out.

S: Yeah, he'd been preparing for some time.

M: I mean we're here in the land of Doctor Death here in Michigan, right?

S: You mean Dr. Kevorkian?

M: Yeah. I mean, I'm not a big dude on the issue. But it seems to me that if somebody has lived their life and they are terminally ill, or they've gotten to that point where, it's their decision what they want to do.

S: Yeah.

M: And whether it is Doctor Death coming with some cyanide drip, or whether it is getting blown up by an e-meter, who the fuck cares?

S: Right. Well, the thing is he was very… because he could see no light at the end of the tunnel for freedom for him. Except body death. You know what I mean?

M: I know.

S: He wanted to come back there so bad.

M: I know. See, I was on the other side of it and I saw the false reports that were going to him and they were embellished reports.

S: I know. I know that DM and Pat religiously went over any comm before it would ever come up. Before it was ever sent up. I know that from early comm drops all the way back. They would pull folders out of the comm and edit things.

M: You mean like edit other people's communications.

S: They were doing all kinds of crap.

…The will thing. I'm trying to remember who was in there. I think Ray, Ray was there. I don't remember if Gene was there or not. Annie was there. Pat was there. I was there.

M: You said he [Pat] briefed you beforehand; what did he tell you?

S: He basically told me, he said, "We want Scientology in capable hands. We don't want the wrong people to get control over the copyrights. Whoever controls the copyrights controls Scientology. And we need to have the leadership in Scientology; the copyrights need to go to RTC, and that's the reason for this will. And all you need to do is witness, Sarge. You don't need to read it or anything."

So I wasn't allowed to read it. I had to go into the Bluebird and I witnessed LRH signing it. But, in my personal opinion, LRH was in no condition to be reading that.

M: Okay, so tell me specifically. You said you walked in. Did you sit down or just stood there? You said LRH was pacing up and down.

S: Yeah. And I was standing toward the entrance and he was pacing up and down in the back saying, "Let's get this over with. I've got a headache. Let's get this over with. I've got a headache." And I think Pat was trying to arrange pencils or papers and putting the… everything, I don't know.

M: On the kitchen…

S: On the little table, yeah. And so LRH sat down at the little table and he signed it and his hand was shaking like this [shakes hand erratically]. He was not in good shape. And I don't know whether I was second or third. I think there was more than one witness. I think Annie might have been a witness. And I signed also. And the death certificate, I signed that.

M: So there was no discussion?

S: The whole thing seemed really screwy to me, okay? See, LRH was probably briefed, otherwise. But at this point, Marty, I gotta be honest with you. He didn't give a shit at this point. Just so you know. That was not his high priority right now.

M: I understand that.

S: "This has to be done, sir." "Okay, let's get it over with. I've got a headache. Let's get this over with." I mean he was not in a… he didn't want to do it, okay? But it had to be done, so he went and did it. And I can't imagine him reading that in that condition. I cannot imagine that. Now, it is possible, Marty, that he dictated a second will earlier on, they put it all together, and he just signed what he dictated earlier. Maybe that's what he was told. But I don't know.

…

M: Can you sum up for me the man L. Ron Hubbard that you knew?

S: LRH was a genius. He had a big temper. And he would lose his temper. And when LRH lost his temper, the windows would rattle. You could hear it a house away. Because he didn't hold things in. He let his anger out. He did not sit on his anger. But then, 30 minutes later he's walking around the messengers saying "Hello" to people. He let the anger out. A lot of people misinterpret that anger. I was on his lines. I was around him. I've seen him yell at people a lot. Because he lost his temper. And he would yell and scream. He never touched anybody. He would vent at them. He was a very powerful man, okay? Not just a big body. He had a lot of intention. And when that was unleashed, everybody would kind of shrivel up, because of the power of the man. But he was also a very nice man. The reason I am saying this is because in all the times I screwed up he never once yelled at me. All the times I was on his lines, and I fucked up, I *never* got that. He was always kind to me, always nice to me… There were times when he got upset that I was a little afraid and everybody would get afraid because he was a powerful man, right. But he was also one of the nicest people I have ever met. I had so much respect for that guy. And I was there right at the end at Creston.

CHAPTER TWENTY-FIVE

EPILOGUE

Wisdom is knowledge plus: knowledge – and the knowledge of its own limits. – Viktor Frankl, *Man's Search for Ultimate Meaning*

Several months after Ron's passing, the advice that resulted in Mary Sue Hubbard being dethroned and my being nearly expelled was finally followed. All of the Flynn litigation was settled for the sum of $2.6 million. To recap, we had seen the wisdom in 1981 of settling it for $1.6 million. Instead of doing so, we spent more than $100 million fighting it tooth and nail, keeping Ron captive in his mobile home bus all the while, only to win the right, five years later, to pay a million dollars more than the original settling price to be rid of it.

In an ironic way, the 100 million might have been a good investment. It resulted in a war-hardened, small group at the reins of Scientology, just as Ron had intended. It resulted in the world at large being frightened of us again, just as Ron had advised. It resulted in a number of firm judicial precedents confirming Scientology was entitled to First Amendment protection as a religion, just as Hubbard directed. Whatever anybody wants to say about L. Ron Hubbard's personality, there is no denying he could get what he wished like a force of nature – even when he was no longer around to witness it.

Ultimately, our aggressive investigation and litigation tactics resulted in the demise of all criminal prosecution threats. The most serious of them, the IRS Criminal Investigation Division probe, lived two years beyond Hubbard's death. The IRS continued to attempt to make a case against Broeker, Miscavige and the church. Miscavige convinced himself that that case died because his personal attorney, the late Gerald Feffer of the D.C. law firm Williams & Connally, had called in chips with his friend, then Assistant Attorney General Roger Olsen. But later freedom of information act request documents revealed otherwise. The case died because when Department of Justice lawyers studied the Armstrong op videos we had obtained and publicized, they concluded that Armstrong, and Flynn's stable of witnesses by association, were worthy of the lowest credibility ratings possible. They could not make a credible case when their critical witnesses had such a *lack* of credibility – at least not under a criminal standard of proof.

Conversely, Robert Mueller's and Bracket Denniston III's attempt to put me behind bars died because of the opposite credibility finding with respect to me. I testified for the government (on the extortion count) and for the defense (on the fraud count) in the U.S. vs. George Kattar case. Veteran Federal District Court Judge McNaughton quipped that he had never seen such a circus, with the government and the criminal defense attempting to bolster a single witness' credibility on one count and discredit him on another, all in the same trial.

Because of the issues in the case, the government had to present to me the transcripts of all electronic surveillance they had conducted on me during my years investigating the check case. The FBI special agent in charge of the matter, Jim Burleigh, was required to hand them over to me personally before I went on the stand. There was a three feet high stack of pages of wire tap transcripts. When Burleigh presented them, he looked down and said sheepishly, "We tried our best, but we just couldn't get you to take the bait." Kattar was convicted of extortion and acquitted of fraud and was ordered to pay back the 25 grand he obtained through extortion. This affair pretty much marked the end of the Department of Justice's obsession with and paranoia over L. Ron Hubbard and Scientology.

A number of former Canadian Guardian's Office personnel and the Toronto church were convicted in Canada. Both Miscavige and I testified on the church's behalf. While we could not prevent the church conviction, we did obtain a written ruling from the court that the church had reformed and taken responsible action to clean out the Guardian's Office.

We took our aggressive, offensive tactics to new heights in combatting the IRS over tax exemption. Seven years after Ron's passing, the IRS capitulated and granted religious, tax-exempt status to all churches of Scientology.

I spent another 18 years in the church of Scientology after L. Ron Hubbard's death. During the final seven years I was posted as the church's second highest ecclesiastical official, Inspector General Religious Technology Center. I have recounted most of the significant events of that period on my blog, *Moving on up a Little Higher* (markrathbun.wordpress.com) and in interviews (most notably video interviews with the *Tampa Bay Times*, available on its website) and in my books *What Is Wrong With Scientology?* (Amazon Books, 2012) and *The Scientology Reformation* (Amazon Books, 2012). The reason I am not chronicling those later years in detail here is that for all intents and purposes in the broader scheme of things, what happened after L. Ron Hubbard is of little importance. Ron created the church of Scientology, and Scientologists for that matter, in his own image. As time passes, each generation produces progressively weaker harmonics of the original, larger-than-life L. Ron Hubbard.

As has been ably reported by Janet Reitman in her book *Inside Scientology* (Houghton Mifflin, 2011) and by Lawrence Wright in his book *Going Clear* (Alfred A. Knopf, 2013), L. Ron Hubbard was a very capable marketing man. What they did not acknowledge as much, but did not totally discount, was Ron's ability to solve problems – including those of the mind and spirit. Ron had a knack for finding out what was bothering people, putting together methods to address those things, and then selling those methods as services – the end-all that people just had to get their hands on.

The Reitman and Wright books detailed how Ron was continually creating new rundowns, new levels and new packaging to keep the Scientology public enthused over the latest in the mind and spirit. It was the formula that created continuing expansion of the Scientology empire during L. Ron Hubbard's life. A strong customer base was established and continually kept interested and buying as new, essential route-to-total-freedom items were rolled out.

Because Ron so unequivocally mandated that *only* Ron could discover, create and memorialize mental and spiritual technology (the *only* stock-in-trade of the church of Scientology) upon Ron's death the church's expansion pattern also died.

Consequently, David Miscavige took on an unenviable task when he was handed the reins of Scientology Inc. And those reins *were* handed to him, whether begrudgingly or not, by Annie Tidman Broeker (Loyal Officer 2) when she sided with Miscavige against her then-husband (Loyal Officer 1) Pat Broeker. Miscavige had no choice but to radically change Scientology's 40-year expansion pattern. The movement had been built and held together primarily through the promise and continual roll-out of new technology. Now Miscavige had to keep that movement going, but with no possibility of introducing new technology. For a while he seemed to have somewhat of a grasp of marketing, but all the marketing in the world could not keep an organization thriving when it had nothing new to sell. At least not an organization whose viability depended on continual emanation of new technology to sell. And by firm religious belief and church doctrine, he was powerless to create any new technology.

The final, highest level of Scientology spiritual attainment that L. Ron Hubbard authored was called OT VIII, Truth Revealed. In June of 1988, after a great deal of pre-release hype, OT VIII was unveiled and delivery began. By the summer of 1990, virtually all of the Scientologists who had completed the previous highest level (OT VII), and who had been kept interested and excited about the next hot one coming from Ron, had participated in the last hurrah – OT VIII.

Two years to the month (June 1990) after the release and first delivery of OT VIII, Scientology's international statistics hit their peak. For the first time in the then 40-year history of Scientology, statistics began to decline across the boards for a significant period of time: at this writing, it's 23 years and counting. I have spoken to more than a dozen witnesses to those statistics, all former high-ranking members who can and have attested to these facts.

During that 1990 statistic-peaking period, David Miscavige desperately tried to coerce the highest technical man in Scientology – Ray Mithoff – to divine something from L. Ron Hubbard's personal counseling records that could be called the latest, unreleased technical breakthrough in Scientology. Ray could divine nothing. Miscavige went through the folders himself and was none the wiser. As he couldn't get a blue spark out of Mithoff, Miscavige accused him of not listening to Ron when he audited him during the last days of his life. Mithoff had come to Creston to give Ron end-of-life assist type auditing, designed to help a spiritual being let go of the dying body. Miscavige claimed that Ron "must have said *something* about what comes next." Surely, there must have been some direction, some advice, anything that might clarify where to go after OT VIII. In defense, after enough positive suggestion through threat and denigration, Ray finally broke down and said Ron did mention something about not going in a certain direction auditing-wise after OT VIII, but he couldn't remember what he said exactly. Miscavige, clutching at straws, turned this into an accusation, "Ray was told by LRH where to go with OT IX and X and can't remember what he said."

In a twisted sort of way, Miscavige drew a measure of solace from Ray's coerced utterance. Miscavige had a "reason" for being caught up the creek without a paddle, and had someone to blame: the first graduate of the level (OT VIII, also known as *Truth Revealed*) that handles "the reason for amnesia on the whole track" had amnesia. Of course Miscavige and Mithoff (by Miscavige's demand) were creating the idea that there was anything to remember in the first place.

Undeterred, by the mid 1990s Miscavige was engaged in alternate plans. If he could not roll out new technology, he would roll out new packaging and make people think he was presenting new technology. To great fanfare, at a cost of millions in promotional glitz, Miscavige announced to the faithful the unveiling of the "Golden Age of Tech." Hundreds of binders were presented, full of detailed drills to be performed so one could make Ron's tech *really* work. Miscavige denigrated all previous Scientology results, announcing to long-term veteran auditors that in fact they were unable to apply even the most fundamental principles of Scientology. All auditors' previous training certificates (including those issued by Ron himself) were cancelled; everybody would need to start their training over at square zero utilizing Miscavige's new drills.

By the year 2000, Miscavige's repackaging tactics had driven church statistics down even further. However, in keeping with his efforts to mimic the man whose shoes he was attempting to fill, by then Miscavige had constructed an iron-clad echo chamber for himself. All staff, including me, were well trained to parrot back to Miscavige the brilliance of his measures, along with creative exaggeration to prove their effectiveness. And so, as the new millennium began, Miscavige was feverishly at work on Golden Age of Tech II (the specifics of which were hard to divine, since Miscavige was continually changing his idea of what that would entail). He was also at work on a ten-year project to re-issue all of Hubbard's books and lectures, edited to – in his view – read more easily. He announced that this was part of what he would unveil to Scientologists as the "Golden Age of Knowledge."

And so, since 1990, apparently most of Ron Hubbard's thousands of pages of advices on church management have been effectively abandoned. Miscavige replaced them with a communist-Russia-style, five-year plan form of management. The dictator announces a grandiose five-year campaign (christened as a new "Golden Age") and all Scientology staff drop whatever they were doing, to frantically pursue the latest end-all. And following further in the tradition of communist Russia, the church has become renowned as a bloviating hype mill that churns out little more than catchy, hollow sales pitches to the faithful and ominous threats to its detractors.

As more and more veteran staff – remembering what Scientology once was under Hubbard's guidance – became disaffected with Miscavige's new Scientology world order, Miscavige's efforts to stamp out dissent became more and more desperate. By January of 2004, Miscavige had literally created a prison for *all* international-level Scientology managers. Eighty people were forced to live and work 24 hours a day in management's temporary quarters – consisting of makeshift offices in conjoined double-wide trailers. Miscavige called the prison "the hole." He organized group confessions resembling something out of Maoist China; each manager was forced to confess thought crimes against Miscavige. He physically beat anyone whose admitted crimes were not salacious enough to suit his deteriorating appetite. Eventually Miscavige forced the managers to beat and physically haze one another.

In the last week of January '04, Miscavige called me to his offices at the Scientology headquarters. He lambasted me for having failed to beat a longtime, close associate of mine named Mike Rinder (chapter 21) for his failure to confess to thought crimes to Miscavige's liking. He grabbed me by the throat and smashed my head against the steel wall of his office lobby. While I was slightly unconscious from the blow, he cupped his hand and slammed it against the side of my head, tearing the ear drum. Miscavige then sentenced me to hard time in the hole. One night while in the hole, I snapped and did throw Rinder to the ground, then bounced him off the floor while holding his lapels. Rinder quietly spoke to me, "Marty, I don't want to play this game anymore." Right then and there, I backed up from the body and observed myself. I saw what I had become, and it appalled me. I loosened my grip, got up and walked away. I planned my escape, and within days I had clandestinely departed the base on my motorcycle, never to return.

I moved to South Texas to be as far away from Hemet, California and Clearwater, Florida as possible. At 48 years of age, I began a new life – sans Scientology – for the first time in my adult years. Classic literature attracted me. It seems the classics mainly focus on the two human virtues I found wanting during my life in Scientology, forgiveness and unconditional love. Consequently, I found the love of my life, Monique, and we have created a wonderful family. After a couple of years I gravitated toward investigating and writing exposés on corruption for two newspapers in the Corpus Christi area. One was left wing, the other right wing. Neither editor ever attempted to edit me; I was single-minded about sniffing out and exposing corruption, and as far as they were concerned that brought greater circulation. But as my local reputation grew as a tough son of a bitch, I again began to question who I really was. I recognized that much of what I was investigating and writing about was the type of corruption I had participated in within the church. I realized that I had left unfinished business behind.

In 2008, I met with Scientologists for the first time since leaving the church in 2004. Marc Pesch (see chapter 9) and his wife Amy Scobee came to visit Monique and me for a week. In hearing their stories about injustices at the hands of Miscavige, I became curious as to what had become of things since I left. I met up with Mike Rinder who had left in 2007. Mike told me that the atrocities that led to my leaving staff had gotten far worse since I had left. Miscavige began orchestrating actual torture in the 'hole' as recently as a year earlier. I realized a couple of things. First, if Miscavige were not exposed for the culture of violence he had created at the Scientology headquarters, who knew but that Scientology might go down in a fiery conflagration ala Waco or Jonestown. Second, irrespective of the inevitable meltdown I believed Scientology management would experience, I also believed Miscavige would take with it the elements of Scientology which I still found worthwhile. In the 1990s I had finally trained and audited to the highest levels of Scientology – completing virtually all of those grades and levels outlined in Chapter Five. I became Scientology's go-to troubleshooter when it came to technology. I audited all Scientology's major executives, as well as all of its A-list celebrities. Irrespective of all the insanity, war and crime I had seen Scientology's darker aspects engender, I never doubted the workability of Scientology's core auditing technology. In 2008 I believed that while period needed to be put to Scientology's abuses, it would be the ultimate travesty if the baby (Scientology auditing technology) were thrown out with the bath water (Scientology control and dominance technology).

I envisioned an independent form of Scientology rising outside of the walls of Scientology Inc. A Scientology that eschewed the absolutism and aggression which was a reflection of the Cold War crucible in which its founder's character had been molded. My blog, *Moving on up a Little Higher* (markrathbun.wordpress.com), served to promote this idea and encourage people to practice Scientology in a sane, integrated manner. There has been a tremendous response, both positively encouraging and negatively violent. The blog has resulted in a number of former church members practicing a more tolerant, peaceful form of Scientology around the world. As this book is published, the blog nears its ten millionth visit.

The response from Miscavige and the church has put our aggression campaigns of the '80s and '90s to shame. For four continuous years there have been teams of private investigators following Monique and me wherever we travel. They have made multiple visits to Monique's family (including her father, when he was recovering from a heart transplant), business associates and friends in attempts to drive a wedge between us and deprive us of employment. Teams of Scientologists (Minute Men calling themselves Squirrel Busters) have accosted us in our driveway, at the beach, and at restaurants. The church rented a home a block away from ours, occupied by teams of Scientologists who overtly harassed us every time we left our home, even to take our evening walk. Scientology Inc. leased another home directly across the street from our home. It was outfitted with numerous surveillance cameras which recorded every movement at and in our home, for three years. My phone records have been stolen, our financial records have been breached, and our computers hacked by the church. This treatment did not deter us. We knew that in fact Miscavige's obsession with me and my wife was playing into my objectives. While all of the church's resources were tied up in attempting to destroy us, independent Scientologists were being afforded a pass to get the independent Scientology show on the road.

Ultimately, however, I came to see the same virus befall independent Scientology as had forever crippled corporate Scientology. I wrote a book that spelled out in detail answers to the question its title asks: *What Is Wrong With Scientology? (*Amazon Books, 2012*).* I concluded the book with three pieces of advice for Scientologists concerned with preserving the relevancy of the subject into the future. Those advices were "integrate or disintegrate, evolve or dissolve, and transcend or descend." I suggested that Scientologists not take the OT III/Xenu space opera construct literally – to do so was not necessary to evolve and transcend above the state of Clear. Also, to take such dogma literally created an us-versus-them and judgmental world view and mentality. The advice met with violent disagreement from the more active independent Scientologists. They went as far as declaring me to be in a condition of Treason for failing to follow in the steps of Ron and Simon Bolivar by applying the policy letter *Responsibility of Leaders* (and its seven points about power) and for having an 'opinion' contrary to L. Ron Hubbard's as to the existence of levels beyond OT VIII. Of course with the Treason condition comes the Enemy formula and its attempt to impose on me the process of finding out who I really am all over again.

It was a tad too late for that. All the assignment from the independent field did for me was to prompt me to research the aspects of Scientology itself (as opposed to only the organization) that created such judgmental and obsessively controlling thinking. That lead to understanding that that which I had created the independent movement to prove – that Scientology itself is not the cause of the abuses of Scientologists – was not honestly provable. I have spent the better part of the past several years studying Eastern thought and religion, psychotherapy, psychology, biology, and science in general – all while engaging in the practice of those parts of Scientology that I find to be workable. In the course of my study I have found an abundance of parallels between Scientology and the subjects of religion, philosophy and psychotherapy. I have found that as continually, vehemently and certainly as Hubbard asserted that Scientology stood alone, immaculately conceived by himself, it was just as certain in reality that this line of segregated teaching was false. And this evidence pointed to the one, overriding flaw in Hubbard's teaching. Ego.

As philosopher Ken Wilber so eloquently postulated in his Kosmic Consciousness series of interviews (*Sounds True* production) an ideal path of spiritual transcendence includes both psychotherapeutic and spiritual practice. He noted that some yogis and gurus undoubtedly have attained spiritual planes that we mortals can only dream of – while at the same time acting as functional invalids in everyday life. In order to create a foundation for wholesome spiritual growth, which according to every validated spiritual tradition includes transcending one's ego, it is necessary to sort out one's ego in the first place. Straightening out one's sense of self and his relationship to others (the realm of psychotherapy) makes for a rounded individual who only then has the rationality and equanimity to fully view and so transcend that self.

As developmental psychology established many years ago, when a person evolves from an immature level of consciousness to a more responsible, fulfilling one, the subject of one level becomes the object of the subject of the next-highest level. The subject and object of this formula of course refers to oneself. And so it goes with spirituality. The power of Scientology is that to a certain level it can psychotherapeutically straighten an individual out, all the while acknowledging and enhancing his sense of spirit.

Scientology at its best, when practiced with no religious fear indoctrination, is what any positive psychotherapy or religious practice seeks to be. L. Ron Hubbard put it this way in 1958 when he most honestly and accurately described the Scientology state of Clear:

A thetan already has a basic personality, and this is what we are trying to uncover in Scientology in order to make a Clear. And it is as easy as that…a Clear could be said to be basic personality revealed.

Ironically, one of the 20th century's most influential psychologists, quoting a famous philosopher, may have put it even more accurately – according to my observations. Carl Rogers wrote:

The best way I can state this aim of life, as I see it coming to light in my relationship with my clients, is to use the words of Sören Kierkegaard – "to be that self which one truly is."

What that means to an individual was well described by another psychologist who was also a contemporary of Hubbard's. Abraham Maslow wrote:

Self-actualized people have a wonderful capacity to appreciate again and again, freshly and naively, the basic goods of life with awe, pleasure, wonder, and even ecstasy, however stale these experiences may be for other people.

Perhaps the greatest attribute of being Clear is the certainty attained about one's spiritual nature. Ken Wilber described that very recognition as the most powerful hallmark of higher consciousness, in any tradition. It comes with a realization about one's immortality, and the concomitant loss of fear of death. That is certainly something I experienced, and witnessed others experience, in Scientology auditing.

And so it is with a Scientology Clear. Until, that is, he is further indoctrinated with appeals to fear and promises of a super human egoic state of perpetual causation over matter, energy, space, time and life. The problem with Scientology, as reflected in the messianic role its founder adopted for himself, is that once it straightens out the ego, rather than helping one to transcend it, it seeks to create an inter-galactic super ego. Perhaps this was the Aleister Crowley OTO magic influence – the idea of conjuring of super human powers.

After codifying the route to Clear and routinely seeing its positive results, Hubbard continued to perceive phenomena containing energy – and confirmed it with the e-meter – that continues to affect one's psyche. Such phenomena can be contacted and communicated with, resulting in a person feeling brighter and more awake. Thousands have attested to that. Why Hubbard chose to complicate it with a dramatic creation mythology, and all the baggage that comes with its adoption, is anyone's guess. As related by Sarge, Hubbard certainly believed in the cosmology he preached to the day he died. In accordance with the history of Scientology, as I have seen and recounted it herein, I have developed some ideas about how those beliefs took root. It seems that the more that psychiatric and medical associations and governments closed in on Hubbard during the '60s, the more he despaired at explaining that aggressive reaction to his route to Clear. His fertile science fiction oriented imagination and Cold War world view created a larger-than-Earth explanation. Governments and psychiatrists were merely the vehicles for dark, inter-galactic forces who put humankind into its miserable condition in the first place.

In 1963 Hubbard postulated that in between lifetimes, spirits are transported to nearby planets for psychiatric-style shocking and implantation of amnesia. He issued policy to drive home the point that a Clear thus should no longer feel free; instead, he should be scared:

If we fail, we've had it. It's not just a matter of getting killed. It's a matter of getting killed and killed and killed life after life forever more. Even if you have no great reality on this now, you will soon enough. But probably you already understand it. Those guys up there mean business. We've got to match or better their energy level and dedication or we lose.

He went so far as to advise violence for fellow Scientologists who did not take the threat seriously:

We haven't any time for doubts and maunderings. The next time you hear somebody whining, "Well I just don't know, whine, whine," kick his teeth in.

By 1967 Ron had created the OT III Xenu explanation of hell on Earth. In 1968 he instructed his most advanced students, at the highest level of Scientology auditor training (Class VIII) that the Xenu myth was to be taken literally. With that, he asserted, comes the recognition that no thought on this planet is original. All modern civilization and progress is merely a dramatization of what was implanted into beings 75 million years before. All technological advances, all religions have been merely humanity's playing out a script that was forcefully imposed on us as spirits, all that time ago.

He concluded that briefing with the conclusion that humanity thus does "*not respond to reason*," and so "*You are the people the planet obeys. You are the people who own the planet.*"

The levels above Clear seek to create that commanding personality who believes – and acts like – he owns Earth. Super egos, loyal officers in an ongoing space opera where we prepare ourselves for following wherever the Admiral of the Sea Organization leads us. And herein lies the schizophrenia built into Scientology. A person who worked for years to attain an unrepressed and self-determined Clear state of self-actualization was indoctrinated to believe that in fact, whether he perceives it or not, he is repressed and no longer self-determined because the source of his oppression is an agency other than himself. Since he cannot be made to understand this through "reason" he will be commanded to "obey." And so, at this level Scientology is no longer a study of knowing how to know. It is no longer a vehicle for coming to greater levels of understanding. It is something to be imposed upon the populace to obey, by way of command by those who really own the world.

These commands are accepted without question by Scientologists, corporate and independent alike. That is so even though the very act of buying into the power of these inter-galactic mythologies is diametrically opposed to the axioms of Scientology, which allow for achievement of the self-actualized condition of Clear and beyond. Even after recognizing all that, in completing this retrospective narrative, those original workable axioms ring more true to me than ever. I see that they apply to me today just as they applied to L. Ron Hubbard until the day he died. Those axioms are probably most succinctly and accurately summed up as follows:

The freedom of an individual depends upon that individual's freedom to alter his considerations of space, energy, time and forms of life, and his roles in it. If he cannot change his mind about these, he is then fixed and enslaved amidst barriers such as those of the physical universe and barriers of his own creation. Man thus is seen as enslaved by barriers of his own creation. He creates these barriers himself or by agreeing with things which hold these barriers to be true.
– L. Ron Hubbard, *The Creation of Human Ability*

Irrespective of L. Ron Hubbard's ultimate ability or inability to fully apply these truths to himself, I am thankful for his articulation of them. I have applied them to myself and find myself no longer afraid, no longer enslaved, and no longer creating barriers against myself. I found out who I truly was when I achieved Clear in 1989. I subsequently was indoctrinated into forgetting that. Part of that indoctrination was the acceptance of a universe view that justified any treatment of others that seemed necessary to forwarding the aims of the Scientology organization. The ends justified the means, and any means that were necessary were acceptable. I came to realize that that imposed viewpoint was self-defeating for Scientology and for those who assumed it. It kept them locked in a struggle to become more powerful, wedded to the necessity of building an indestructible super ego that could fight the good fight like a real Loyal Officer, a warrior.

Twenty years later, while embarking upon study outside of Scientology in order to better understand Scientology, and while counseling people to rebuild their lives after the church of Scientology, and while defending myself and my family against the full force of the Scientology organization, I found out again who I really am.

I am the same guy who got blown out of his mother's womb by high voltage electrodes before birth and stuck around for more. I am the same guy who found solace in the words of Jesus, the chants of Krishna, and the Zen of basketball. I am the same guy who fished his brother out of a mental institute and then joined a religious cult. I am the same guy who fought vigorously through his prime years in L. Ron Hubbard's defense. I am the same guy who graduated from Scientology and yet continued to use that of it which demonstrably works.

I finally came to appreciate the wisdom of a saying by the ancient Zen Master Pai-chang:

One is not different from who one used to be; only one's course of action is different than before.

OTHER BOOKS BY MARK RATHBUN

What is Wrong with Scientology (2012, Amazon Books) The first critical treatment of Scientology that seeks to identify and correct what is wrong with it rather than to merely expose or advocate against the subject. As the first simple, accurate description of the philosophy from its introductory to its most advanced levels, the book will inform those interested in Scientology as no other available work has.

The Scientology Reformation (2012, Amazon Books) Why Scientology must be reformed. An insider's account of the abuses at the top levels of Scientology management. It answers the most frequently asked questions about Scientology today, including 'what is the future of Scientology'?

Visit Rathbun's blog, *Moving On Up A Little Higher* at markrathbun.wordpress.com

45202567R00185

Made in the USA
San Bernardino, CA
02 February 2017